DK BACKPACK BOOKS

1,001 FACTS ABOUT

ANCIENT EGYPT

MUMMIFIED
HEAD

ANUBIS, THE JACKAL
GOD OF EMBALMING

FOOT CASE FROM
A MUMMY

OUTER AND INNER
MUMMY CASES

[DK] BACKPACK BOOKS

1,001 FACTS ABOUT
ANCIENT EGYPT

Written by SCOTT STEEDMAN
with additional material by MARILYN INGLIS

GODDESS
HATHOR

LOTUS FLOWER
DRINKING CUP

SPHINX
SCULPTURE

DORLING KINDERSLEY

LONDON, NEW YORK, MUNICH,
MELBOURNE, DELHI

Project editor Clare Lister
Senior designer Adrienne Hutchinson
Senior editorial co-ordinator Camilla Hallinan
Senior design co-ordinator Sophia M Tampakopoulos Turner
DTP designer Jill Bunyan
Category publisher Sue Grabham
Production Linda Dare
With thanks to the original team:
Project editor Linda White
Art editor Ann Cannings
Senior editor Hazel Egerton
Senior art editor Jacquie Gulliver
Editorial consultant Angela Thomas
Picture research Giselle Harvey
Additional material created by Book Creation Services

First published in Great Britain in 2003
by Dorling Kindersley Limited
80 Strand, London WC2R 0RL
A Penguin Company

A CIP catalogue record for this book is available from the British Library.

ISBN 0 7513 4422 2

Colour reproduction by Colourscan, Singapore
Printed and bound in Singapore by Star Standard

See our complete catalogue at
www.dk.com

CONTENTS

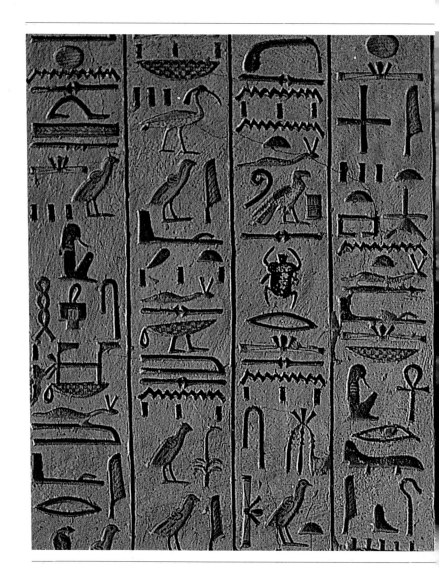

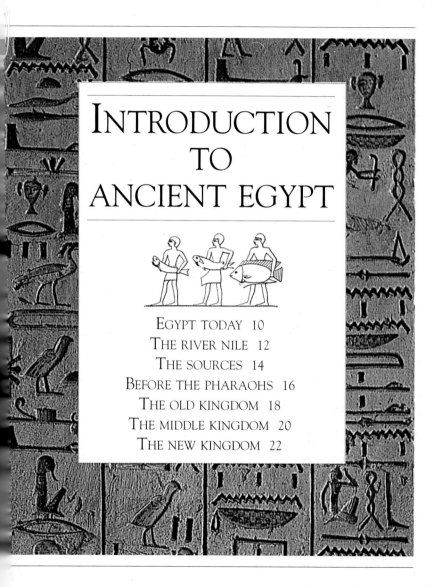

INTRODUCTION TO ANCIENT EGYPT

EGYPT TODAY

THE RIVER NILE and the Sahara Desert dominate Egypt. Until recently, the Nile flooded every year, bringing fertile black soil to the farmland on its banks. The ancient Egyptians called this lush strip the "black land", the land of life. The scorching desert was the "red land", the land of death.

CAIRO
Egypt's capital, Cairo, is the largest city in Africa, with a population of over 11 million. It was founded by Muslims in A.D. 969, more than a thousand years after the last pharaoh.

SAILING ON THE NILE
The Nile is the longest river in the world, flowing 6,670 km (4,145 miles) from the highlands of East Africa to the Mediterranean Sea.

PYRAMIDS AND SPHINX
These famous monuments are both in Giza, on the outskirts of Cairo. They were built 4,500 years ago, during the period known as the Old Kingdom.

FACTS ABOUT EGYPT

• The Sahara is the world's largest desert.

• Egypt is Africa's second biggest country (population: 55 million).

• Egypt has been a Muslim country since A.D. 642.

• The Aswan High Dam, built in 1969–70, ended the annual floods.

QUEEN HATSHEPSUT'S TEMPLE
Millions of tourists come to Egypt every year to visit its great monuments and museums. This is Queen Hatshepsut's mortuary temple at Deir el-Bahri on the west bank of the Nile near Luxor.

KING'S COFFIN
The Egyptians had elaborate beliefs about life after death. Pharaohs and the elite were mummified and buried with a wealth of treasure in decorated tombs. These are a rich source of information on ancient life.

MODERN MAP WITH OLD SITES
Build-ups of silt in the north has altered Egypt's coastline. Other changes are the Suez Canal and Aswan Dam.

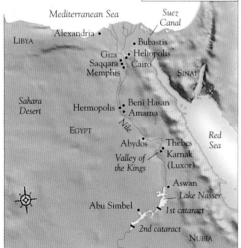

Mediterranean Sea
Suez Canal
LIBYA
Alexandria
Bubastis
Giza • Heliopolis
Saqqara • Cairo
Memphis
SINAI
Sahara Desert
Hermopolis • Beni Hasan
• Amarna
EGYPT
Nile
Abydos • Thebes
Valley of the Kings
Karnak (Luxor)
Red Sea
Aswan
Lake Nasser
Abu Simbel •
1st cataract
2nd cataract
NUBIA

11

THE RIVER NILE

EGYPT HAS BEEN CALLED "the Gift of the Nile". All the water for drinking, bathing, and watering crops came from the great river. The Nile was also Egypt's main highway. The dominant wind blew from north to south, so boats could float downstream with the current or sail upstream against it.

ANCIENT WAYS
Egyptians still grow crops and raise livestock on the banks of the Nile, as they have been doing for more than 7,000 years.

Steering oar

Sun canopy

Steersman

TOMB MODEL FOR USE IN THE AFTERLIFE

Man rowing

FISHING NET

Prow

FISH HOOKS

BOAT
A text from c.1100 B.C. records "Merchants sail up and downstream, eager to convey goods from one place to another and to supply whatever is needed anywhere".

HUNTING AND FISHING
The Nile teemed with life. Men hunted birds in the marshes and caught fish with nets or hooks and lines. Children were taught to be afraid of crocodiles and hippos, which could overturn boats.

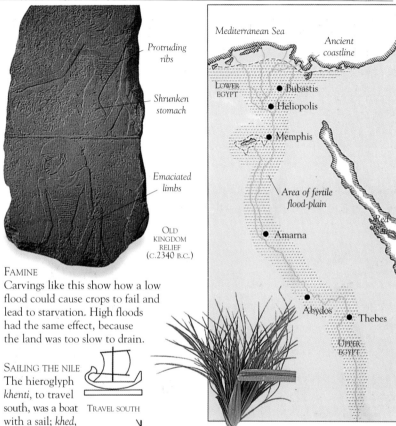

FAMINE

Carvings like this show how a low flood could cause crops to fail and lead to starvation. High floods had the same effect, because the land was too slow to drain.

Protruding ribs

Shrunken stomach

Emaciated limbs

OLD KINGDOM RELIEF (C.2340 B.C.)

SAILING THE NILE

The hieroglyph *khenti*, to travel south, was a boat with a sail; *khed*, to travel north, was a boat with the sail down.

TRAVEL SOUTH

TRAVEL NORTH

PAPYRUS

This reed plant once flourished in Egypt's river marshes. The ancient Egyptians turned the pithy stem into a kind of paper for writing and painting.

Mediterranean Sea

Ancient coastline

LOWER EGYPT

Bubastis

Heliopolis

Memphis

Area of fertile flood-plain

Red

Amarna

Abydos

Thebes

UPPER EGYPT

UPPER AND LOWER EGYPT

Ancient Egypt was divided into Upper and Lower Egypt. North, or Lower Egypt, is the Delta – a flat, green area of marsh and grassland. Upper Egypt, in the south, is a steep river valley – a hot, dry land where the desert is never far away.

13

THE SOURCES

OUR KNOWLEDGE of ancient Egypt comes from buildings, objects, and writings. Many disappeared over the centuries. Thieves stole treasures, and the desert sands invaded temples and tombs. But a hot, dry climate preserved monuments well. Egyptologists study these, and other sources, for clues to Egypt's past.

MYSTERIOUS LAND
Sources can never give a complete picture of the past. This is the Queen of Punt, a land somewhere to the south. We still do not know exactly where.

GUTENBERG BIBLE
Jews and Christians learned about Egypt from the Old Testament of the Bible (the Jewish Torah). It tells the story of the Jews' exile in Egypt, where many worked as slaves for the pharaoh.

THE FIRST PRINTED BIBLE

The body is coated head to toe in resin

NAPOLEON IN EGYPT

When the French general Napoleon invaded Egypt in 1798, he brought a team of scholars and artists who made detailed studies of temples, tombs, and mummies. This sparked off the West's fascination with Egypt.

An owl stood for "m" "Mouth" or "r" Bandages

HIEROGLYPHS

Egyptian monuments, statues, and other artefacts are covered in hieroglyphs, a type of picture-writing. In 1822, French linguist Champollion discovered how to read them and opened up a huge new source of information.

Mummy case

Skeleton

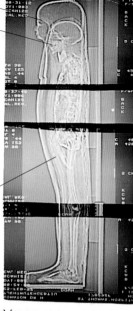

MUMMY SCAN

During the 19th century, mummies were unwrapped, often as public events. This was destructive and disrespectful. Now modern scanners can create 3-D X-ray images of a mummy.

Linen bandages

MUMMIFICATION

The Egyptians went to incredible lengths to preserve their bodies for eternity. Mummies give us all sorts of information about health, diet, and disease. This woman's teeth were worn down by a lifetime of chewing coarse bread. We can even identify the plant oils used to preserve her skin.

15

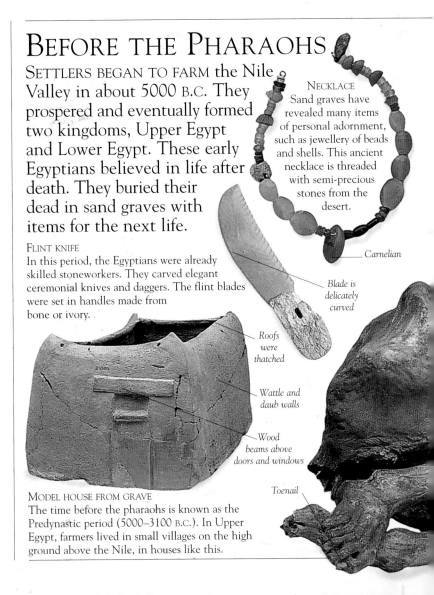

BEFORE THE PHARAOHS

SETTLERS BEGAN TO FARM the Nile
Valley in about 5000 B.C. They
prospered and eventually formed
two kingdoms, Upper Egypt
and Lower Egypt. These early
Egyptians believed in life after
death. They buried their
dead in sand graves with
items for the next life.

NECKLACE
Sand graves have
revealed many items
of personal adornment,
such as jewellery of beads
and shells. This ancient
necklace is threaded
with semi-precious
stones from the
desert.

Carnelian

FLINT KNIFE
In this period, the Egyptians were already
skilled stoneworkers. They carved elegant
ceremonial knives and daggers. The flint blades
were set in handles made from
bone or ivory.

Blade is
delicately
curved

Roofs
were
thatched

Wattle and
daub walls

Wood
beams above
doors and windows

Toenail

MODEL HOUSE FROM GRAVE
The time before the pharaohs is known as the
Predynastic period (5000–3100 B.C.). In Upper
Egypt, farmers lived in small villages on the high
ground above the Nile, in houses like this.

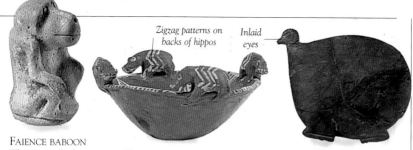

Zigzag patterns on backs of hippos

Inlaid eyes

FAIENCE BABOON
This is made from a glazed earthenware called faience, which first appeared in Egypt during this period.

HIPPO BOWL
Early potters used Nile silt and clay. The river was also a source of inspiration. This bowl is decorated with hippos.

SHEEP SHAPE
This sheep-shaped stone palette was for grinding make-up. Others are in the form of hippos, turtles, and falcons. These mysterious objects probably had a magical purpose as well.

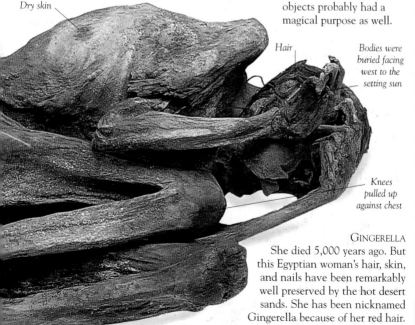

Dry skin

Hair

Bodies were buried facing west to the setting sun

Knees pulled up against chest

GINGERELLA
She died 5,000 years ago. But this Egyptian woman's hair, skin, and nails have been remarkably well preserved by the hot desert sands. She has been nicknamed Gingerella because of her red hair.

THE OLD KINGDOM

EGYPT WAS UNIFIED for the first time in about 3100 B.C., more than 400 years before the start of the Old Kingdom, or "Pyramid Age". Under the stable rule of powerful pharaohs, the country's economy and culture flourished. Art and architecture reached a peak with the building of the great pyramids at Giza.

DOUBLE CROWN
As a symbol of his power, the pharaoh wore the *pschent* or double crown. This combined the White Crown, worn by the kings of Upper Egypt, and the Red Crown of Lower Egypt's kings.

RULER OF TWO LANDS
The union of Egypt is shown here by the entwined lotus (symbol of Upper Egypt) and papyrus (Lower Egypt). One of the pharaoh's official titles was "Ruler of the Two Lands".

Painted limestone

Papyrus plant

Lotus

KING KHAFRA'S THRONE (DETAIL)

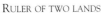

ROYAL COUPLE
These beautiful statues are Prince Rahotep and his wife Nofret. They were found near the pyramid of his father, King Sneferu. The statues are so lifelike it is hard to believe they are 4,600 years old. The eyes are rock crystal, with irises of purple amethyst.

18

FIRST PHARAOH?

Legend tells that Egypt was united by Menes, a king from Upper Egypt who conquered the north. Experts believe he may be King Narmer (here wearing the White Crown). On the other side of this palette, he wears the Red Crown.

NARMER'S PALETTE

King Narmer

STEP PYRAMID

The first pyramid was built at Saqqara for King Djoser in c.2680 B.C. This huge stepped structure is 60 m (198 ft) high. Like most pyramids, it is a tomb. Djoser and his family were buried in chambers far beneath.

KHUFU SMITES ENEMY CHIEF

MIGHTY KINGS

Kings Khufu, Khafra, and Menkaura, builders of the Pyramids of Giza, were among the most powerful. They must have directed Egypt's entire economy into building their tombs.

Royal beard

GOD-KING

The Egyptians believed that the pharaoh was the son of the sun god Ra. The king was also associated with the sky god, Horus, seen here as a falcon protecting Khafra.

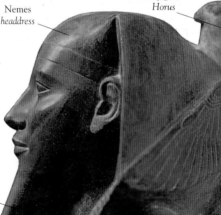

Nemes headdress

Sky god, Horus

THE MIDDLE KINGDOM

THE OLD KINGDOM COLLAPSED in about 2160 B.C., and Egypt was rocked by war and chaos. It was eventually reunited by Mentuhotep, who founded the Middle Kingdom in 2040 B.C. Peace and prosperity returned. Strong pharaohs strengthened government and foreign trade, and Egypt invaded Libya and Nubia. Art revived, and pyramids were built again.

SENUSRET I
This dynamic king took the throne after sharing it for ten years with his father, Amenemhat I. Senusret I fought the Libyans and Nubians and built many grand temples. The earliest known literary texts were written in his court.

ETERNAL STONE
This noble died in about 1850 B.C. Statues like this were placed in local temples, so relatives did not have to travel to a tomb with offerings.

Spells cover coffin inside and out

MUMMY CASE
Middle Kingdom coffins were painted with magical spells to help the soul on its journey through the underworld to the next life. During the Old Kingdom, these spells – known as the Pyramid texts – had been carved in royal tombs.

AMENEMHAT III

During his long and peaceful reign (1854-1808 B.C.)
this powerful pharaoh built temples, border forts, two
pyramids, and undertook a land reclamation scheme.

BLACK PYRAMID

This is the first pyramid of
Amenemhat III, which he
built at Dahshur. Like all
Middle Kingdom pyramids,
the core is of mud bricks
rather than stone. These have
collapsed in a shapeless heap.

UNDER THE BLACK PYRAMID

Kings built mazes of false passages and
hidden doors to try to conceal their
burial chambers from robbers. It did not
work. The Middle Kingdom collapsed
in 1750 B.C., and all the pyramids were
looted during the chaos that followed.

*Pyramid
enclosure wall*

*Extent of
rubble*

*King's burial
chamber*

Entrance

*False eyes allow
mummy to "see" out*

OSIRIS

GOD OF THE DEAD

The worship of Osiris, god of death
and rebirth, spread across Egypt in
the Middle Kingdom. He offered all
Egyptians, not just those close to the
pharaoh, the hope of an afterlife.

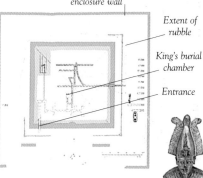

21

THE NEW KINGDOM

THE GREATEST PERIOD of Egypt's history was the New Kingdom (c.1550–1086 B.C.). Warrior kings, such as Ahmose I and Thutmose III, expanded the empire into Nubia, Libya, and the Middle East. Many temples were built, and pharaohs were buried in painted tombs in the Valley of the Kings.

WAR CROWN
The pharaoh's new image was as a war leader. He adopted the Blue Crown, or war helmet, and was seen as a living form of a warrior god.

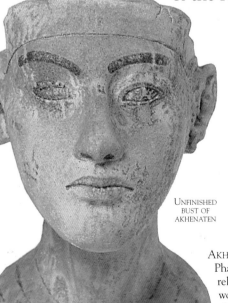

UNFINISHED BUST OF AKHENATEN

RAMSES THE GREAT
In his 67 years on the throne, Ramses II built more monuments than any other pharaoh. This is the massive rock-cut temple of Abu Simbel. The four statues of Ramses II are each 20 m (65 ft) high.

AKHENATEN, HERETIC PHARAOH
Pharaoh Amenhotep IV introduced a new religion, the first in history based on the worship of one god (the Aten). He even changed his name to Akhenaten. After his death, his name was scorned, his city abandoned, and the gods were reinstated.

WAR CHARIOT
To expel Asian invaders,
the first pharaohs of
the New Kingdom built an
efficient army. This included corps of war
chariots, copied from the Asian enemy.

TOMB OF SENNEDJEM (DEIR EL-MEDINA)
The Egyptians gave up on pyramid tombs, which were
too easy to find and rob. Instead, they were buried in
tombs cut deep into the rock in barren spots like the
Valley of the Kings and the Valley of the Queens.

MASS GLASS
Factories, mass-producing
colourful glass vessels, were
set up near many palaces.
Glass was also cast to
decorate jewellery, furniture,
and even mummy cases.

TUTANKHAMUN'S SECOND COFFIN
The tombs in the Valley of the Kings were robbed long ago.
The only one found intact belonged to an obscure boy-king
called Tutankhamun. The glittering treasures
inside amazed the world.

Coloured glass

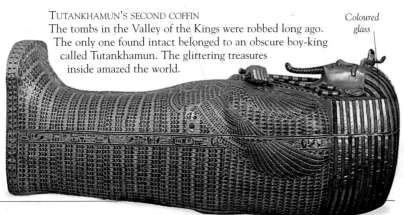

EGYPTIAN SOCIETY

THE PEOPLE OF EGYPT

AT THE TOP of Egyptian society was the pharaoh. He commanded the army and ruled the country through a network of nobles, officials, and scribes. Skillful craftsworkers were kept busy building and decorating temples and tombs. But most Egyptians were peasants who worked the land.

AT THE PHARAOH'S SIDE
In life as in death, the king was surrounded by his nobles. This noble's tomb is in the shadow of King Khufu's Pyramid.

Tomb of Seshemnufer

SERVANT GIRL
Many women worked as servants in the houses of the rich. This wooden palette is in the shape of a serving girl, carrying a large pot on one shoulder. It is a make-up container; the top slides open and closed.

A KEEPER OF RECORDS
Scribes were important because they were among the few who could read and write. They recorded many details of everyday life.

FACTS ABOUT PEOPLE

• A massive tomb recently discovered in the Valley of the Kings (1995) shows that it contains at least some of Ramses II's many sons.

• When the pharaoh praised one man's work, the man died of shock.

HARVEST SCENE
Farming life followed the seasons. As soon as the summer's crop was ripe, farmers rushed to harvest it before the Nile flooded the land again. These oxen are treading the grain.

OFFICIAL
The state was highly bureaucratic. Every town had officials. These civil servants collected taxes, regulated businesses, and organized loans and marriage contracts.

CRAFTSMEN
Most craftsmen were employed in workshops run by royal palaces or temples. This carpenter is building a ship for a wealthy patron.

MUSICIAN
The Egyptians believed in enjoying life. Dancers and musicians performed at the royal courts and at private dinner parties. They also entertained the bustling crowds during festivals and celebrations.

KING AND CAPTIVE
The pharaoh was seen as a living god. He led in battle and protected Egypt from famine, disease, and chaos. This is symbolized by this statue of pharaoh Ramses IV gripping a captive enemy.

PEASANTS AND SERVANTS

THE VAST MAJORITY of ancient Egyptians were peasant farmers. They worked in the fields by the Nile, channelling the floodwaters and planting and harvesting crops. Many others worked as servants or labourers. Few of them could read or write. But they enjoyed more freedom than slaves, who were rare.

FOREIGN SLAVES
Slaves were never an important part of Egyptian society and were rare until the New Kingdom. Most slaves were foreigners, captured during Egypt's wars abroad. Here, a scribe registers foreign captives.

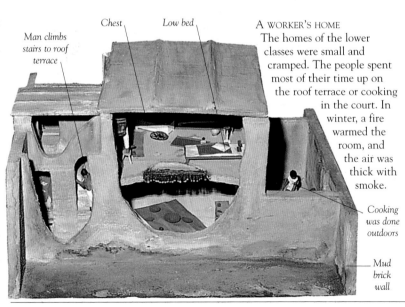

Man climbs stairs to roof terrace

Chest

Low bed

A WORKER'S HOME
The homes of the lower classes were small and cramped. The people spent most of their time up on the roof terrace or cooking in the court. In winter, a fire warmed the room, and the air was thick with smoke.

Cooking was done outdoors

Mud brick wall

TRAMPLED UNDER FOOT
These bound Libyans, painted on the soles of shoes, symbolized Egypt's power over foreigners. Slaves could be bought and sold like cattle, but they could also rent land and earn their freedom.

SERVANT GIRL
Most domestic servants were just poor. But some were female slaves who had escaped debt by selling themselves into slavery. The purchaser agreed to protect and feed the slave – and might later free her.

Quern (grind stone)

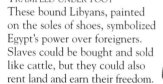

A BEATING
Peasants who did not pay their taxes were beaten. More serious criminals were whipped or had their noses cut off and then sent to the mines of Sinai or Nubia.

GRAPE PICKING
Harvest time was very busy. These men are picking grapes and carrying them in buckets to the press. The squeezed juice was turned into wine.

WOODEN MODEL OF SERVANT GRINDING CORN

MODEL WORKER
Egyptians believed that, in heaven, they would work for the gods in the *Field of Reeds*. The rich were buried with model *shabti* figures, to do the hard work for them.

MIDDLE CLASSES

EGYPT'S EFFICIENT administration was run by an educated middle class of scribes and officials. Military officers ran the army, while priests organized prayers and offerings in the temples. Lower on the social pyramid were craftsworkers and traders – but they still had a much better standard of living than the peasant farmers.

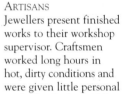

MEDICAL DOCTOR
This is one of just two known images of a doctor at work. Many priests and scribes were also doctors. Some specialized in treating the eyes, teeth, or the head. One priest had the title "Doctor to the King's Belly".

ARTISANS
Jewellers present finished works to their workshop supervisor. Craftsmen worked long hours in hot, dirty conditions and were given little personal credit for the beautiful works of art they produced.

A variety of trees

Sistrum
(ceremonial rattle)

Incense cone

The garden pool would have been stocked with fish

PRIEST

In countless temples throughout the land, teams of priests and priestesses made offerings to the gods in the name of their pharaoh. In return, they were rewarded with land and a generous income.

Shrine of god Atum

Papyrus

Vents to catch cool breeze

SERVANT

Well-off middle-class families had servants to cook, clean, and help them wash and dress. This servant is placing an incense cone on his master's head, ready for a night out.

This official carries a wooden staff, which was a symbol of authority

SCRIBE

In most towns and villages, the only people who could read and write were scribes, which made them powerful and influential people. Art often shows them sitting cross-legged. This scribe is Pes-shu-per, c.700 B.C.

WELL-TO-DO COUPLE

This detail from a papyrus shows the scribe Nakhte and his wife in the garden of their villa. A platform protects the house from high floodwaters. The couple are wearing elaborately pleated clothes and heavy wigs.

OFFICIAL

The government was run by state officials, ranging from the *Vizier*, the top statesman, to local officials who ran the day-to-day affairs in each district, or *nome*.

31

THE ARMY

EGYPT'S FIGHTING forces evolved from the Old Kingdom tradition of mustering troops when an emergency arose to the large, well-equipped army of the New Kingdom. In supreme control was the pharaoh. Below him, ranking officers commanded corps of soldiers, who fought on foot or in chariots.

WAR GALLEY
Armed with axes and bows, the navy fought sea battles from ships. These had figureheads of gods and names like "Wild Bull", "Star of Egypt", or "Soul of the Gods".

STING OF BATTLE
The pharaoh thanked soldiers for bravery in battle by giving them gold flies, made in the royal workshops by the best jewellers. Worn around the neck, the fly meant that a soldier had "stung" the enemy.

BATTLE FORMATION
In the periods of disorder that followed the Old Kingdom's collapse, many regional princes owned armies. This model, c.2000 B.C., from the tomb of Prince Mesehti may represent his private army.

STANDARD TACTICS
The pharaoh and his council of war decided on strategy. Every unit of the Egyptian army carried a standard so that they were easy to identify on the battle field. Orders were given by war trumpet.

PEACE WORK

In peacetime, the army was put to work digging ditches, mining, or hauling stone for temples and pyramids. The navy went on trading expeditions. This wall carving from Queen Hatshepsut's temple shows a trip, *c.*1496 B.C., to the Land of Punt. The fleet returned with baboons and incense trees.

Domed houses on stilts

Many different trees and plants

BORDER FORT

During the Middle Kingdom, massive mud-brick forts were built to protect Egypt's border with Nubia. Egyptian art never shows these forts under seige.

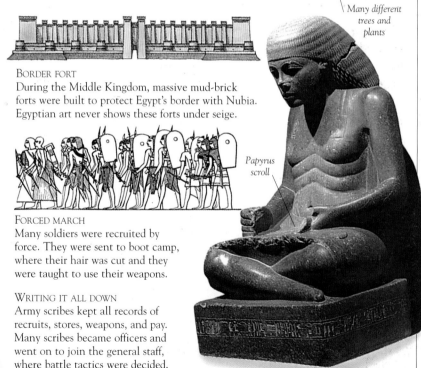

Papyrus scroll

FORCED MARCH

Many soldiers were recruited by force. They were sent to boot camp, where their hair was cut and they were taught to use their weapons.

WRITING IT ALL DOWN

Army scribes kept all records of recruits, stores, weapons, and pay. Many scribes became officers and went on to join the general staff, where battle tactics were decided.

EGYPTIAN WOMEN

WOMEN HAD CLEARLY DEFINED roles. They were responsible for looking after the house and bringing up the children. Many did a lot of back-breaking labour, such as working in the fields. But, by law, women had the same rights as men. A wife could even take her husband to court if he treated her badly.

A DELAYED BEATING
Egyptian criminals were beaten. But an exception was made with pregnant women, so as not to hurt the innocent unborn child. Punishment had to wait until after the birth.

Coffins fit inside each other

BRINGING UP BABY
A woman's main job was raising children. Mothers carried babies in slings. If a wife did not bear a son, her husband would take a mistress, and the family would adopt the child.

GOLDEN PRIESTESS
"Priestess" was one of the few titles women could have. Another was "Player of Music in the Temple". These golden coffins belong to Henutmehit, a priestess of the city of Thebes, c.1250 B.C.

MARRIED COUPLE
This happy-looking couple are Katep and his wife Hetepheres, c.2500 B.C. Some unions were arranged, but other Egyptians married for love. Men could have several wives, but the marriage contract protected the wife and children, so most men could only afford one.

Woman's pale skin suggests she stayed in the home

NEFERTITI
This statue of the beloved wife of king Akhenaten was found in a sculptor's workshop in Amarna. After her husband's death Nefertiti may even have ruled on her own under a false name.

BREAST MILK JUG
Mothers breastfed their babies openly. One carving even shows Queen Nefertiti nursing her daughter. Excess milk may have been kept in jugs like this. Mothers with a short supply prayed to the goddess Isis.

Woman carries basket on head

A WOMAN KING
Hatshepsut was the first woman to become a true pharaoh (1479–1457 B.C.). Like other pharaohs, Hatshepsut had herself portrayed as a sphinx.

Ceremonial beard

Face of Hatshepsut

Base fitted in stand

WOMAN'S WORK
Many women were household servants. Others worked as wet nurses, bakers, weavers, singers, dancers, musicians, and even doctors. But women never held public office.

35

THE PHARAOH

EGYPTIANS BELIEVED their pharaoh was a living god. He alone could unite the country and maintain the cosmic order, or *Ma'at*. They believed that, when he died, he would achieve eternal life – not just for himself, but also for his people. The pharaoh's power was absolute. He led the army, set taxes, judged criminals, and controlled the temples.

HORUS
The pharaoh was associated with the gods of the sun and sky, especially the falcon-headed sky god Horus.

Thutmose IV

ROYAL NAME
A pharaoh's name was written inside a cartouche. This oval loop symbolized the king's power over "all that the sun encircles".

KING OF THE NILE
Hapy was the god of the Nile flood. He was portrayed as a king, wearing the royal *nemes* headdress and false beard. The woman's breasts were symbolic of his waters, which gave life to Egypt.

ANKH
The ankh was the symbol of life. In art, only gods or kings carry this symbol. Many paintings show a god or goddess giving life to a pharaoh by touching his mouth with the ankh.

SYMBOLS OF THE PHARAOH
Tutankhamun carries a crook and flail and wears the striped *nemes* headcloth and ceremonial beard. The vulture and cobra on his brow represent Upper and Lower Egypt, respectively.

The Uraeus
(said to spit fire at the king's enemies)

Vulture goddess Nekhbet

Nemes headcloth

PEPY II
This pharaoh ruled for 94 years. Every 30 years the pharaoh was recrowned in the *Sed* festival, a jubilee celebration. The highlight was a race in which the king ran a course to prove his fitness to rule.

False beard

Crook

OSTRICH-FEATHER FAN
The pharaoh was almighty. Servants fanned him, and visitors kissed the ground before him. But anyone touching him without permission could be sentenced to death.

37

THE ROYAL HOUSE

IMPORTANT OFFICIALS were called "Friends of the Pharaoh". They had titles like "Fanbearer on the Right of the King" and "Master of the Horse". Many of them lived at the palace. On great state occasions, they would be joined by high priests and officials from all over Egypt.

ROYAL SPORT
The sport of kings and their courts was hunting. Noblemen killed birds with throwing sticks. The cartouche of pharaoh Akhenaten is painted on this fragile example, which was probably only ever used for ceremonial purposes.

18TH DYNASTY THRONE

RAMSES III AND HAREM
The pharaoh lived in a harem, a court of many wives and other women. They washed and dressed him many times a day and catered to his every need.

POWER OF THE THRONE
The pharaoh's might was visible throughout the palace. This throne has bound captives under the seat, showing the king's control over foreigners and his role as defender of Egypt.

TUTANKHAMUN'S OFFICIALS
A painting in Tutankhamun's tomb shows the court officials dragging the king's coffin at his funeral. In his lifetime, they would have helped the king in the day-to-day affairs of state.

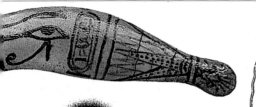

PREGNANT QUEEN

This is the only known image of a pregnant queen. She is the mother of King Thutmose III. One king could have many wives. To keep the dynastic line pure, pharaohs often married their sisters and cousins – and sometimes even their own daughters.

A PRINCE

It was very important for the pharaoh to have an heir. If his chief wife had no sons, a boy born by one of his other wives became heir. If he had no sons, the next pharaoh could start a new dynasty.

RAMESSIDE QUEEN

COURT OFFICIAL

This is Sennefer and his wife. He was "Prince of the Southern City" (Thebes) and "Administrator of Granaries" in c.1400 B.C. Sennefer's wife was a royal wet-nurse.

GODDESS QUEEN

The pharaoh's chief wife ruled beside him as his queen. She was also looked upon as a god on earth. The king represented the all-powerful sun god, while she was associated with Hathor, goddess of love, and Isis, the mother goddess.

39

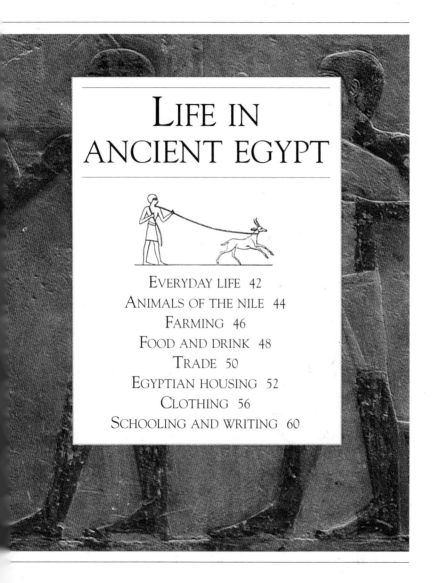

LIFE IN ANCIENT EGYPT

EVERYDAY LIFE

EGYPTIAN LIFE revolved around three seasons. During the flood, *akhet* (July to October), farm work stopped. *Peret*, the time of ploughing and sowing, began when the waters went down in November. The busiest season was *shemu*, the harvest. From March to June, farmers worked hard to bring in the crops before the river rose again.

IRRIGATION DEVICE
Farmers used *shadufs* to raise water from the river. They irrigated the land by using a system of canals and dykes.

PYRAMID
Thousands of farmers had nothing to do during the flood season. So they joined the pharaoh's skilled labour force to work on huge building projects like temples or pyramids. This is the remains of the Meidum pyramid, built around 2550 B.C. for the pharaoh Sneferu.

Limestone core of pyramid

Farmland on edge of desert

HUNTING IN THE MARSHES

Work and play centred on the Nile. This tomb carving shows cattle being herded across the river. The calf being helped into a boat is about to be grabbed by a crocodile.

In the Old Kingdom, silver was far rarer than gold

THE SIDELOCK OF YOUTH

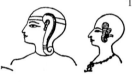

Children often ran around naked in the hot climate. They are usually shown with a distinctive hairstyle.

RINGS

Both men and women enjoyed wearing jewellery, which was often made from precious metals. These swivel-top rings have scarab beetles one side and good-luck designs the other.

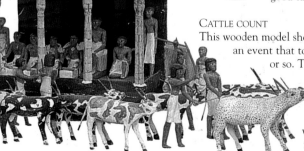

CATTLE COUNT

This wooden model shows the cattle count, an event that took place every year or so. This was a means of assessing a person's wealth. The cattle are driven past scribes, who write down the numbers for the owner's tax records.

43

ANIMALS OF THE NILE

IN ANCIENT TIMES, a great variety of animals thrived in Egypt. The desert was home to lions, wolves, antelopes, wild bulls, and hares. The river marshes echoed with the loud cries of exotic birds. Crocodiles lazed on the banks, while hippos wallowed in the water. At night, owls, jackals, and hyenas came out in search of food.

CAT MUMMY
Sacred to the goddess Bastet, cats were popular pets. Cats were often mummified and buried in cat-shaped coffins after they died.

CROCODILE GOD
Many people were killed by the huge Nile crocodiles. The animal was worshipped as the god Sobek.

ANIMAL GAMES
This comical papyrus gives us a glimpse of ancient Egyptian humour. Like the lion and antelope playing senet, the animals are all doing things that are wildly out of character.

Senet was a popular board game

Mouth poured perfume

Ripples for scales

FLASK
Fish such as perch and catfish were caught up and down the river. This fish-shaped glass flask poured perfume from its mouth.

WILD SHEEP
This figurine may once have graced the dressing table of a wealthy lady. It is a cosmetic container in the shape of a wild sheep, an animal that still roams the fringes of the Sahara today.

Lid of container

Crouching cat

Water-plant design

HIPPO
This animal was feared because it overturned boats. In legend, it was associated with the evil god Seth, so killing a hippo was a symbolic victory over evil. The wealthy hunted them with spears.

Jackals herd goats

A cat tends a flock of geese

Lion and ox play

FARMING

EGYPTIAN LIFE was based on farming the rich flood plain of the Nile. The main crops were emmer wheat, barley, and flax. Farmers also grew beans, lentils, onions, leeks, cucumbers, and lettuce in garden plots, and fruits like grapes, dates, figs, and pomegranates. Animals raised for meat included cattle, pigs, sheep, goats, geese, and ducks.

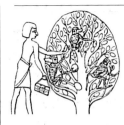

PICKING FIGS
Ancient Egyptians loved sycamore figs. So did baboons, which were trained to climb the trees and pick the fruit.

Scribes making tax records

Wooden chest

Tomb owner

Man with jars of water

Man drinking water from jar

Mother with baby

Workers cutting grain with sickles

Men carrying grain in basket

PLOUGHING THE FIELDS

This wooden tomb model shows a man ploughing. The wooden plough is being pulled by two oxen. The ploughman used a hoe if he needed to break up any heavy clumps of soil. Another man would have followed behind, sowing seed.

Man guides plough

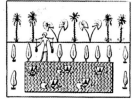

The wooden blade cuts through the soil

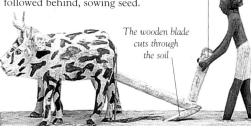

WATERING THE CROPS

A network of dykes, pools, and irrigation channels criss-crossed the farmland. Here, a man is carrying buckets of water hung on a yoke across his shoulders.

Workers winnowing

HARVESTING GRAIN

This is a harvesting scene from a tomb. Below, workers cut the grain and load it into baskets. Above, other workers are winnowing – throwing the grain into the air to separate it from the chaff. Scribes record the quantity.

Protective headcloth

LENTILS

DATES

Girls squabbling about left-over wheat

Linen kilt

WHEAT

CROPS

The fertile soil by the Nile enabled Egyptian farmers to grow a large variety of crops. Harvested grain was stored in granaries and used to make bread and beer.

FOOD AND DRINK

BREAD AND BEER were the two staples in an Egyptian's diet. Both were made in a similar way, using wheat or barley. Bakers also made a whole variety of cakes and pastries, often sweetened with dates or honey. There were many fruits and vegetables, but potatoes and citrus fruits were unknown. The wealthy enjoyed lavish banquets – feasting on meat, washed down with wine. Poor people were more likely to dine on fish and beer.

HONEY
Egyptians were the first people known to keep bees. Honey was collected to sweeten cakes, beer, and wine.

Wooden syphon

BEER STRAINER

Holes for straining

GRAPES

BREWING BEER
Women made beer. They mixed bread dough with yeast and left it to ferment in large vats. A few weeks later, they filtered the mash. The mature beer was seasoned with spices or dates. It was very thick and had to be strained before drinking.

GRAPES AND WINE
Wall-paintings show workers picking grapes and squeezing them in a press. The wine matured in tall amphorae, inscribed with the year, type of grape, region, and vineyard owner.

WINEPRESS

FOOD OFFERINGS

Egyptians brought food to temples and tombs to make sure the gods and spirits of the dead were well fed. This tomb carving shows bearers bringing a selection of offerings.

BREAD

EVERYDAY FARE

Fruit, vegetables, and grain were grown in plenty. The Egyptians ate bread with every meal. Until the New Kingdom, when bakeries became common, most housewives made their own bread. Loaves came in many shapes, some made specially for religious rites such as offerings for the dead. This bread was placed in a tomb more than 3,000 years ago.

Baboons could not resist figs

MODERN FIGS

MODERN DATES

AT THE BUTCHERS

This tomb model shows an ox being slaughtered. The meat would be roasted, boiled, or stewed. Rich Egyptians ate a lot of meat, which was often wild game from the hunt. Antelope, gazelle, porcupine, hare, and fowl such as quail and crane were all on the menu.

ANCIENT PALM TREE FRUIT

Ostrich plumes and eggs were often among the tributes sent to pharaohs from lands in the south.

TRADE

FOR MOST OF ITS HISTORY, ancient Egypt was the richest country in the world. The Egyptians grew more than enough food. So the surplus grain, along with linen, papyrus, and dried fish, was exported in exchange for luxury items such as incense, silver, and fine cedar wood. Horses came from Asia to the east, while, to the south, Nubia and Punt were a source of gold, ivory, ebony, and incense.

Ebony

Red jasper

Incense

Gold rings

Giraffe tails

NUBIAN GIFTS
These Nubian envoys are taking gifts to the Egyptian court. Nubia was rich in copper, gold, and semi-precious stones. Merchants also supplied Egypt with exotic goods like incense and wild animals, brought from lands farther south.

Live baboon

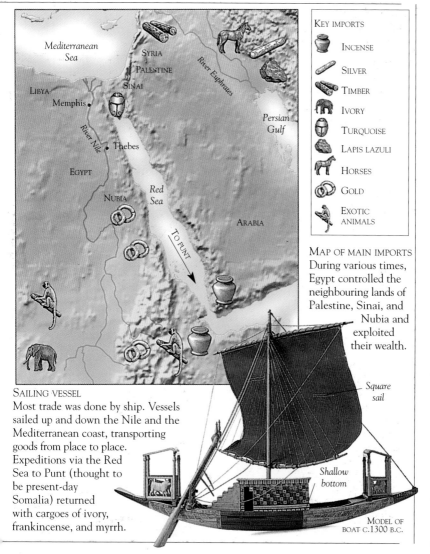

KEY IMPORTS

- INCENSE
- SILVER
- TIMBER
- IVORY
- TURQUOISE
- LAPIS LAZULI
- HORSES
- GOLD
- EXOTIC ANIMALS

Mediterranean Sea

SYRIA

PALESTINE

SINAI

River Euphrates

LIBYA

Memphis

Persian Gulf

River Nile

Thebes

EGYPT

NUBIA

Red Sea

ARABIA

TO PUNT

MAP OF MAIN IMPORTS

During various times, Egypt controlled the neighbouring lands of Palestine, Sinai, and Nubia and exploited their wealth.

SAILING VESSEL

Most trade was done by ship. Vessels sailed up and down the Nile and the Mediterranean coast, transporting goods from place to place. Expeditions via the Red Sea to Punt (thought to be present-day Somalia) returned with cargoes of ivory, frankincense, and myrrh.

Square sail

Shallow bottom

MODEL OF BOAT C.1300 B.C.

51

EGYPTIAN HOUSING

EGYPTIAN HOMES were built to stay cool. From pharaoh's palace to worker's hut, most houses were made from mud bricks. Many dwellings had roof terraces, where people could take the air in hot weather. Wealthy families lived in large villas with lush gardens and fish-stocked pools. In the cities, the poorer people lived in simple homes, crammed together in a maze of alleys, passageways, and squares.

MAKING BRICKS
Wet Nile mud was mixed with sand and straw, squeezed into a wooden mould, and then dried in the sun.

ANCIENT FRESCOES
The walls and ceilings of rich people's houses were painted with colourful designs, often composed of geometric patterns and plant motifs.

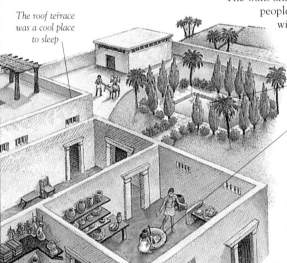

The roof terrace was a cool place to sleep

Decorative pond

Kitchen area with open fire for cooking

INSIDE A HOUSE
In a typical house of a well-off Egyptian, the main living area was placed some way from the kitchen to avoid cooking smells. Some bedrooms had their own bathing facilities and lavatories.

Flat roof

Chair

Stairs to
upper
storey

Colonnaded
entrance

Food was stored and
cooked in courtyard

Bed

SIMPLE HOME
This pottery house (c.1900 B.C.) was placed in
a tomb for the owner's use in the next life and
shows architectural details that existed in
houses of the period.

HOUSE FACTS

• Mud bricks were
sometimes stamped with
the name of the reigning
pharaoh.

• A workman's week
was nine days long – the
10th was a day of rest.

• Windows were small
to keep out hot sunlight.

A VILLAGE ON THE NILE TODAY
Egyptian houses are still made of mud bricks. Some
towns now sit on hills because they have been rebuilt
again and again on the ruins of older settlements.

In the home

Egyptian houses were sparsely furnished. Tables were rare, and many pictures show people squatting cross-legged on the floor rather than sitting on stools. Most people slept on benches built into the walls; only the wealthy had real beds. The pieces of furniture that have survived have simple, elegant lines. Many are exquisitely crafted, with inlays of gemstones, glass, and precious woods.

NOBLE CHAIRS
Only a wealthy Egyptian household would have chairs. Like tables, these were usually low and wide. Legs were often carved to look like lions' paws or bulls' hooves.

Special base holds jar steady

JAR STAND
Lamps and jars often sat on wooden stands. Oil lamps were the only means of artificial light. Oil was expensive, so many poorer people went to bed early and rose at dawn.

Carved decoration

Bow

Painted legs

Firestick

End of stick fits into groove

String

SERVANT LOOKING AFTER FIRE

Fanning flames

FIRE
This is the only type of Egyptian fire-making device found. A stick was pushed into a wooden base, while a bow looped around the stick was moved quickly back and forth. The friction set the base on fire.

Base

Grooves blackened by fire

LION HEAD
Walls and furniture were decorated with images of gods, especially ones that protected the household. This lion head may represent Bes, a guardian of sleep, who is half lion, half dwarf.

Cup in shape of open lotus

Ducks

CONTAINERS
The first vessels, from over 7,000 years ago, were clay pots. Later, carved stone jars were produced. Faience, a coloured and glazed earthenware, first appeared *c.*3200 B.C. This faience vase and cup from Thebes were made *c.*1450 B.C.

HEADRESTS
Instead of pillows, Egyptians slept on headrests. They were made from stone, wood, or bone. Much more comfortable than they look, headrests are still used in many parts of Africa.

Curved surface supports head

Wide base

String mesh netting

All six of Tutankhamun's beds have clawed feet

TUTANKHAMUN'S BED
Of the six beds discovered in Tutankhamun's tomb, this is the most spectacular. The carved ebony frame is completely covered in gold, and embossed panels are decorated with plant motifs. Another of his beds folded up for travelling.

55

CLOTHING

EGYPTIANS WORE simple linen clothes. Men dressed in short kilts, leaving their chests bare or draping a cloak or a strip of linen over their shoulders. Women wore long, tight-fitting dresses. On cool evenings they might put on a long-sleeved gown as well. In later periods, tunics and dresses with complicated pleats became popular. Both women and men wore wigs.

Damp cloth was pressed into grooves

PLEAT BOARD

PRESSED PLEATS
Grooved boards like this may have been used to pleat the clothes of well-to-do Egyptians.

COARSE LINEN
Ordinary Egyptians wore coarse linen, while the rich dressed in a lighter, finer cloth. Finest of all was the semi-transparent "royal linen". The Egyptians knew about dyes, but most linen was left a natural white.

Interwoven flax fibres

OFFICIAL ATTIRE
This is Mereruka, *vizier* to King Teti in about 2340 B.C. He is wearing the short kilt typical of the Old Kingdom. The kilt was tied at the waist, often in an elaborate bow.

ROYAL DRESS
Egyptians were not prudish about their bodies. Kings are often shown in tiny kilts, and queens wore near transparent dresses. For important ceremonies, the king wore a long kilt and an elaborate cloak with countless pleats.

COURT LADY
Clothes were draped rather than cut to fit. The fringed, finely pleated dress of this noblewoman leaves one shoulder bare and reaches well below her ankles. Her heavy, braided wig is crowned with a circlet of flowers.

WEAVING LINEN
Women combed the stems of the flax plant to remove the spiky heads. Then they separated the fibres from the stalk and spun them on a spindle, weighted by a whorl. The spun threads were woven on a loom to make cloth.

Whorl

SPINDLE

FLAX COMB

Twine strap

DRESS FACTS
• Priests dressed statues of gods each morning and undressed them at night.

• Some peasants and fishermen worked naked.

• The wealthy used professional laundries. Poorer people did their washing in the river.

Rotating spindle twists fibres

SANDALS
Most Egyptians went barefoot. But priests and wealthy people wore sandals. These were made from leather or reeds like papyrus that flourished in the marshes by the River Nile.

CLOTHING

57

Jewellery and make-up

The Egyptians went to great lengths to look good. Men and women rubbed oil into their skins, painted their eyes with thick make-up, and sprinkled their clothes with sweet-smelling perfumes. At parties, women crowned their wigs with incense cones. These melted slowly, pouring scent onto their hair and clothes. The wealthy wore gold jewellery that sparkled with semi-precious stones.

Malachite

Galena

COLOUR
Green eye paint came from malachite, black eye *kohl* from galena, and red for lips was made from iron oxide.

Iron oxide

EARRINGS

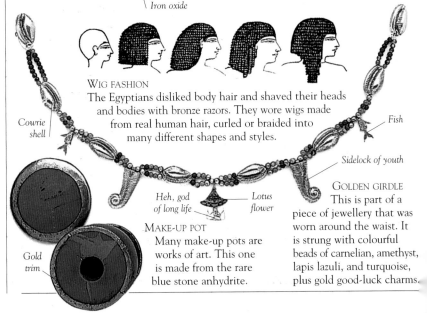

WIG FASHION
The Egyptians disliked body hair and shaved their heads and bodies with bronze razors. They wore wigs made from real human hair, curled or braided into many different shapes and styles.

Cowrie shell

Fish

Sidelock of youth

Heh, god of long life

Lotus flower

MAKE-UP POT
Many make-up pots are works of art. This one is made from the rare blue stone anhydrite.

Gold trim

GOLDEN GIRDLE
This is part of a piece of jewellery that was worn around the waist. It is strung with colourful beads of carnelian, amethyst, lapis lazuli, and turquoise, plus gold good-luck charms.

COSMETIC PALETTE
This make-up container is carved and painted to look like a bunch of flowers. The buds are circles of ivory, dyed a soft pink. The swivelling top hides a hollow where cosmetic cream was stored.

BRACELET
Cobras protect the sky god Horus on this bracelet made for a prince.

Top swivels sideways

Polished metal surface

Handle in shape of serving girl

Glass container with applicator

Lotus-style headdress

Duck   *Leaves*

METAL MIRROR
The Egyptians did not have glass mirrors. Instead, they admired their reflections in polished discs of copper or bronze. The bright, shining surfaces reminded the Egyptians of the sun they worshipped.

MAKE-UP FOR EYES
Kohl was kept in pots and applied with thin metal tools. Even children wore *kohl*, which also protected against eye infections.

59

SCHOOLING AND WRITING

MOST EGYPTIAN CHILDREN did not go to school. To be a goldsmith or a painter, a boy trained in a workshop or with a team of workers building a tomb. Scribes were given a more formal education, starting at age nine and lasting about five years. They had to study hard and were beaten if they were lazy. But it was worth it – scribes were among the only people who could read or write, and this gave them status.

Layers placed at right angles

MAKING PAPYRUS
Paper was made from papyrus reed. The soft pith was cut into strips, placed in two layers, then pounded together to form a strong sheet.

Hieratic text always reads right to left

THREE SCRIPTS
Egyptian picture-writings are called hieroglyphs, the Greek word for "sacred carvings". Scribes later developed two other scripts, hieratic and demotic, which were much quicker to write.

Hieroglyphs read either left to right or right to left. They were written downwards in columns or in horizontal lines

When figures face left, reader starts on left-hand side

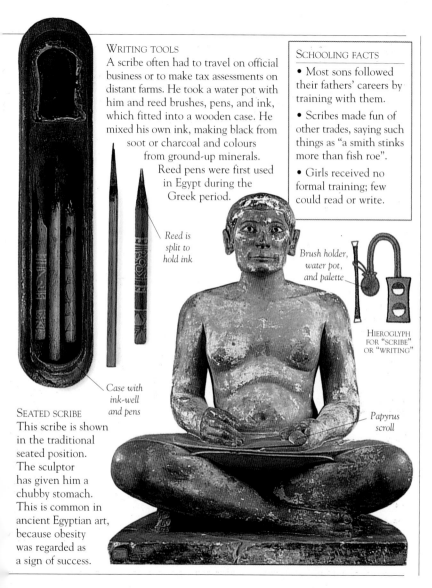

WRITING TOOLS

A scribe often had to travel on official business or to make tax assessments on distant farms. He took a water pot with him and reed brushes, pens, and ink, which fitted into a wooden case. He mixed his own ink, making black from soot or charcoal and colours from ground-up minerals. Reed pens were first used in Egypt during the Greek period.

Reed is split to hold ink

SCHOOLING FACTS

• Most sons followed their fathers' careers by training with them.

• Scribes made fun of other trades, saying such things as "a smith stinks more than fish roe".

• Girls received no formal training; few could read or write.

Brush holder, water pot, and palette

HIEROGLYPH FOR "SCRIBE" OR "WRITING"

Case with ink-well and pens

Papyrus scroll

SEATED SCRIBE

This scribe is shown in the traditional seated position. The sculptor has given him a chubby stomach. This is common in ancient Egyptian art, because obesity was regarded as a sign of success.

Deciphering hieroglyphs

For nearly 1,500 years, no one could read hieroglyphs, the ancient Egyptian picture-writing. The French scholar Jean-François Champollion spent most of his life trying to break the code. He made his first breakthrough in 1822, while studying the Rosetta Stone, and soon experts were able to read the inscriptions that cover many Egyptian artefacts.

The text is a message of thanks to Pharaoh Ptolemy V

Demotic

The loop represents eternity

ROYAL NAMES

A pharaoh's name was written inside an oval loop called a cartouche. This piece of jewellery contains the cartouche of Senusret II.

Sa	Ankh	N	Ra	Nefer
Son	Life	Water	Day	Beautiful

PICTURES FOR WORDS AND SOUNDS

One hieroglyph can stand for either a word or a sound. For instance, a scribe would draw a goose both for the sound "sa" and the word "son".

A name of a pharaoh can be recognized because it is written within a cartouche

Hieroglyphs

JEAN-FRANÇOIS CHAMPOLLION (1790–1832)
A brilliant linguist, Champollion had mastered 12 languages by age 16. The first hieroglyphs he deciphered were pharaohs' names. By 1824, he had translated most of the symbols and begun to unravel Egyptian grammar.

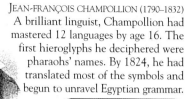

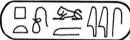

"PTOLEMY" IN HIEROGLYPHS

"PTOLEMY" IN DEMOTIC

ΠΤΟΛΕΜΑΙΟΣ

"PTOLEMY" IN GREEK

THE ROSETTA STONE
Inscribed in 196 B.C., the Rosetta Stone was unearthed again in 1799. The text is repeated in hieroglyphs, demotic, and Greek. Champollion could read Greek, and so he used this text to translate the other two scripts.

CRACKING THE CODE
The English physicist Thomas Young was the first to recognize the hieroglyphs for Ptolemy and Cleopatra on the Rosetta Stone. But Champollion made the great breakthrough when he realized that some symbols stood for ideas while others were simply sounds.

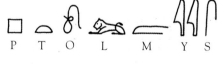

P T O L M Y S

K L E O P A T R A

Greek

The Stone is a slab of black basalt, found near Rosetta in the delta

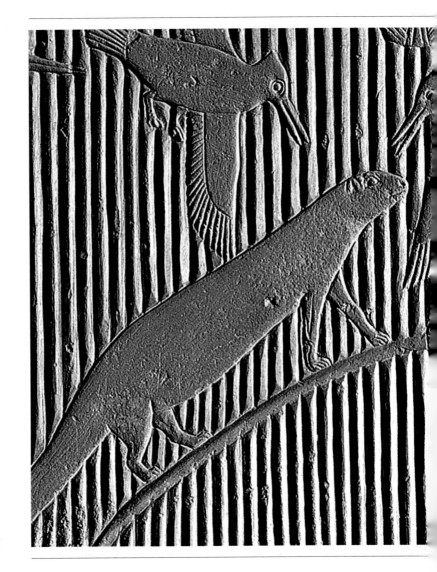

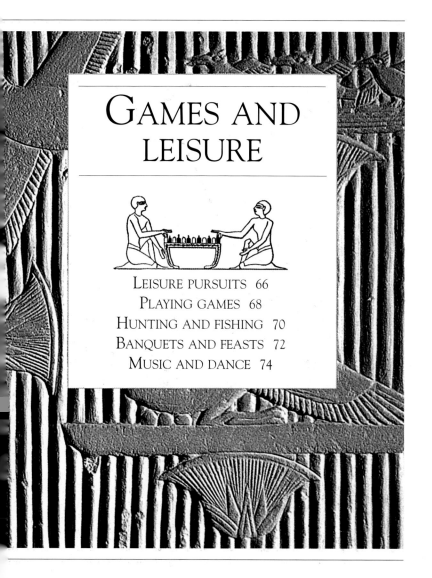

GAMES AND LEISURE

LEISURE PURSUITS

THE EGYPTIANS LIVED LIFE to the full. At public festivals and private parties they feasted and drank, entertained by singers, dancers, and musicians. Children played out in the sunshine, while adults revelled in sports like hunting and fishing. In quieter moments they wrote poetry or enjoyed board-games.

ANGLING
Egyptians were the first people to fish for pure pleasure. Nobles are often shown in armchairs, lazily dangling lines into their well-stocked garden pools.

ENTERTAINERS AT A BANQUET
Party scenes show how much the Egyptians liked music and dance. In this tomb painting, c.1400 B.C., one woman plays a double flute while others clap along or dance to the beat. In Egyptian art, it is very unusual to see faces front on.

LEISURE FACTS

• Egyptians swam backstroke and crawl. Upper-class children were given lessons.

• Farmworkers and fishermen had their own working songs.

• Festival revellers sailing on Nile barges sometimes "mooned" the crowd on the shore.

STONE THROWER
This is the earliest known example of a sling. It dates from about 1900 B.C. and was found in the town of Kahun in the Faiyum Oasis. The sling was probably used to scare birds away from Kahun's vineyards and lush gardens. One end of the cord was looped around a finger to keep hold of the sling after firing.

Woven cord

Loop for finger

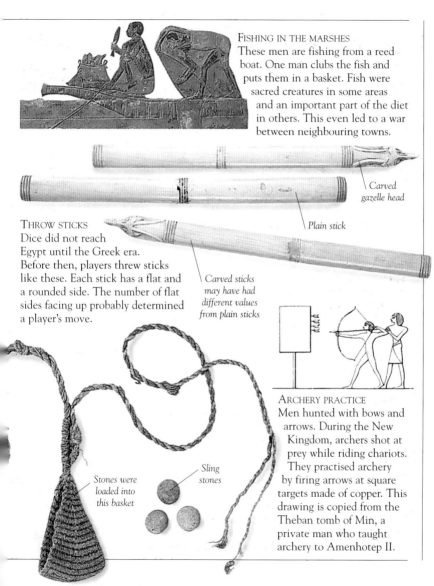

FISHING IN THE MARSHES
These men are fishing from a reed boat. One man clubs the fish and puts them in a basket. Fish were sacred creatures in some areas and an important part of the diet in others. This even led to a war between neighbouring towns.

Carved gazelle head

Plain stick

THROW STICKS
Dice did not reach Egypt until the Greek era. Before then, players threw sticks like these. Each stick has a flat and a rounded side. The number of flat sides facing up probably determined a player's move.

Carved sticks may have had different values from plain sticks

ARCHERY PRACTICE
Men hunted with bows and arrows. During the New Kingdom, archers shot at prey while riding chariots. They practised archery by firing arrows at square targets made of copper. This drawing is copied from the Theban tomb of Min, a private man who taught archery to Amenhotep II.

Stones were loaded into this basket

Sling stones

PLAYING GAMES

IN THE WARM EGYPTIAN CLIMATE, boys and girls spent a lot of time outdoors, swimming, dancing, riding donkeys, and enjoying games of leapfrog and tug-of-war. They played with balls, dolls, toy animals, and pets such as cats, birds, and monkeys. The most popular board-game for adults was called senet. Tutankhamun liked it so much he was buried with four complete boards.

TOPS
Children spun these pottery tops with a twist of the fingers or a quick tug on a piece of string wrapped round the toy.

CLAY BALLS
Balls made of papyrus, cloth, and leather have all been found. These brightly painted clay balls were once filled with seeds or tiny lumps of clay to make them rattle when thrown.

String to move lower jaw

CAT TOY
Pulling the string on this carved wooden cat makes it open and close its mouth. Other ancient animal toys have glass eyes, movable legs and arms, and tails that wag.

CATCHING AND JUGGLING
This scene is copied from a Middle Kingdom tomb. These jugglers may have been professionals or people playing for fun or ritual.

HORSES AND MUMMIES

This wooden horse could be pulled along with a string through its nose. Nile mud animals, birds, and even tiny mummies lying in their coffins have been found. These may be toys made by children or votive offerings.

Senet

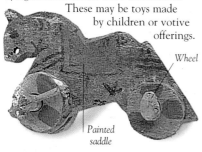

Wheel

Painted saddle

A GAME OF SENET

Senet was played by moving counters on a board of 30 squares – some were dangerous to land on, others were lucky. Unfortunately, the rules have been lost.

Fighting with wooden sticks

TOURNAMENTS

Men competed in games of boxing, wrestling, and fencing. King Ramses III held the first recorded fencing tournament in *c*.1250 B.C. Egyptian and allied soldiers fought with wooden sticks.

SNAKE GAME

This was one of the earliest Egyptian board-games. The playing surface is the shape of a coiled snake. Players started at the tip of the tail and tried to move balls towards the snake's head at the centre.

Winning position

Hieroglyph of pharaoh's name

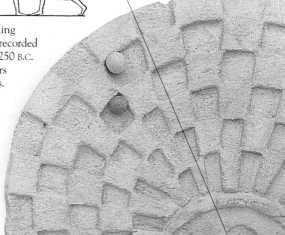

HUNTING AND FISHING

THE MAIN SPORT for well-to-do Egyptians was hunting. In early times, nobles stalked antelope, bulls, and lions on foot; later they hunted from horse-drawn chariots. Pharaohs were proud of their kills. Amenhotep III boasted of 102 lions in ten years as king, and Thutmose III claimed 120 elephants during one trip to Syria.

MAN WITH ANTELOPE
A man returns from the hunt. Trained dogs or even hyenas were used to catch antelope or to chase them into traps.

HUNTING WITH NETS
Marsh hunters netted both fish and wild-fowl. They snared birds by baiting nets with corn or maggots.

FISHING FROM RAFTS
Egyptians fished for food and fun. During the Old Kingdom, fish were usually netted or speared. Later, angling became popular. The fishermen in this tomb relief are using hooks and nets to catch the fish.

Papyrus thicket

Throwing stick

Wife

Duck decoy

Daughter steadies raft

HUNTING HYENAS

Hyenas got into game reserves and were killed along with animals kept there as quarry. They were also hunted as a menace to domestic flocks.

FOWLING

Nobles preferred to hunt birds with a throwing stick. It was like a boomerang and killed a bird by breaking its neck. This man has brought his family, including pet cat, on the hunt.

HIPPO HUNTING

These three men are spearing hippos from a papyrus raft. Spearheads were attached to long pieces of rope, so that the dying hippo could be hauled onto land.

71

LUTIST
Hosts hired
musicians to
play and sing
at the feast.

BANQUETS AND FEASTS

EGYPTIANS HELD FEASTS to celebrate births, marriages, and religious festivals, or just to entertain friends. The wealthy enjoyed holding dinner parties. Cooks prepared a huge meal, flavoured with imported herbs and spices. Dressed in their best clothes, guests sat on chairs or cushions on the floor, eating food with their fingers and drinking large quantities of wine.

Acrobat

Wine amphorae

Food is piled high on tables

AFTER-DINNER ENTERTAINMENT
Dinner parties were one of the main sources of employment for dancers, acrobats, and other entertainers. They performed after the meal was finished.

NEW KINGDOM BANQUET
This scene shows Egyptian hospitality at a dinner party. An army of servants ply the guests with food, wine, and presents.

TOO DRUNK TO WALK
Guests sometimes drank too much; some even vomited into bowls. These drunk men are being carried home from a party.

FOOD FOR THE FEAST
Pictures showing food offerings give us a good idea of the types of foods that wealthy hosts could serve their guests.

Scantily clad serving girl

Pleated clothes

Necklace presented as gift

Married couples sit arm in arm

Chair legs shaped like lions' paws

Incense cones

Servants offer wine and lotus flowers to guests

This group of women sitting together are probably unmarried

MUSIC AND DANCE

NO EGYPTIAN CELEBRATION would have been complete without music and dancing. At parties, singers performed to the music of harps, lutes, drums, flutes, and tambourines. Festival crowds chanted and clapped, carried along by the vibrant rhythm of Egyptian orchestras, while dancers leapt and twirled. Work, too, was often accompanied by music.

WOMAN PLAYING THE HARP
This model of a harpist was placed in a tomb to entertain guests at parties in the afterlife. In tomb pictures, harpists are often blind men.

SINGING ALONG
Singing played an important role in Egyptian music. These young women sing and dance, while beating tambourines and hand-held drums.

Double crown of Egypt

CYMBALS
We do not know how Egyptian music sounded because it was never written down. The people played a wide range of instruments, suggesting that their music was varied. These bronze cymbals were used for rhythm and beat.

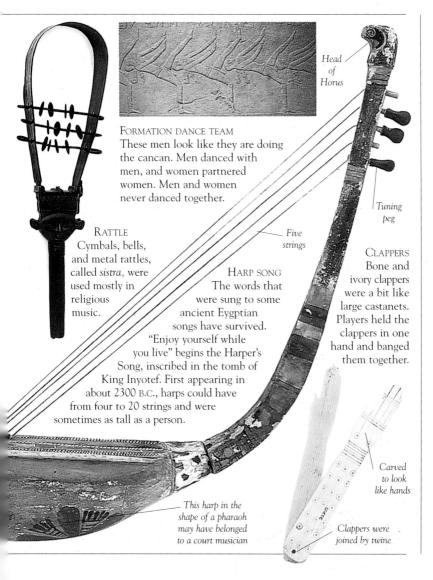

Head of Horus

Tuning peg

FORMATION DANCE TEAM
These men look like they are doing the cancan. Men danced with men, and women partnered women. Men and women never danced together.

RATTLE
Cymbals, bells, and metal rattles, called *sistra*, were used mostly in religious music.

Five strings

HARP SONG
The words that were sung to some ancient Eygptian songs have survived. "Enjoy yourself while you live" begins the Harper's Song, inscribed in the tomb of King Inyotef. First appearing in about 2300 B.C., harps could have from four to 20 strings and were sometimes as tall as a person.

CLAPPERS
Bone and ivory clappers were a bit like large castanets. Players held the clappers in one hand and banged them together.

Carved to look like hands

This harp in the shape of a pharaoh may have belonged to a court musician

Clappers were joined by twine

75

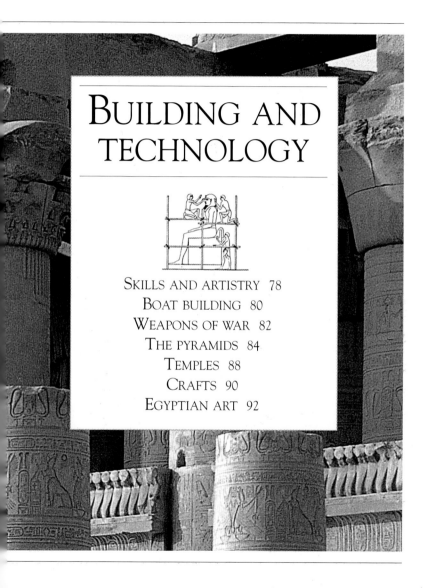

BUILDING AND TECHNOLOGY

SKILLS AND ARTISTRY

THE ANCIENT EGYPTIANS were very practical people. The great pyramids, tombs, and temples that still stand today show how they had mastered many architectural and engineering problems. These monuments were built and decorated by teams of skilled craftsmen, who worked year round for the pharaoh.

PLUMB LINE
Tools like this were used to make sure lines were vertical and to create grids for painting and carving on walls.

MUD BRICK

USING A MOULD
Wooden tomb models show scenes of ancient Egyptians at work. This man is busy moulding a mud brick.

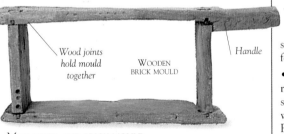

Wood joints hold mould together

WOODEN BRICK MOULD

Handle

MUD BRICK AND BRICK MOULD
The Egyptians built most of their buildings with bricks. Workmen used moulds like this to shape a mixture of Nile mud, sand, and straw. Bricks were not fired, just left to dry in the hot sun.

TECHNOLOGY FACTS

• Pharaoh Khafra had 23 life-size statues of himself made for just one temple.

• The first strike in recorded history was staged by craftsmen working in the tomb of Ramses III in 1150 B.C.

• The new capital at Amarna was the first planned city in history.

78

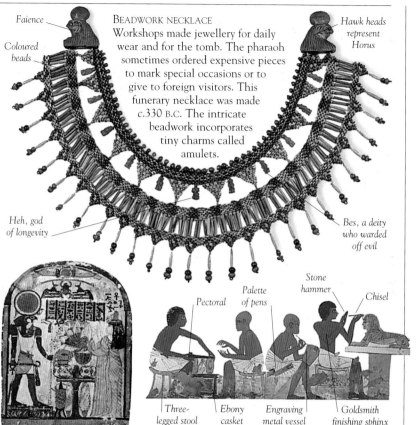

BEADWORK NECKLACE

Workshops made jewellery for daily wear and for the tomb. The pharaoh sometimes ordered expensive pieces to mark special occasions or to give to foreign visitors. This funerary necklace was made c.330 B.C. The intricate beadwork incorporates tiny charms called amulets.

Faience

Coloured beads

Hawk heads represent Horus

Heh, god of longevity

Bes, a deity who warded off evil

Pectoral

Palette of pens

Stone hammer

Chisel

Three-legged stool

Ebony casket

Engraving metal vessel

Goldsmith finishing sphinx

TOMB ART

Some of the greatest art was made for the tombs of kings and nobles. On this wooden funerary stela, a priestess raises her hands in adoration of Ra-Horakhty the falcon-headed sun god.

METALWORK

There are many paintings of craft workshops. In this detail, two jewellers finish a pectoral (pendant) and place it in a casket. To the right, a man engraves an inscription, while another is working on a golden sphinx. Other scenes in the same tomb show controllers weighing gold and checking finished articles. In reality, this workshop must have been noisy, dirty, and very hot.

79

BOAT BUILDING

EGYPT'S HIGHWAY was the Nile. Everything from grain and cattle to coffins and building stone was transported by water. Only the best boats were wooden, because wood was very rare. Most travellers and fishermen punted through the shallows on rafts made from bundles of reeds.

ADZE
Blade

STEERING OAR
The Egyptians steered their boats with special oars mounted on the stern (back). This brightly painted example was found in a boat pit near the pyramid of the pharaoh Senusret III (c.1850 B.C.). The Eye of Horus was a symbol of protection.

String

Bow

BOW DRILL

Drill bit

WOODWORKING TOOLS
A carpenter's tools have changed little since ancient Egyptian times. Saws, chisels, and axes have all been found. This adze was used for hacking and planing, while the bow drill bored holes for pegging pieces of wood together.

Man uses adze to smooth hull

CARPENTERS AT WORK
Boat building is an ancient craft. This tomb scene from Saqqara dates from about 2300 B.C. The Egyptians had not yet discovered iron, and all tools and pegs were made of copper and wood.

Sun canopy

Attendant

Mummy

Oars

MODEL BOAT
Egyptians put model boats in tombs in the belief that the boat would carry the dead person's mummy to the afterlife.

Prow carved to look like a bundle of papyrus

Five pairs of oars

Priest

Steersman

Royal cabin

Steering oars

Stern

KHUFU'S BOAT
The best preserved boat is the funeral barge of King Khufu. It was found in 1954 in a sealed pit next to his tomb, the Great Pyramid at Giza. Made from 651 pieces of cedar, the boat is 43.5 m (143 ft) long.

NILE SAILBOAT

SEA-GOING SHIP

SAILING
Large sails were used to travel upriver against the current. Going downriver, the sail was dropped and the boat was rowed.

CARGO BOAT

WEAPONS OF WAR

THE ARMIES of the Old and Middle Kingdoms were small, and citizens were often called up to fight. In the New Kingdom, a more professional, permanent army was established, with corps of infantry, scouts, and marines. Chariots held two soldiers; one handled the horses and the other fired arrows at the enemy.

LONG SWORD

SHORT SWORD

DAGGER

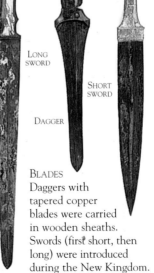

GODDESS OF WAR
War goddess Sekhmet has a lion's head and a woman's body. She was said to stand by the pharaoh in battle, armed with arrows "with which she pierces hearts".

BLADES
Daggers with tapered copper blades were carried in wooden sheaths. Swords (first short, then long) were introduced during the New Kingdom.

FIGHTING FORMATION
Foot soldiers trained to fight in strict formation, moving together and presenting the enemy with a wall of shields. These soldiers wear kilts and carry spears.

ARROWHEADS

For thousands of years arrowheads were made from stone (especially flint), bone, or the hardwood ebony. Bronze was not used until c.1800 B.C.

FLINT HEADS

BRONZE HEADS

CHARIOTS

Introduced from the Middle East in c.1650 B.C., chariots revolutionized warfare. Here, Tutankhamun fires arrows at Nubian enemies from the raised platform of his chariot.

ARCHER

Massed units of archers led the assault. On foot or riding in chariots, they showered the enemy with arrows. Many archers came from Nubia, which Egyptians called "the Land of the Bow".

SILVER SHAFTED AXE

CEREMONIAL AXE

AXES

Battle-axes were used all across the Middle East. The ceremonial axe was probably awarded to a warrior for bravery.

ARCHER'S AID

An archer wore this guard on the wrist of his bow hand to protect himself from the lash of the bowstring.

SOLDIER ON HORSE

The army relied on charioteers rather than on a cavalry. This rare picture is from the Greek era.

BATTLE AXE

MERCENARIES

The Egyptians supplemented their own forces by relying on foreign mercenaries, who were allowed to retain their own weapons and costumes.

GIZA

▲ TRUE PYRAMID
▲ BENT PYRAMID
▲ STEP PYRAMID

THE PYRAMIDS

ALREADY ANCIENT by Tutankhamun's times, the Pyramids of Giza have awed people ever since they were built – more than 4,500 years ago. Pyramids are tombs made to house the mummies of kings. Their massive size and the precision of their construction are amazing.

ALL THE PYRAMIDS
The biggest and best-preserved pyramids are the three at Giza. There are more than 80 others in Egypt – mostly ruins, all but buried by shifting desert sands. The first pyramids had stepped or bent sides. Then came the classic (true) shape.

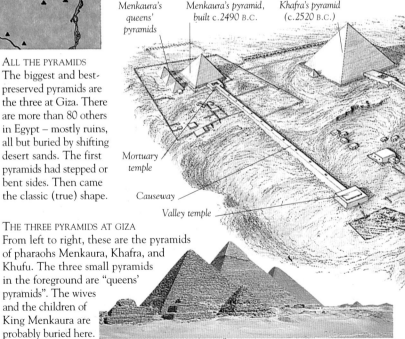

Menkaura's queens' pyramids

Menkaura's pyramid, built c.2490 B.C.

Khafra's pyramid (c.2520 B.C.)

Mortuary temple

Causeway

Valley temple

THE THREE PYRAMIDS AT GIZA
From left to right, these are the pyramids of pharaohs Menkaura, Khafra, and Khufu. The three small pyramids in the foreground are "queens' pyramids". The wives and the children of King Menkaura are probably buried here.

THE SPHINX

This massive stone figure of a lion with the head of a king crouches before the pyramid complex at Giza. The Sphinx's face is believed to be a likeness of pharaoh Khafra.

PYRAMID FACTS

• The Pyramids of Giza are one of the seven wonders of the ancient world and the only one still standing.

• The four sides of the Great Pyramid are aligned exactly with true north, south, east, and west.

• A dream told Thutmose IV to free the Sphinx from the sands that buried it.

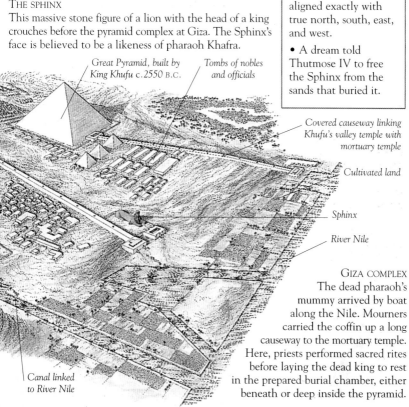

Great Pyramid, built by King Khufu c.2550 B.C.

Tombs of nobles and officials

Covered causeway linking Khufu's valley temple with mortuary temple

Cultivated land

Sphinx

River Nile

Canal linked to River Nile

GIZA COMPLEX

The dead pharaoh's mummy arrived by boat along the Nile. Mourners carried the coffin up a long causeway to the mortuary temple. Here, priests performed sacred rites before laying the dead king to rest in the prepared burial chamber, either beneath or deep inside the pyramid.

How were pyramids built?

Egyptologists estimate that it took 100,000 men 20 years to build the Great Pyramid at Giza. But how was it built? The most popular theory is that workers slid the massive blocks of stone up ramps onto the pyramid. As little real evidence exists, we will probably never know for sure.

SQUARING OFF
One tomb painting shows masons using chisels and mallets to smooth down blocks of stone.

RAMPS OR LIFTING MACHINES?
An ancient Greek traveller wrote that workers had used lifting machines to raise stones. But he was told this 2,000 years after the pyramids were built. Ramps are less work and so more likely.

Four times as many men

WERE THE PYRAMIDS BUILT LIKE THIS?
This model illustrates how the Egyptians may have built the pyramids. Workers unload the stone blocks from boats, then slide them up a long ramp to the top of the pyramid.

Mud-brick ramp is built higher as pyramid grows

Stacks of stone blocks

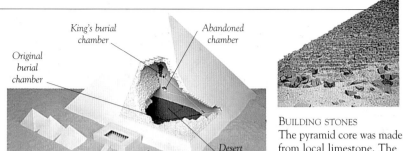

King's burial chamber

Abandoned chamber

Original burial chamber

Desert bedrock

INSIDE THE GREAT PYRAMID
A complex network of passages and dead-end chambers lies within Khufu's pyramid. Workers sealed the shaft leading to the burial chamber with huge blocks of stone.

BUILDING STONES
The pyramid core was made from local limestone. The outer layer – mostly gone now – was high-quality limestone brought by boat from Tura on the east side of the Nile, south of Giza.

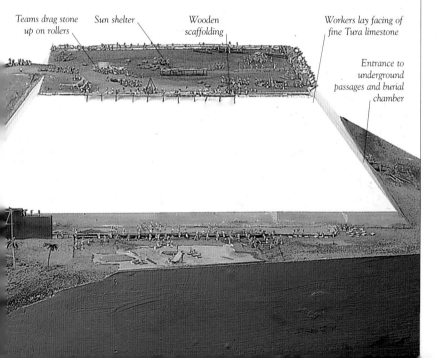

Teams drag stone up on rollers

Sun shelter

Wooden scaffolding

Workers lay facing of fine Tura limestone

Entrance to underground passages and burial chamber

TEMPLES

EGYPTIAN TEMPLES were awesome structures with massive stone walls and rows of columns carved with hieroglyphs and religious images. A temple was the home of a god. Ordinary people could only enter the outer court. In dark rooms at the temple's heart, priests performed sacred rituals.

TEMPLE OF LUXOR
Ramses the Great enlarged this temple and added two obelisks and six colossal statues.

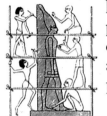

KING-SIZE SCULPTURE
Sculptors used wooden scaffolding to carve the towering statues of kings. Only the pharaoh could be shown as large as the gods in temple statues.

SON OF THE SUN GOD
The pharaoh was believed to be the son of sun god Amun. This "Birth Room" at Luxor Temple has a series of carvings that illustrate Amenhotep III's divine birth.

Elevated roof

Papyrus-shaped columns

Pictures of gods

COLOSSI OF MEMNON
These giant figures are all that is left of the temple of Amenhotep III, the biggest ever built. A stela records that it was "inlaid with gold throughout, its floors paved with silver".

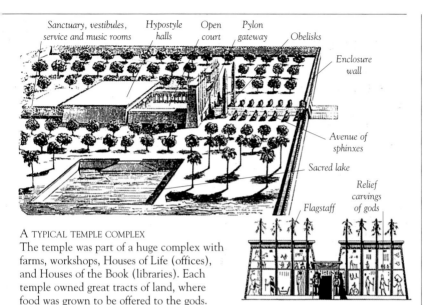

Sanctuary, vestibules, service and music rooms — Hypostyle halls — Open court — Pylon gateway — Obelisks — Enclosure wall — Avenue of sphinxes — Sacred lake — Relief carvings of gods — Flagstaff

A TYPICAL TEMPLE COMPLEX

The temple was part of a huge complex with farms, workshops, Houses of Life (offices), and Houses of the Book (libraries). Each temple owned great tracts of land, where food was grown to be offered to the gods.

PYLON GATEWAY

People entered the temple through a pylon gateway, which was often flanked with seated statues and obelisks. High above, on wooden flagstaffs, flew the gods' flags.

Hall contained 134 columns

HYPOSTYLE HALL AT KARNAK TEMPLE

This powerful temple owned land all over Egypt, and its priests virtually ruled the country at several periods. This is a reconstruction of Karnak's Great Hypostyle Hall. A temple symbolized the creation of the world, which is why the hall's cluster of columns were shaped like plants.

89

CRAFTS

IN LARGE WORKSHOPS, skilled craftsmen made pots, carved wood to make mummy cases and furniture, cured hides to produce leather, and worked metal and glass to make jewellery and everyday items such as magic amulets, tools, bowls, and even early drainpipes.

Glazed with bright pattern

STRIPED GLASS VESSEL
Glass beads were made before the pharaohs. But glass was not mass-produced until c.1400 B.C. The glass was not blown, so vessels were uneven.

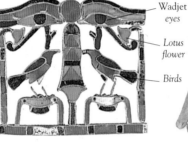

Wadjet eyes

Lotus flower

Birds

Antelope's head

GOLD PECTORAL
The finest jewellery was made in royal workshops. This gold pectoral – a large pendant worn on the chest – is inlaid with gemstones and coloured glass.

IVORY ANTELOPE
From predynastic times, the Egyptians used ivory from elephants and hippos to carve a variety of everyday objects. These carvings were often shaped to fit the cylindrical shape of the tusk or tooth. This skilfully crafted toilet dish was made in about 1300 B.C.

POTTERY WORKSHOP
By Old Kingdom times, pots were being made on potters' wheels. After a few days drying in the sun, pots were smoothed and then fired in kilns.

FORMING
LIP OF CUP

SHAPING
OUTER SURFACE

CUTTING CUP
FROM CLAY BASE

STARTING
A NEW CUP

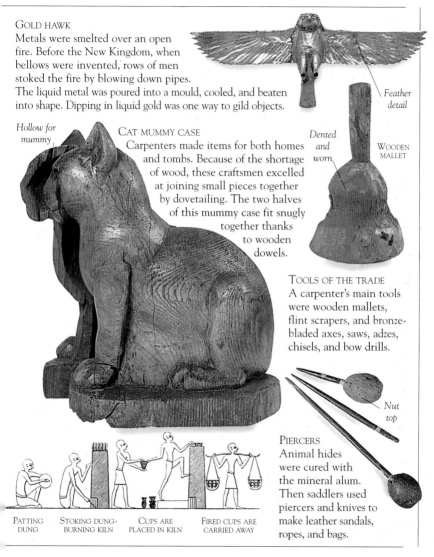

GOLD HAWK
Metals were smelted over an open fire. Before the New Kingdom, when bellows were invented, rows of men stoked the fire by blowing down pipes. The liquid metal was poured into a mould, cooled, and beaten into shape. Dipping in liquid gold was one way to gild objects.

Feather detail

Hollow for mummy

CAT MUMMY CASE
Carpenters made items for both homes and tombs. Because of the shortage of wood, these craftsmen excelled at joining small pieces together by dovetailing. The two halves of this mummy case fit snugly together thanks to wooden dowels.

Dented and worn

WOODEN MALLET

TOOLS OF THE TRADE
A carpenter's main tools were wooden mallets, flint scrapers, and bronze-bladed axes, saws, adzes, chisels, and bow drills.

Nut top

PIERCERS
Animal hides were cured with the mineral alum. Then saddlers used piercers and knives to make leather sandals, ropes, and bags.

PATTING DUNG | STOKING DUNG-BURNING KILN | CUPS ARE PLACED IN KILN | FIRED CUPS ARE CARRIED AWAY

EGYPTIAN ART

THE BEAUTIFUL ART of ancient Egypt was produced by teams of anonymous painters and sculptors. They worked in tombs, temples, palaces, and houses. Their art is highly stylized; figures are almost always depicted in formal poses, and it is difficult to recognize individuals because most subjects are given perfect features.

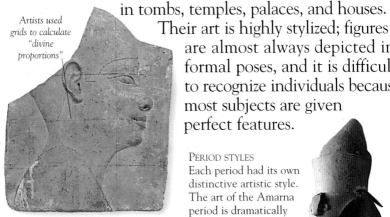

Artists used grids to calculate "divine proportions"

GRIDLINES
Artists began by drawing a grid. Then they sketched in figures and objects, scaled up from examples in pattern books. Master designers checked and made corrections before work began.

PERIOD STYLES
Each period had its own distinctive artistic style. The art of the Amarna period is dramatically different. This statue of King Akhenaten has the heavy hips and long, oddly distorted face that are typical of the time.

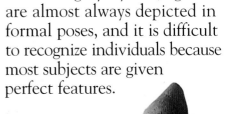

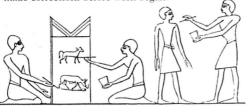

IN A PAINTER'S WORKSHOP
Painters worked on wooden panels or straight onto statues or walls. They applied the paint in flat blocks of colour, with no shading or gradations of tone.

SOME CHARACTERISTICS OF EGYPTIAN ART

Artists portrayed everything in its most recognizable form. For example, the human body was shown in profile, but the eyes and chest were face forwards. Hieroglyphs were like a caption to the picture.

SKETCHING

Artists worked out ideas with scale models or rough sketches on ostraca (fragments of stone or broken pottery).

ART FACTS

• Tools and paints were so precious that foremen issued them each morning and locked them away at night.

• Fragments of a gigantic statue were found at Tanis. The big toe is the size of a man.

MUMMY CASE

The imagery of religious art had deep meaning to the Egyptians. The gods and symbols painted on mummy cases and tombs were to help the dead avoid the dangers of the underworld.

93

Sculpture and carvings

Ancient Egypt was rich in stone, and sculpture was the most important artform. Copper or bronze tools were used to carve softer materials like limestone and fine woods. These could then be coated with a plaster mixture called *gesso* and painted in bright colours. Hard stone, such as granite, was carved with pounders made of stone. Metal was cast or else beaten into shape.

RAISED RELIEF
This is an example of raised relief, in which the background is cut away to leave the figures raised above the surface.

Ready for crown

Drawn guidelines

SUNK RELIEF
In sunk relief, the outlines of the figures are first gouged out. Then the details within each figure are modelled at various depths. This is a sunk relief of Pharaoh Thutmose III (c.1450 B.C.).

THE FACE OF QUEEN NEFERTITI
Unfinished statues give us many clues about the way sculptors worked. This half-finished bust, marked with guidelines, was found in the ruins of a workshop in the abandoned city of Amarna.

TWO HEADS OF KING USERKAF

Each stone has its own qualities, making it suitable for certain purposes. Here are two heads of the same king. The colossal one is carved in granite, the smaller one in schist.

Pink speckled Aswan granite

LOST WAX METHOD

This bronze figure of King Thutmose IV was made by the lost wax method. The figure was modelled in beeswax. This was then coated in clay and heated until the wax melted. Finally, liquid metal was poured into the clay mould.

Eyes are set in copper

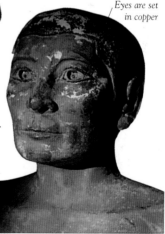

LOOKING LIFE-LIKE

Some statues have inset eyes. This man's eyes are made from calcite with brown obsidian irises. The effect is so life-like that the eyes seem to follow you around a room. This is the head of the seated scribe, shown on page 61.

GRANITE PHARAOH

Kings' statues were usually carved from hard stone, as they were made to last. This 3,500-year-old granite statue of King Sobkemsaf proves that they did.

RELIGION

WORSHIP AND BELIEFS

LIKE OTHER ANCIENT PEOPLE, Egyptians believed that all events were controlled by the gods. By wearing amulets (lucky charms) and giving offerings to the gods, the Egyptians hoped for a happy life. They also hoped the gods would help them to live on after death.

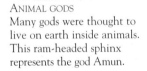

ANIMAL GODS
Many gods were thought to live on earth inside animals. This ram-headed sphinx represents the god Amun.

PROTECTED BY THE GODS
This mummy case is covered in images of gods and magic symbols meant to help the dead person in the afterlife. A Greek wrote that Egyptians were "religious beyond measure, more than any other nation".

Spell for the soul of the dead person

Tomb

Mummy is made ready for the tomb

REPRESENTING THE PHARAOH
The gods were kept happy by priests, who made offerings and conducted rituals in the name of the pharaoh, the sun god's representative on earth. Here, priests perform rights to help the dead person achieve eternal life.

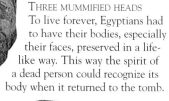

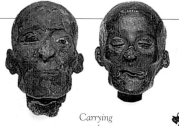

THREE MUMMIFIED HEADS
To live forever, Egyptians had to have their bodies, especially their faces, preserved in a life-like way. This way the spirit of a dead person could recognize its body when it returned to the tomb.

Servant with fan

Carrying pole

CARRIED AWAY
A rich man was buried with this model of a sedan chair carried by three porters. He expected them to come to life after his tomb was sealed.

FACTS ABOUT RELIGION
• The sacred Apis Bull was treated like a god, kept in a luxurious part of the temple, fed the best food, and buried like a pharaoh when it died.
• Many Egyptians were buried with 365 *shabti* figures – one to help on each day of the year.

VIEW OF HEAVEN
In the ideal world shown on his funerary stela, Iy smells flowers with his family. The stela would keep his name alive as he lived these scenes in the afterlife.

MYTHS AND LEGENDS

THE EGYPTIAN CREATION STORY has many versions – most begin in an ocean of chaos. There were hundreds of other myths and legends. But because everyone knew the stories, they were never written down, and few have survived. Luckily, the story of god-king Osiris and his victory over death was recorded by a Greek writer.

ATUM

IN THE BEGINNING
One creation myth tells of a time when Nun, the eternal ocean, filled the universe. When the waters subsided a primeval hill appeared, on which stood the creator god – the sun god Atum.

Isis nurses the infant Horus, her son by Osiris

THE GODS ARE CREATED
Atum's children, Shu (air) and Tefnut (moisture) created Geb (earth) and Nut (sky). At first Geb and Nut were joined, but Shu came between them – so separating heaven and earth. Geb and Nut had four children – Osiris, Seth, Isis, and Nephthys.

ISIS AND HORUS
Osiris became king and took sister Isis as his queen. Jealous brother Seth killed Osiris and cut up the body. Isis collected the pieces and made them into the first mummy. Osiris lived on as god of the underworld.

Corn, not a body, fills the bandages

Wadjet Eye amulets were placed on mummies

WADJET EYE
When he grew up, Horus set out to avenge his father's death. Eventually, he vanquished Seth and took the throne. But in their many fights he lost an eye. This Eye of Horus, or *Wadjet* Eye, became a symbol of victory over evil.

MURDER OF A BROTHER
Seth held a banquet where he showed off a beautiful casket, saying he would give it to whoever fitted inside. When Osiris climbed in, Seth locked it and threw it in the Nile. Isis found the casket, but Seth seized it and cut up Osiris' body.

OSIRIS
This is a corn mummy in the shape of Osiris. At first he was a fertility god, responsible for the floods that brought new life to Egypt every year. As the first king to survive death, he became a god of rebirth.

SACRED SHAPES
According to legend, the rays of the sun fell first of all upon the primeval mound, or *ben-ben*. This sacred shape was recreated in obelisks and may have been the reason for the structure of pyramids.

SUN TEMPLE

101

THE SUN GODS

SOURCE OF ALL HEAT AND LIGHT, the sun was worshipped from earliest times. This life-giving force took many forms, each represented by a different god or personality. The rising sun was a scarab beetle; at noon it was Ra, the orange disc itself; while in the evening it took the form of a ram. Satirical literary texts depict the setting sun as a dribbling, decrepit old man.

AMUN-RA
During the New Kingdom, power moved to Thebes in the south. Theban priests merged their local god Amun, a creator god, with the powerful sun god Ra. Throughout the land, Egyptians worshipped Amun-Ra as chief god.

Akhenaten and his family worship Aten

AKHENATEN, THE SUN KING
To break the power of the Theban priesthood, King Amenhotep IV banned all gods but Aten, the sun in its purest form. It was depicted as a disc with rays that touched with human hands. The king changed his name to Akhenaten and built a new city dedicated to Aten at Amarna.

WINGED SCARAB

The scarab is a beetle that rolls up balls of dung to lay its eggs inside. Egyptians believed that a giant scarab made the sun in the same way and then rolled it over the horizon and across the sky.

Scarab god clasps the sun in its claws

Prayers to the sun god

SAILING THROUGH THE NIGHT

When the sun set in the West, the Egyptians believed it sailed through the underworld on a boat before rising again in the East. Here, the god Nun steers the boat safely through the waters of chaos.

IMHOTEP

The cult of the sun began at Heliopolis. Here, King Djoser's chief minister Imhotep designed the first pyramid – possibly as a stairway, so the dead pharaoh could join the sun god in the sky.

SUN STRUCK

Heliopolis means "Sun City". In its temple, priests kept a triangular stone, the *ben-ben* – believed to be the first object struck by the sun's rays when the world was created. This tomb cap is carved in the same magical shape.

RA-HARAKHTY

Sun gods are usually depicted with the disc of the sun on their heads. The god on the far right is Ra-Harakhty, a falcon-headed sun god and a version of the sky god Horus.

103

GODS AND GODDESSES

EGYPTIANS HAD A DIZZYING number of gods – one ancient text lists 740. But only a small number were worshipped in the same place at the same time. All the forces of nature were represented by gods or goddesses. Temples were dedicated to state gods or important local deities and controlled by an elite priesthood. Ordinary people were excluded.

Ptah is depicted with a tight skull cap pulled over his shaven head

Flail

PTAH
The cult centre of this god was Memphis, capital city during the Old Kingdom. By New Kingdom times Ptah had become a state god. He is always shown as a man, wrapped up like a mummy. He was a creator god and a patron of craftsmen.

WOLF GOD WEPWAWET
This god from Lycopolis in Middle Egypt was associated with war and life after death. On this stela, the dead man bows before Wepwawet in the hope that the god will help him to live forever.

MIN
The fertility god Min wears two tall plumes on his hat and holds a flail – an agricultural tool. One of his symbols was lettuce, which the Egyptians considered a fertility food.

MAAT

The basic laws of the universe – justice, truth, and order – were represented by the goddess Maat. Her name meant "straight". She wore the *Feather of Truth* on her head. Maat is often shown as a doll, held by the sun god Ra.

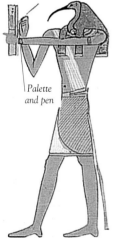

Palette and pen

HATHOR

Some gods had different roles in different parts of Egypt. Hathor, goddess of love, music, and dance, was shown as a woman or a cow. In the Delta she was associated with the sky and held the sun between her horns. In Thebes she was a goddess of death.

THOTH

Many gods were associated with animals. For example, Thoth, the god of writing and wisdom, was depicted as an ibis – a bird that the Egyptians thought was wise. Here he is shown as an ibis-headed man writing with a scribe's pen and palette.

KHNUM

This ram-headed creator god is sometimes shown moulding people on a potter's wheel. At Aswan, Khnum was guardian of the Nile and worshipped as "he who brought the flood".

BASTET

Worship of the cat goddess Bastet began at Bubastis, in the Delta. In later times she became popular all over Egypt, and her annual festival was a national celebration.

MAGIC AND POPULAR RELIGION

THE STATE GODS played little part in normal life. If they had a sick child or a son at war, Egyptians asked protection from more down-to-earth gods. People wore amulets (lucky charms) and recited prayers and spells to ward off disease or disaster.

Taweret was shown as a pregnant hippo

OFFERING SHRINE

Like most ancient people, the Egyptians tried to please the gods by giving offerings of food and drink. They did this at temples, in chapels set up next to tombs, or in small shrines inside the home.

Lotus-bud shape

BES

Part dwarf and part lion, Bes was a popular household god. He carried a knife and a musical instrument, whose sweet sounds warded off bad spirits.

TAWERET

Childbirth was dangerous, both for the mother and the baby. Egyptians prayed and put their faith in Taweret, the goddess of childbirth.

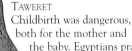

MAGIC WAND

This magical stick was made from a hippo tusk. It is carved with powerful symbols, and it could be used to create a defensive barrier around a part of the house. These wands were also used to protect a child or a sick person.

MEDICAL TOOLS
Egyptians believed in magic, but they were also highly skilled at medicine. This temple carving shows a range of medical instruments, including forceps. One papyrus lists over 700 prescriptions for different ailments, grouped according to the sick organ.

HOUSE CHARM
This stela asks god Horus to protect the family from the dangers of daily life. He tramples on two crocodiles and grips snakes, lions, and scorpions in his hands. Above Horus' head, Bes pokes his tongue out at evil spirits. Magic spells cover the stela's sides.

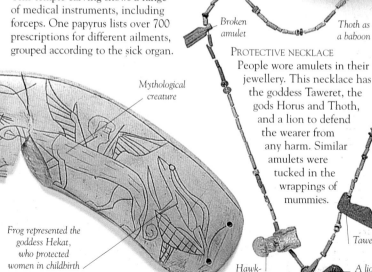

Mythological creature

Frog represented the goddess Hekat, who protected women in childbirth

Broken amulet

Thoth as a baboon

PROTECTIVE NECKLACE
People wore amulets in their jewellery. This necklace has the goddess Taweret, the gods Horus and Thoth, and a lion to defend the wearer from any harm. Similar amulets were tucked in the wrappings of mummies.

Taweret

Hawk-headed Horus

A lion for defence

PRIESTS AND RITUALS

ANCIENT EGYPTIAN PRIESTS were called "servants of the gods". Their job was not to preach to the people, but to keep the gods happy and fulfilled. They did this by performing elaborate rituals in the sacred inner sanctums of temples, where only senior priests and the pharaoh were allowed to enter.

Cup for burning incense

PURE ONE
To show their purity, priests shaved their heads and bodies and washed many times a day. This man burns incense and sprinkles water from the sacred lake. In the inner sanctum of the temple, the priest chanted "I am a Pure One" as he approached the gold statue of the god.

Hair in sidelock of youth

Offering table

Bucket held water from sacred lake

CHILD PRIEST
There were many different classes of priests. This one wears his hair in a sidelock of youth, not because of his age, but to show that he is acting as the loving son of the god.

SITULA (SACRED BUCKET)

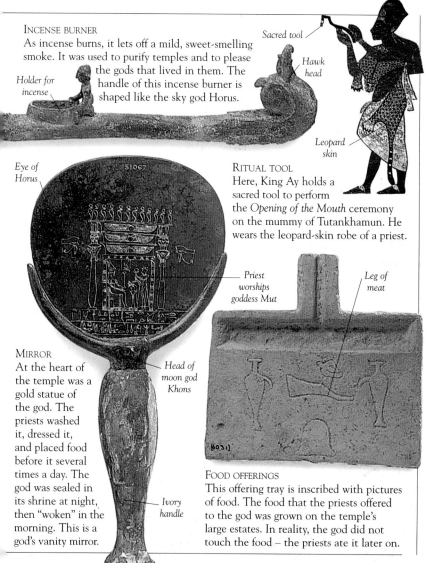

INCENSE BURNER
As incense burns, it lets off a mild, sweet-smelling smoke. It was used to purify temples and to please the gods that lived in them. The handle of this incense burner is shaped like the sky god Horus.

Holder for incense

Sacred tool

Hawk head

Leopard skin

RITUAL TOOL
Here, King Ay holds a sacred tool to perform the *Opening of the Mouth* ceremony on the mummy of Tutankhamun. He wears the leopard-skin robe of a priest.

Eye of Horus

Priest worships goddess Mut

Leg of meat

MIRROR
At the heart of the temple was a gold statue of the god. The priests washed it, dressed it, and placed food before it several times a day. The god was sealed in its shrine at night, then "woken" in the morning. This is a god's vanity mirror.

Head of moon god Khons

Ivory handle

FOOD OFFERINGS
This offering tray is inscribed with pictures of food. The food that the priests offered to the god was grown on the temple's large estates. In reality, the god did not touch the food – the priests ate it later on.

DEATH AND BURIAL

THE EGYPTIANS WANTED TO LIVE forever. To achieve this, they believed that a dead person's body had to be preserved, or "mummified". The mummy was then buried with elaborate rites and a book of magic spells to help it in its journey through the treacherous underworld.

Pieces of gold leaf

GIRL MUMMY
This is the body of a girl who died over 2,000 years ago, aged eight or nine. Her body was coated in oils and resins to stop it from decaying and then covered in gold leaf – maybe because Ra, the sun god, was believed to have a skin of gold.

Ba *bird*   Mummy

THE MUMMY'S SOUL
Egyptians believed that a person's spirit took several forms. One of these was the Ba, similar to a soul. The Ba – depicted as a bird – left the body at death. Only when it returned would the person live forever.

TOMB OWNERS

Statues of the dead were placed in the tomb chapel to make sure that the gods knew who was buried there. Loved ones visited the chapel to put offerings before the statues.

Husband and wife

A HUMBLE HEAVEN

The Egyptians' idea of heaven was a rural paradise, presided over by the god Osiris. They called it the *Field of Reeds* – a place where the sun shone and people worked in the fields, planting and harvesting their crops. In fact, it was just like Egypt – except grain grew a foot taller.

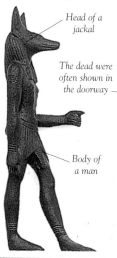

Head of a jackal

The dead were often shown in the doorway

Body of a man

ANUBIS

The god of death and embalming was the jackal-headed Anubis. He was thought to guard mummies and necropolises (burial grounds). A priest wearing an Anubis mask supervised the ritual practices that surrounded the process of embalming (preserving).

FALSE DOOR

Tomb walls contained false doors – gateways between the worlds of the living and the dead. The spirits of the dead were thought to come and go through these doorways.

FUNERAL PROCESSION

Mourners wailed and splashed their faces with mud, as priests dragged the mummy to the tomb. Before sealing the mummy in, the priests performed sacred rites and repeated magic spells.

PREPARING A MUMMY

TO STOP IT FROM ROTTING away, a body was preserved by embalming. After the internal organs were removed, the corpse was washed, dried out with natural salts, and then coated with oils and resins. Finally, it was wrapped in many layers of tight linen bandages. The whole process took 70 days.

PROTECTIVE EYE
Cuts made in the flesh were covered with plates like this one. It bears a sacred symbol, the Eye of Horus, to protect the body.

RITUAL KNIVES
The internal organs were removed through an incision cut in the abdomen. The brain was drawn out with a hook passed through the nose.

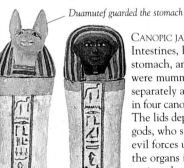

Duamutef guarded the stomach

CANOPIC JARS
Intestines, lungs, stomach, and liver were mummified separately and put in four canopic jars. The lids depicted gods, who stopped evil forces using the organs in spells against the dead.

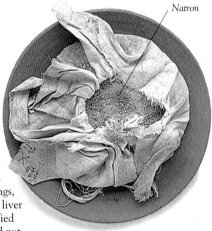

Natron

PRESERVING SALT
To stop decay, a body must be thoroughly dried out. The Egyptians did this with dry crystals of natron, a natural salt found by desert lakes. The procedure took 40 days.

KEEPING HER HAIR
This skull of a woman is 3,500 years old. Skin and flesh have rotted away, leaving nothing but hair and bone. Every hair was saved and then placed in the tomb, because a lost strand could be used in spells against her.

Plaited hair

Teeth can give clues about age and diet

Linen bandages

MUMMY OF A BOY
A mummy could be wrapped in more than 20 layers of bandages. As each one was added, it was brushed with oils and resins.

WRAPPED UP
Before wrapping, the dried body was stuffed with linen and sawdust to restore shape. Sunken cheeks might be padded out and artificial eyes put in.

OPENING THE MOUTH
During mummification there were constant prayers and rituals. The most important was the *Opening of the Mouth*, held just before burial. It was meant to restore the mummy's senses.

MUMMY LABEL
Embalming was done by special priests. They made sure body parts were not mixed up by tying labels to the mummies.

113

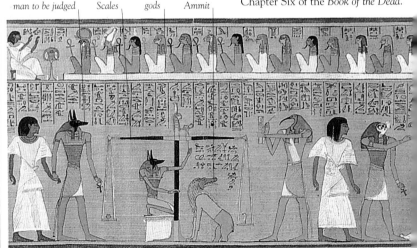

JOURNEY TO THE AFTERLIFE

TO REACH HEAVEN, the Egyptians believed that a dead person had to travel through *Duat*, the underworld, where monsters and lakes of fire awaited. To fight them, the mummy was forearmed with a collection of magic spells, written in the *Book of the Dead*. The book included a map of *Duat* and many prayers to ward off evil.

BOX OF WORKERS
Shabtis are model workers placed in the tomb. They are inscribed with Chapter Six of the *Book of the Dead*.

Anubis takes dead man to be judged

Scales

Jury of gods

Monster Ammit

STILL TALKING

This tomb model of a man and wife chatting shows how Egyptians expected life to be much the same after death. They crammed their tombs with jewellery, clothes, food, games, make-up, and anything else they might need in the afterlife.

Ptah-Sokar-Osiris wearing Atef crown and false beard

Base of statue

Scroll

EXTRA PROTECTION

Amulets – magic charms worn like jewellery or put into the wrappings – also helped protect a mummy from evil. The *djed* pillar was thought to give strength.

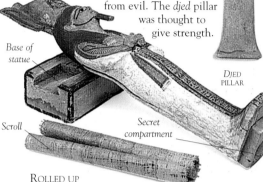

DJED PILLAR

Secret compartment

ROLLED UP

The Book of the Dead was written on scrolls of papyrus and put in the tomb. This statue of composite god Ptah-Sokar-Osiris has a hidden compartment where the scroll was kept.

Osiris, god of the underworld, presides over judgement

Goddess Nephthys with sister Isis

WEIGHING THE HEART

The final test came in the *Hall of the Two Truths*. Here, Anubis weighed the dead person's heart to see if it was heavy with sin. If it was lighter than the *Feather of Truth*, the person lived forever. If not, the heart was thrown to the monster Ammit, "Devourer of the Dead".

HEART PROTECTOR

Pectorals are amulets that were laid on the mummy's chest to guard the heart, a symbol of life. Many were inscribed with pleas like "See, this heart of mine, it weeps and pleads for mercy".

115

MUMMY CASES

THE FINISHED MUMMY was laid in a coffin, or mummy case. Like the tomb, this case was seen as a "house" for the dead person's spirit. Mummy cases changed gradually through the course of history, but from the earliest days the Egyptians covered them with magic symbols and pleas to the gods.

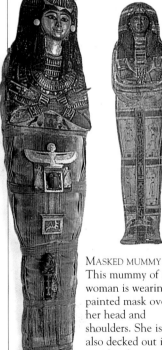

WOODEN CASE
For a long time all mummy cases were wooden. In later times many inner cases were made of cheaper cartonnage – layers of papyrus or linen, pressed together like papier mâché.

Mummy was sealed inside while cartonnage was still wet

LACED IN TIGHT
Many mummies were buried in two or three cases – one inside the other like Russian dolls. The tight-fitting inner case was laced up at the back.

Reed matting tied with twine ropes

MASKED MUMMY
This mummy of a woman is wearing a painted mask over her head and shoulders. She is also decked out in a wide selection of protective amulets.

BABY COFFIN
The earliest coffins, from about 3000 B.C., were simple reed baskets. This later example (c.1400 B.C.) contains the body of a baby. Bone deformities indicate death due to serious illness.

SAFELY INSIDE
The priests in charge of embalming secure a mummy in its case. Wooden cases were held together with thick pegs.

LOOKING GOOD
The mummy case usually presented an idealized portrait of the dead person. Analysis of this youthful-looking mummy shows that he was about 50 when he died.

FACTORY FACE
This is a wooden portrait from a coffin. Sometimes the face was made separately and pegged onto the case. These carved features were often mass produced. Regional styles allow experts to identify the area of Egypt.

WOODEN BOX
A pharaoh or an important official had an extra stone coffin, or sarcophagus. These massive structures were extremely heavy and difficult to move. This priest (Hor) had an extra wooden box instead.

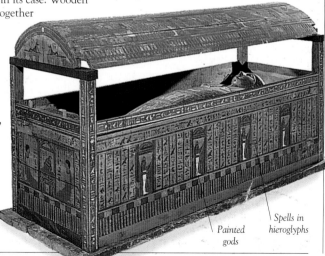

Painted gods

Spells in hieroglyphs

117

Animal mummies

Beetles, birds, cats, crocodiles – the Egyptians mummified an amazing array of creatures. Some were beloved household pets. But most animals were mummified because of their association with particular gods. In later times, millions of animals were bred just to be mummified and buried in special cemeteries dedicated to the gods. Four million ibis mummies were found in one cemetery, each in its own pot.

Painted face

Geometric wrappings, a feature of the Roman period

IBIS
This large wading bird is still common in the marshes by the Nile. It was sacred to Thoth, the god of writing and wisdom and patron of scribes.
Biologists have used mummies and ancient pictures of ibises to show that the species has not changed in 5,000 years.

CAT MUMMY
Egyptians were the first people to keep cats as pets. The earliest written mention dates from 2100 B.C. They probably tamed African wild cats, a species that was the ancestor of all modern pets. Cats were linked with goddess Bastet.

Anubis, god of embalming

FOUR FALCONS
The falcon was king of the Egyptian skies and was seen as a representative of the sky god Horus. This case contains four falcon mummies and is painted with funerary scenes.

Carved falcon, symbol of the sky god Horus

UNWRAPPED CROCODILE
Crocodiles were sacred to the water god Sobek. Priests kept pet crocodiles in luxury, feeding them on the best meat and wines.

Ears are flattened against skull

Fur

PRESERVED FISH
Other animals found as mummies include fish, vultures, owls, baboons, rats, snakes, mice, dogs, geese, scarab beetles, shrews, lizards, rams, and huge bulls.

UNDER THE LINEN
The legs of this unwrapped cat mummy have been tucked in to make a compact shape. Many of these cats were bred by priests just to be mummified and sold to worshippers visiting the temples.

Case has door at back

Each case contained a cat mummy

Tail curled up between legs

CAT CASES
These cat mummy cases all come from Bubastis, sacred city of Bastet. In later times, the festival of Bastet was an important yearly event. Huge celebrations were held in honour of the goddess, and hunting lions was forbidden.

119

VALLEY OF THE KINGS

DURING THE NEW KINGDOM, the capital city moved to Thebes in the south, and pharaohs were buried in the desolate Valley of the Kings. These royal tombs were hidden, cut deep into the rock. Steep steps and cramped passages led to the burial chamber, where the pharaoh's mummy lay surrounded by fabulous treasures.

VALLEY VIEW
The ancient Egyptians called the Valley of the Kings *The Great Place*. Neighbouring Valley of the Queens was known as *The Place of Beauty*. This view across the Nile shows the temple of Queen Hatshepsut.

OVERSEER
The workers who built the kings' tombs lived in the nearby village of Deir el-Medina. A few, like the overseer Sennedjem, had beautifully painted tombs.

STAR-STUDDED CEILING
The Egyptians decorated tomb walls with exquisite paintings and reliefs. This is their view of the northern sky at night, from Sety I's tomb. Animals represent constellations, which are named in hieroglyphs.

Red spots represent bright stars

Egyptians could tell the time from the position of constellations

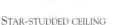

TOMB OF RAMSES IX
This pharaoh tried accused tomb robbers. One confessed "We took gold and jewels and the precious metal of his coffins. Then we found the queen and took everything that was hers and set fire to the coffins".

VALLEY TODAY
In ancient times, the valley was guarded. In spite of this, thieves had looted almost every tomb by 1000 B.C. Today, tombs in the valley are threatened by ground water, pollution, and endless crowds of tourists.

MAN AT WORK
This sketch shows a bald, unshaven mason using a chisel and mallet. Building the tombs was hot, thirsty work.

The Egyptians called this constellation Mes

Crocodile rides on hippo's back

The sun disc

Tutankhamun's tomb

In 1922, the English archaeologist Howard Carter found the tomb of a little known pharaoh, buried 3,200 years earlier in the Valley of the Kings. Crammed inside were priceless treasures that amazed the world. As Carter said, "There were rooms full of gold, everywhere the glint of gold".

Crook and flail, symbols of the pharaoh's power

Squatting baboon gods

INNER COFFIN
The dead pharaoh was buried in three mummy cases, one inside another. The outer two shine with gold leaf, but the inner case is made from solid gold and inlaid with gemstones. This coffin weighs an incredible 110 kg (245 lb).

BURIAL CHAMBER
The outer coffin has now been returned to the stone sarcophagus in Tutankhamun's burial chamber. The walls are painted with gods and scenes from the underworld.

SHRINE DETAIL
The sarcophagus was housed in four wooden shrines, fitting one inside another. All four glittered with gold-leaf decoration.

122

MUMMY MASK

The most famous treasure is the portrait mask, which covered the pharaoh's head as he lay in state. He wears a falcon-headed collar, false beard, and striped *nemes* headdress. Made from solid gold inlaid with gemstones, this masterpiece weighs 10.2 kg (22.5 lb).

PAINSTAKING WORKER

Carter catalogued every detail of his work. It took him ten seasons to clear the tomb. By the time of his death, in 1939, he had published three volumes of notes.

MUMMY

The king's mummy was inside his inner coffin. In separate miniature coffins were two tiny mummies, probably his stillborn twin daughters.

THE GOLDEN THRONE

This is made of carved wood inlaid with intricate designs. The back panel shows the king and his wife.

PILED HIGH

Here, the throne can be seen as it was found. The tomb's four rooms were piled high with treasures. It had been prepared in a hurry, probably because the king died suddenly. Later the entrance was blocked by accident, so the tomb was forgotten for more than 3,000 years.

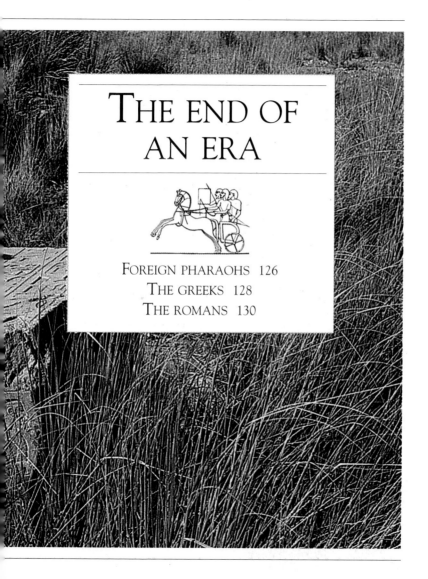

THE END OF AN ERA

FOREIGN PHARAOHS

THE SPLENDOURS of the New Kingdom
ended with the death of Ramses XI in
1069 B.C. The empire was gone, and Egypt
was once again split by war and chaos. In
the centuries that followed, the country
was invaded by its powerful neighbours.
Egyptian culture still
thrived, but life by the
Nile was not as stable.

POWERFUL PRIESTS
The priests of Amun
at Karnak Temple
near Thebes became
so powerful that they
were able to challenge
the authority of the
pharaoh. This helped
lead to the collapse
of the New Kingdom.

TEMPLE OF AMUN
AT KARNAK

CAPTIVE ENEMY
Egypt's traditional
enemies came from
what is now the
Middle East. They
included Babylonians,
Hyksos, Hittites, and
the Persians, who ruled
Egypt twice (525–359
and 343–332 B.C.).

LIBYAN MUMMY
This is the mummy
case of a Libyan called
Pasenhor. Many Libyans
settled in the Delta, and
their chiefs ruled Egypt
from 945 to 715 B.C. The
Libyan pharaohs were
resident kings, who wrote
in Egyptian scripts and
worshipped Egyptian gods.

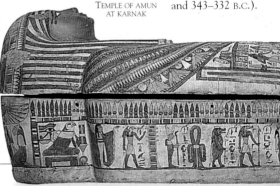

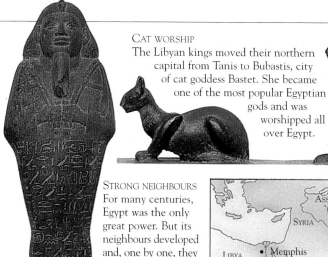

CAT WORSHIP

The Libyan kings moved their northern capital from Tanis to Bubastis, city of cat goddess Bastet. She became one of the most popular Egyptian gods and was worshipped all over Egypt.

STRONG NEIGHBOURS

For many centuries, Egypt was the only great power. But its neighbours developed and, one by one, they overran its borders. Libyan and Nubian kings lived like native Egyptians, but Assyria and Persia ruled Egypt as a colony.

NUBIAN KING

This is Taharqo, one of the Nubian kings. They ruled Egypt from 747 to 656 B.C. Their empire was bigger than Egypt at its height.

Egyptian gods

FACTS ABOUT THE ERA

• The Nubian pharaohs were buried in pyramids in the desert of Sudan.

• The Persians introduced the camel.

• According to legend, Alexander the Great was mummified and laid in a glass coffin floating in honey. It has never been found.

127

THE GREEKS

ALEXANDER THE GREAT conquered Egypt in 332 B.C.
He built a new capital city, Alexandria, on the coast.
When he died, his general Ptolemy founded a dynasty
that ruled Egypt for 300 years. The new rulers spoke
Greek and followed Greek law. But they respected the
local culture, which
continued to flourish.

TEMPLE OF ISIS AT PHILAE
The Greeks built many great temples
in Egypt, dedicated to the Egyptian
gods. On the walls, the Ptolemies
were shown as pharaohs. But these
Greek rulers rarely left Alexandria on
the Mediterranean coast, and there
were regular revolts against them.

ALEXANDER THE GREAT (356–323 B.C)
This great war leader was born in
Macedonia, part of the Greek empire.
Shortly after he became king, at age
20, he conquered the entire Persian
empire, including Egypt, Syria, and
Mesopotamia. His huge empire broke
up after he died suddenly of a fever.

128

FOUR DIFFERENT SCRIPTS

Greek became the official language under the Ptolemies. Hieroglyphs were only used for religious inscriptions; priests wrote in demotic. Many documents were still written in hieratic. This detail from the Rosetta Stone shows the same text in Greek and demotic.

GREEK MUMMY MASK

The invaders adopted many local traditions. The mix of Greek and Egyptian art and religion created many new hybrids. This mummy mask has realistic Greek-style features and the headdress of a wealthy Egyptian.

Lotus flowers

Body of lion

Greek-style sculpture of an Egyptian icon

CLEOPATRA FROM TEMPLE OF HATHOR, DENDERA

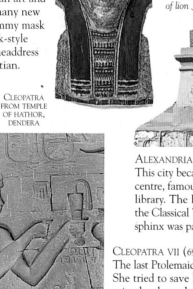

ALEXANDRIA

This city became an important cultural centre, famous for its lighthouse and library. The library – the greatest in the Classical World – burnt down. This sphinx was part of the library complex.

CLEOPATRA VII (69–30 B.C.)

The last Ptolemaic ruler was Cleopatra VII. She tried to save Egypt from the Romans, using her legendary charm to seduce first Julius Caesar and then Mark Anthony. But, when Roman general Octavian invaded Egypt in 30 B.C., she killed herself.

THE ROMANS

EGYPT BECAME A ROMAN state after
the conquest by Octavian in 30 B.C.
The Roman capital was Alexandria,
but the emperors ruled from Rome and
took little interest in local traditions.
Not surprisingly, there were regular
uprisings. In A.D. 642,
Egypt was invaded by
Muslim armies.

AUGUSTUS (63 B.C.–A.D. 14)
Octavian, Egypt's conqueror,
became Emperor Augustus
Caesar. He made Egypt the
granary of Rome, forcing the
country to export huge
quantities of wheat to feed
the rest of the Roman empire.

Real rings

MUMMY CASE
Mummification of
the dead continued
under the Romans.
Some mummy cases
show the dead person
dressed in their best
clothes. This Roman
woman is wearing a
colourful toga, sandals,
and wig. Her jewellery
even includes real
gold rings.

PORTRAIT
During Roman times,
a portrait, painted on
a wooden panel, was
often put over the face
of the dead person and
secured by bandages.
Painted from life, this
portrait may have
hung in the house
until the sitter died.

130

GOLD PARTS
Shaped pieces of gold leaf were placed over tongues, eyes, and other body parts of Roman mummies in the belief that these would restore the various functions in the afterlife.

Bunch of flowers

besst.

Gold tongue to allow mummy to speak

MUMMY MASK
This Roman mummy mask is probably one of many made in a factory from an original model. Typical of the period, he is holding a candle and a bunch of flowers, which are both symbols of rebirth.

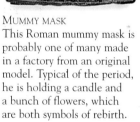

HADRIAN (A.D. 76–138)
The only emperor to take much interest in Egypt, Hadrian was fascinated by its culture. He brought these statues back to grace his villa near Rome. He also founded a new city, named Antinoopolis, at the spot by the Nile where his lover drowned.

This area of the villa was inspired by Canopus, an Egyptian town

Pair of ducks *Crocodile* *Songbird on water plant* *Ibis*

NILE SCENE
Alexandria was a centre of art. Workshops there produced many frescoes and mosaics, which were exported all over the Roman empire. This Nile-scene mosaic comes from a villa in Pompeii, Italy.

131

New

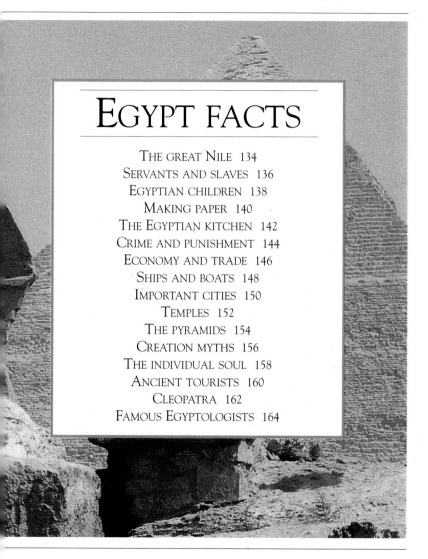

EGYPT FACTS

THE GREAT NILE

THE RIVER AND AGRICULTURE

Almost every aspect of life in ancient Egypt was affected by the annual inundation (flood) of the Nile, the longest river in the world.

- The White Nile, the Blue Nile, and the Atbara (in present-day Sudan) all flow into the Nile (which was called Iteru in ancient Egypt).

- The Nile divided into seven channels in the Delta (the most fertile part of ancient Egypt), before it flowed into the Mediterranean Sea.

- Floodwaters began to rise in June at 4–8 cm (1.5–3 in) per day, and deposited silt (rich muddy soil) on the land.

- The calendar was divided into three seasons that corresponded to the phases of the river – the flood season, the growing season, and the drought season.

THE NILOMETER

Nilometers were located in temples, and fulfilled a mainly religious function. Priests divined the wills of the gods according to the Nile tides. Nilometers were huge stone staircases that went down into the river and measured the level of the water and how fast it was rising during the flood. Nilometers still exist at Dendera, Edfu, Esna, Philae, Kom Ombo, in Cairo, and on Elephantine Island at Aswan.

This Nilometer at Elephantine Island, Aswan was used to measure the depth of the Nile.

THE ASWAN DAM

- The Aswan High Dam, begun in 1960 and opened in 1970, created Lake Nasser, which helped to control the Nile's floodwaters and improve agriculture.

- Many ancient monuments were lost when Lake Nasser was created and over 60,000 Nubians had to be resettled.

- With the support of UNESCO (United Nations Educational, Scientific, and Cultural Organization), 14 temples and monuments were moved to safety, including Philae, Abu Simbel, and Kalabsha.

- The famous rock-cut temples of Abu Simbel were removed, numbered in pieces, and rebuilt in a safe area.

DAM FACTS

Tranjan's kiosk at the Sanctuary of Isis, in Philae, was saved from the floodwaters by the UNESCO campaign.

- Lake Nasser, created by the Aswan Dam, is 500 km (310 miles) long, between 10 and 30 km (6 and 18 miles) wide and 90 m (295 ft) deep.
- The dam is 3.6 km (2.5 miles) long and 111 m (365 ft) high.

HOW FARMERS USED THE FLOODWATERS

- Farmers used the floodwaters in two important ways: the flood deposited fertile soil on the land, and it provided the water to grow crops.

- As the floods were subsiding in October or November, farmers captured water in canals, basins, and reservoirs for later use.

- The rich soil, deposited as silt, supported two crops a year but the second one needed to be watered by hand.

- Crops were watered in a variety of ways. Farmers often carried water in two clay jars slung on a wooden yoke across their shoulders.

- *Shadufs* (buckets on the end of a pole, with a counterweight on the other end) were used during the New Kingdom (*c.*1550–1086 B.C.).

- *Sakkias* (animal-powered water wheels) lifted water on to the fields in the Greek period (332–30 B.C.).

SERVANTS AND SLAVES

WORKERS

- The king, temple officials, and nobles owned most slaves and servants. Servants, unlike slaves, were freeborn, although both often performed the same tasks.

- Servants received food and other goods as payment for their services, but slaves were not paid. They were kept by their masters.

SERFS (SEMEDET)

- Serfs, or farm workers, were freeborn, although most were tied to the land, working for landowners.

- They could own land, but had little opportunity to change their career.

- Each year they were expected to grow a certain amount of grain or other produce, which was handed over as a form of tax.

- During the flood season, farm workers left their fields and livestock to help build the pharaoh's pyramids, temples, and other monuments.

- Punishments were severe for non-payment of taxes. If the crops failed, the workers were still expected to pay.

DOMESTIC SERVANTS

- Large households and organizations had many servants to perform clearly defined tasks.

- Cooking, cleaning, gardening, childminding, weaving, and hundreds of other tasks were done by servants who were paid by the temple, nobles, or the king.

- Middle-class households also had servants or slaves to help with the domestic chores.

- A servant's profession or craft was passed down from father to son and from mother to daughter.

- Servants could leave their master if he was unjust. They were allowed to set up their own business and buy property.

WHO REALLY BUILT THE PYRAMIDS?

- A labour force of thousands of men was needed to build the pyramids.

- Contrary to popular belief, Egypt's pyramids were not built by slaves.

- Most of the workers were farm labourers, who owed their labour as tax and worked on the pyramids when they were not required on the land.

- Prisoners of war and convicts sometimes quarried and mined stone for the pyramids. They were not a significant part of the workforce until the Middle (2040–1750 B.C.) and New Kingdoms (1550–1086 B.C.).

- Artisans such as carpenters, stone masons, sculptors, painters, potters, and cabinet makers also helped.

SLAVE LABOUR

- Most slaves (*hemw*) were foreigners, usually prisoners of war from other countries.

- Prisoners of war were given to the king, to a temple, or to soldiers as a reward for their bravery.

- Slaves could be hired out, sold, or exchanged as goods at any time.

- Egyptians sometimes sold themselves into slavery in order to have a home and food to eat.

- Slaves could be freed by their masters. They were given presents and could also own property with their master's consent.

- Slaves could marry someone who was freeborn, which released them from their status as a slave.

FEMALE SLAVES

- Female slaves worked at spinning, weaving, cleaning, and many other domestic chores.

- Beautiful slave women were highly prized and well cared for. They were sold for high prices to temples to become dancers, singers, or servants.

- Ramses II (c.1279–1213 B.C.) is reputed to have branded his female slaves with his name.

Female attendants helping their mistress.

EGYPTIAN CHILDREN

FAMILY LIFE

- Ancient Egyptians had large families – four to seven children on average. They wanted to make sure there would be someone to perform the religious rituals after they died.

- Boys were expected to help their fathers, and girls their mothers.

- Girls stayed at home until they were about 13, when they got married. Boys left home at puberty, when they were considered to be adults.

- Some marriages were arranged, but people often married for love. Divorce was common – proceedings could be begun by husband or wife.

HOW DID THEY DRESS?

- Young children mostly went naked because of the heat.

- Older boys wore a short kilt made of linen. Girls wore a long straight dress.

- Underwear was a simple linen loincloth.

- Most children went barefoot. Sandals were a luxury, or an indication of status.

- Winter clothes were made of wool and heavier linen.

- Like adults, children's eyes were outlined with kohl (a black cosmetic) for decoration, and for protection against the sun and infection.

GAMES AND SPORTS

Egyptian children had plenty of amusements and played many games. Older children played leapfrog, ball games, tug-of-war, and board-games, while smaller children had pull-along toys, tops, dolls, and balls. Boys practised shooting at targets with bow and arrows, as well as boxing, wrestling, and stick-fighting in preparation for going into the army. Girls were encouraged to do gymnastics, juggling, dancing, and singing. Some children kept pets.

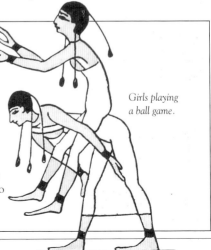

Girls playing a ball game.

THE BOY-PHARAOH

- Tutankhamun came to the throne when he was only nine years old and reigned from 1336 to 1327 B.C..

- He died (or was murdered) when he was 18. An x-ray of his mummified body shows damage to the skull, which may have been caused by a blow to the head, a fall, or damage from the mummification process.

- Tutankhamun's tomb is famous because it was found with most of its priceless treasure intact. It still contained more than 200 pieces of jewellery, 16 model boats, furniture, clothes, cosmetics, and food.

Tutankhamun's mask was made of gold and inlaid with precious stones.

- Souvenirs from his boyhood included a board-game called senet, a tiny bow with which the pharaoh must have learned to shoot, and miniature tables and chairs.

- It took archaeologist Howard Carter (1874–1939) five years to list all the treasures of Tutankhamun's tomb.

GOING TO SCHOOL

- Education was expensive and only boys were allowed to attend school.

- Boys who did go to school went at five years of age and carried on into their teens. Boys whose parents couldn't afford school fees worked and learned their fathers' trades.

- Girls never went to school, but some were taught to read and write at home by one of their parents or an older brother. Most girls learned to spin, weave, and cook.

- Education was a way of advancing in Egyptian society. Many people wanted their sons to become scribes.

- Schools were attached to temples and government offices, with priests as teachers.

- Young students learned hieratic script (used by priests). They wrote on wooden boards or broken bits of pottery, because papyrus paper was too expensive. Students made their own brushes and inks.

- Older students studied hieroglyphics, mathematics, history, languages, geography, astronomy, and law, as well as gymnastics and good manners.

MAKING PAPER

ORIGINS

Our word "paper" comes from the Greek *papyrus*, which is the word for the writing material invented by the Egyptians as well as the reed from which it is made.

- Ancient Egyptians discovered how to make papyrus paper in about 2500 B.C.

- The paper was strong, flexible, white, and very durable.

- Papyrus paper was expensive to produce, and was used only for important texts such as archives, accounts, religious writings, and literature.

OTHER WRITING SURFACES

Students wrote on used bits of broken pottery (*ostraca*) because paper was too expensive. They also wrote on leather, soft stone, and slabs of wood spread with plaster. *Stelae* (stone or wood carved with text, paintings, and reliefs) were used for religious or commemorative purposes.

A cartouche of Ramses II (c.1279–1213 B.C.) from the Temple of Abu Simbel.

THE BOOK OF THE DEAD

- This collection of spells is the most famous Egyptian text. It contains spells for mummification, and a guide to survival in the afterlife.

- Arranged in 190 chapters, the spells are in hieroglyphs on rolls of papyrus, each up to 30 m (98 ft) long.

- Copies of *The Book of the Dead* were placed in coffins with mummies. The magic contained in it was thought to

allow the dead to reach the kingdom of Osiris safely. Osiris was the supreme ruler and judge of the underworld.

- It was called *The Book of Coming-Forth-By-Day* by ancient Egyptians but was renamed *The Book of the Dead* by leading 19th-century Egyptologist Karl Lepsius.

- The finest copies had beautiful illustrations and were made by scribes of the New Kingdom (1550–1086 B.C.).

ANCIENT SCROLLS

- Many papyrus scrolls have been acquired by museums and collectors all over the world. Scrolls are named after their institution or owner.

- Many ancient scrolls contained literary or scientific works. Others were mundane lists, such as censuses, or letters of complaint.

- *The Salt Papyrus*, named after its owner and written in 1200 B.C., contains complaints from workmen about their foreman Paneb.

- Many papyri were devoted to medicine and cures. *The Brooklyn Papyrus* talks about treatments for snakebites.

- Stories and legends were popular subjects in the Middle Kingdom. *The Papyrus Westcar* relates *The Tale of Wonder*, a series of five stories, including that of a magician entertaining the king.

- Papyrus paper was used throughout the Greek and Roman eras and into the Islamic period, until it was replaced by cloth paper made of cotton rags.

- Cloth paper was introduced from the Far East in the 8th and 9th centuries A.D., and was cheaper and easier to produce.

- Egyptologists found more than 15,000 papyri at Oxyrhynchus in what was Upper Egypt between 1897 and 1922.

HOW PAPYRUS IS MADE

- Reeds of papyrus grew in the Nile Delta up to 6 m (20 ft) tall.
- The green outer layers of skin were peeled away (1), then cut into fine strips (2).

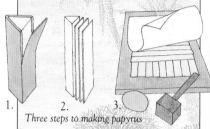

1.   2.   3.

Three steps to making papyrus

- The strips were first laid horizontally then vertically to make a square sheet (3).
- Linen was laid over the sheet and then pounded with a heavy stone or mallet to make the papyrus fibres stick together.
- When the sheets dried, they were joined together to form scrolls (*medjat*), usually with 20 squares to a scroll.
- Some scrolls were as long as 40 m (130 ft).
- When rolled up, the horizontal fibres were on the inside of the papyrus scroll.
- Writing and drawing were done on the inside of the scroll, and sometimes the outside as well.
- Paper made from papyrus was long-lasting.

THE EGYPTIAN KITCHEN

MIDDLE-CLASS AND WEALTHY FAMILIES

- Kitchens in middle-class and wealthy homes were simple rooms at the back of the house, often in a courtyard that kept smells and smoke away from the rest of the house.

- Some kitchens had two sections: a cellar for storing food and fuel, and another area for preparing food.

- Ovens were made of clay in the shape of a cylinder about 1 m (3 ft) high. They had a door at the bottom for ventilating the oven and removing ash.

- Fuel was put on a grill inside the oven. Wealthy families used charcoal and firewood for fuel.

- Cooking took place in a pot that rested on the hole at the top of the oven. The fire below heated the pot.

- The smoke from the oven was vented through one or two holes in the ceiling.

KITCHEN EQUIPMENT

- Larger kitchens had several tables. One was used to prepare meat and fish, another for vegetables. Trestle tables held joints of meat.

- There were many containers. Clay pots and pans were used for cooking, jugs for water, wine, and beer, and jars, trays, and baskets for serving food. Alabaster and other stone crockery was a luxury.

- Knives, choppers, and wooden utensils for stirring were kept on the tables ready for use.

- The storeroom held jars of wine, beer, oils, spices, and honey, and sacks of beans and lentils, grain, and other food.

Clay bowl decorated with hippopotamuses

EATING TOGETHER

Families sat together on the floor to eat. Food was served in baskets, trays, or jars, and everyone helped themselves with their fingers. At parties, servants would pass food around on trays and in baskets. Although there were pottery cups for everyday use, individual plates were used only in wealthy households.

Servant carrying drinks on a tray.

WHO DID THE COOKING?

- In all but the wealthiest households, women and girls were expected to do all the food preparation and cooking – from grinding the flour to making the bread and beer.

- The women also made packed lunches for the men of the household to take to work and to school.

PEASANTS

- A peasant's kitchen was simple and sometimes smelly, with a roof made of branches or straw loosely woven to allow the smoke to escape.

- Ovens were very basic, usually a pot resting on three stones. Cheap fuel was burned underneath the pot.

- Peasants could not afford charcoal or firewood. Instead they burned dried animal dung or straw left over after the crops had been harvested.

- Flat pancakes or bread were baked on a heated stone.

- Peasants lived on a diet of bread, beer, and a few vegetables. Sometimes they ate rabbits, wild birds, and fish.

CRIME AND PUNISHMENT

CRIMINAL OFFENCES

Egyptian law was based on a common-sense view of right and wrong. Crimes included the following, with the least serious shown first:

- Fighting and drunkenness
- Petty theft and burglary
- Corruption by priests and officials
- Stealing from temples and tombs
- Avoiding military service
- Non-payment of taxes
- Murder
- Conspiring to murder the king

THE JUDGES

- The pharaoh was the supreme judge in Egypt but he rarely attended cases. He was represented by his viziers who acted for him in legal matters.

- Beneath the viziers were magistrates. They sat in judgement in the main law courts in Thebes.

- Outside the cities, local councils of elders in each town tried minor cases, such as the non-payment of loans, and imposed penalties.

- Ancient Egyptians also consulted images of gods in temples for answers to their legal problems.

THE POLICE

By the New Kingdom (1550–1086 B.C.) there were three types of law-enforcers – urban police made up of Nubian mercenaries (*medjays*); desert police (*nww*); and border police. The police caught and punished criminals, guarded temples and tombs, and arrested those who hadn't paid their taxes.

An Egyptian policeman with his spear, sword, and shield.

TOMB-RAIDERS

- Tomb-raiding was a common practice in ancient Egypt.

- Hieroglyphic inscriptions in tombs warned tomb-raiders against stealing the treasures. However, this was not enough to protect the tombs.

- Corrupt officials, police, and workmen at burial sites took bribes. Priests were also known to steal from their temples.

- Tomb-raiders removed all the precious metals and jewels and abandoned the mummies.

- One gang of eight operating in Thebes in 1116 B.C. stole 14.5 kg (32 lb) of gold each. Eventually, three of the gang were caught, tried, and executed.

- No tomb was left untouched. Even Tutankhamun's showed some evidence of theft.

Amenhotep II's mummy, shown here in its sarcophagus, was stripped of its bandages by robbers looking for valuable amulets.

PUNISHMENT TO FIT THE CRIME

- Everyone in ancient Egypt received the same punishment for a crime regardless of their status.

- Thieves were fined and beaten.

- Running away from military service was punished by exile to the desert. Prisoners died of thirst if they tried to escape.

- Corrupt judges and officials could have their ears and noses cut off.

- Stealing from tombs was one of the worst crimes and resulted in the death penalty, by either being burnt alive or being impaled on sharp stakes and left to die slowly and painfully.

- Instead of prisons there were labour camps where prisoners dug canals or dragged stones to building sites.

- One of the worst punishments was to work in the Nubian gold mines in the intense heat of the day.

145

TRADE AND BARTER

Egyptian trade was based on a complicated system of exchange, called barter, which was used by the whole of society.

- People were paid in oil, grain, or linen, which they could then exchange for other goods.

- Farmers often bartered some of their produce, such as wheat, barley, or livestock.

- An Egyptian might exchange a pair of sandals for a finely crafted walking stick, or a linen garment for a large quantity of food.

- Trading took place in town and village marketplaces.

- Even taxes were paid using the barter system, through work or produce. This may be how the pyramids were built, with citizens who owed taxes paying them off through labour.

- Travelling by land was time-consuming, so goods were often transported by boat. Traders sailed up and down the Nile and across the Mediterranean.

WEIGHTS AND MEASURES

- There were no coins until the 30th Dynasty (380–343 B.C.). Instead prices were calculated against a scale of value based on weights of metal or stone. These were very precise and were checked regularly by temple and government officials.

Large balance for weighing produce

- The *shat*, *kite*, and *deben* were the weights that were used to establish the value of many goods.

- In later years, copper came to be used for small transactions, while silver and gold were used for things of higher value.

TRADING PARTNERS

Egypt was very wealthy and exchanged gold and surplus food in return for luxury goods from other countries.

- Incense, ebony, ivory, ostrich eggs, feathers, furs, and exotic animals came from Nubia and Punt.

- Silver came from Syria, and copper from Cyprus.

- Olive oil was obtained from Crete.

- Cedar wood came from Lebanon.

- Incense and spices came from Arabia.

- Lapis lazuli, a precious blue stone, came from Afghanistan.

TRADING CENTRES

- Because so many Greeks were interested in trading with Egypt, Naukratis in the Nile Delta became a Greek town.

- Alexandria, founded by Alexander the Great, became the capital and main port during the reign of Ptolemy I (305–282 B.C.).

- Alexandria was the most important trading centre for Egypt, welcoming ships and traders from countries all over the Mediterranean.

- Many exotic goods from central Africa arrived through Aswan.

THE FIRST COINS IN EGYPT

Coins were first introduced in Egypt as currency during the 30th Dynasty (380–343 B.C.). The first coins minted bear the name of the ruler Teos (362–360 B.C.). The end of the barter system in ancient Egypt made it easier to trade with countries already using coins. Coins captured as war prizes from other nations were melted down into ingots (pieces of metal), which were also used as a form of currency.

Early Egyptian coins

ECONOMY AND TRADE

147

EARLY PREDYNASTIC BOATS

- Simple boats used for fishing and hunting in the Delta were made of papyrus reeds lashed together.

- Some boats had upturned fronts, and poles that were used for steering.

OLD KINGDOM

- The first large boats made of wood appeared during this period (2686–2160 B.C.) and had steering oars, a mast, and a long narrow sail.

- They were used to carry blocks of stone to building sites.

- The remains of a boat from the Old Kingdom were found buried near the Great Pyramid at Giza in 1954.

MIDDLE KINGDOM

- Boats of this period (2040–1750 B.C.) looked very similar to earlier ones.

- Small improvements were made to oars, (flatter), masts (collapsible), and cabins (placed at the back of the boat).

THE IMPORTANCE OF SHIPS

Boats and ships were an essential part of everyday life in Egypt.

- Vessels were used for a variety of purposes, including travelling, fighting, fishing, trading, and religious ceremonies.

- Every town along the Nile had a riverside quay and many temples and palaces had private docks.

Gods and kings were thought to travel to the underworld in boats.

- Funerary barques (model boats) were placed in pharaohs' tombs, ready for the pharaoh's journey through the afterlife.

NEW KINGDOM

- During this period (1550–1086 B.C.), many specialized boats appeared.

- Ships' cabins could be built on to the front, back, and middle of the vessel, and the sail was wider than it was high.

- Some boats were manned by as many as 15 oarsmen and one helmsman.

- Some large vessels could carry up to 295 tonnes (300 tons) of cargo on deck.

LATE AND GREEK PERIOD

- The Greek and Phoenician influence on ship-building in Egypt was at its height during this period (661–332 B.C.). This is seen in the long, low hulls and the lion figureheads at the end of the prows.

- Nekau II (610–595 B.C.) created the first full Egyptian navy. It was manned by Greek mercenaries.

- During the Battle of Actium (31 B.C.), the ships of the Roman general Octavian (63 B.C.–A.D. 14) defeated the Egyptian navy of Cleopatra VII (51–30 B.C.).

EGYPTIAN ARMY DEFEATS THE SEA PEOPLES

During the eighth year of the reign of Ramses III (1184–1153 B.C.), a mixed group of Mediterranean people, the Sea Peoples, attacked Egypt from the land and the sea with the intention of settling there. Ramses III's army in Syria-Palestine defeated the land attack, and his army in the Delta destroyed the Sea Peoples' fleet. To celebrate the victory, Ramses had scenes from the battle at the Delta recreated in reliefs on the walls at Medinet Habu, a large royal temple south of Thebes.

A relief on the walls of Medinet Habu showing Ramses's defeat of the Sea Peoples.

IMPORTANT CITIES

MEMPHIS, THE FIRST CAPITAL CITY

- Said to be founded by the 1st-dynasty ruler Menes in 3100 B.C., Memphis was the capital and main port of Egypt until the 4th century B.C.

- The creator-god Ptah and his wife Sekhmet were the deities of Memphis. Ptah's temple was the most important building in the city.

- The Colossus of Ramses II and his temple were built here.

- Pharaohs built most of their palaces, temples, pyramids, and tombs at nearby Giza and Saqqara.

SAQQARA

- Part of the royal cemetery of Memphis, Saqqara was used as a burial site from 3100 B.C. until A.D. 540.

- As well as the famous Step Pyramid, Saqqara has many mastaba (tombs), temples, and other pyramids. There are also underground galleries and shafts that have been used by robbers through the ages.

- Many of the interiors of the pyramids are covered in hieroglyphic inscriptions known as the *Pyramid Texts*. These are short spells to help the dead ruler on his journey to the afterlife.

GIZA

Giza was part of the royal cemetery at Memphis. Many rulers from the Old Kingdom (2686–2181 B.C.) built pyramids here, including Khufu (2587–2564 B.C.), Khafra (2556–2530 B.C.), and Menkaura (2526–2506 B.C.). Khufu's Great Pyramid took nearly 20 years to complete. It is thought to have required a workforce of 30,000 men.

Khafra's pyramid at Giza was guarded by the Sphinx, who had the head of the pharaoh and the body of a lion.

THEBES, CHIEF CITY OF UPPER EGYPT

- Thebes is the Greek name for the ancient town of Waset. It was the official capital of the New Kingdom (c.1550–1086 B.C.), and an important religious centre.

- Thebes was well situated between the Delta and the African provinces. Caravans from Nubia carrying gold, ebony, ivory, ostrich feathers, and gum passed through Thebes. As a result, trade flourished here.

- The Great Temple of Amun-Ra was begun in the Middle Kingdom (2040–1750 B.C.) and built over 2,000 years. It was mainly dedicated to the gods Amun-Ra, Mut, and Montu.

- Many monuments were built under Amenhotep III (c.1390–1352 B.C.) and Ramses II (c.1279–1213 B.C.).

- Ramses II also built the Great Hypostyle Hall (columned hall), measuring 102 m (340 ft) long, 53 m (175 ft) wide, with 134 columns 25 m (85 ft) high to support the ceiling.

- Thebes ruled Egypt for more than 500 years before being invaded by the Assyrians in the seventh century B.C. The two great temples of Karnak and Luxor are all that remain today.

HELIOPOLIS

- The city of On, called Heliopolis (City of the Sun) by the Greeks, was one of the oldest and most important cult centres in ancient Egypt.

- The first sun temple dedicated to Ra was built there in 2600 B.C.

- Now buried under Cairo, some of its monuments have been transported to other places.

- Cleopatra's Needle, an obelisk from Thutmose III's reign (1479–1425 B.C.), was brought to London in 1878.

ALEXANDRIA, CITY OF THE PTOLEMIES

- Alexander the Great founded this city in 331 B.C. on the site of an earlier town called Raqote.

- It became the capital city of Egypt during the Greek (Ptolemaic) period (332–30 B.C.) and was a major centre for trade and learning.

- It was famous for The Great Library of Alexandria, which housed more than 700,000 books, and for the Pharos Lighthouse and many other important monuments and temples.

- By the 1st century B.C., half a million people lived in this city.

TEMPLES

HOUSES OF THE GODS

- Each temple in ancient Egypt was dedicated to the worship of a particular god. ·

- Early temples were made of reeds and mud-bricks. Later temples used longer-lasting and richly decorated stone to preserve the houses of the gods and their priestly rituals.

- Few temples survive from the Old and Middle Kingdoms (2686–2160 B.C. and 2040–1750 B.C.). They were looted and built over.

- The Temple of Amun at Karnak is the most elaborate, and the Temple of Horus at Edfu the best preserved.

TEMPLE COMPLEXES

- The priesthood in ancient Egypt was rich and powerful. Temples had vast tracts of agricultural land with farm labourers who worked it.

- Temple complexes were like small towns, with houses and offices for priests and scribes, and storage areas for agricultural produce.

- Temples also ran schools for scribes, and many had libraries, law courts, and tax and administrative offices.

- Craftsmen making furniture, pottery, paper, leather goods, textiles, and jewellery had workshops within the temple complex.

HOW WERE THEY STRUCTURED?

- All temples were based on a similar structure. They were enclosed by a wall that surrounded a courtyard and a sanctuary – a small, dark room where offerings to the gods were made. Additions in the New Kingdom (1550–1086 B.C.) included pylons (gateways) and hypostyle halls with massive columns.

- A statue of the temple's god was placed in the sanctuary and was thought to contain the spirit of that particular god.

- Priests' rituals involved purifying the sanctuary and offering the gods food, clothing, and cosmetics.

- Ordinary people prayed in the courtyard or outside the walls of the enclosure.

- Many temples were highly decorated, and the walls were brightly painted.

GREAT TEMPLES AND THEIR REMAINS

KARNAK

- The temple complex at Karnak
  was the largest in Egypt. It contained
  a huge number of buildings. The first
  temple was built by Senusret I
  (1965–1920 B.C.), and other temples
  and buildings were added later.

Royal statues in the temple complex at Karnak

- The largest temples were dedicated
  to Amun, the state god, Mut, the
  vulture goddess, and Montu, a local
  war god.
- Karnak's priests employed thousands
  of people.
- By Roman times, Karnak covered
  3 sq km (1.9 sq miles) with
  shrines, halls, pylons, statues,
  and obelisks.

THE WEST BANK – THE RAMESSEUM AND MEDINET HABU

- The West Bank at Thebes
  contains many palaces, temples,
  and tombs, which are all
  interconnected.

- Ramses II
  (1279–1213
  B.C.) built one
  of Egypt's most
  impressive
  mortuary
  temples (where
  the body was
  embalmed).
  It is called the
  Ramesseum, and
  is almost as large
  as St Peter's Basilica in Rome.

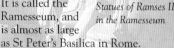

Statues of Ramses II in the Ramesseum

- The remains of a royal palace,
  granaries, storerooms, and a school
  for scribes have also been found in
  the Ramesseum.
- In the 1st century B.C. the traveller
  and historian Diodorus Siculus
  mistakenly called the Ramesseum the
  "tomb of Ozymandias". Centuries
  later, the English poet Percy Bysshe
  Shelley (1792–1822) also wrote
  about it in *Ozymandias of Egypt*.
- The mortuary temple of Ramses III
  (1184–1153 B.C.) at Medinet Habu
  was modelled after the Ramesseum.
  It was built to
  celebrate Ramses
  III's achievements
  – including his
  defeat of the
  Sea Peoples and
  the Libyans.

Colonnade at Medinet Habu

THE PYRAMIDS

FUNCTION, SHAPE, AND SIZE

- Pyramids were funerary monuments, eternal resting places from which the pharaohs protected their kingdoms and subjects in the afterlife.

- The triangular shape gave the impression that the pyramids received the rays of the divine sun.

- Believed to be staircases to heaven, the pyramids reunited the pharaohs with Ra, the sun god and ruler of the heavenly kingdom.

- The average stone block in a pyramid weighs 2.54 tonnes (2.5 tons), and the largest stone slabs weigh 50 tonnes (49 tons).

HEIGHT

Just how tall the pyramids are can be seen in the comparisons below.

Pyramid of Khufu 147 m (482 ft)
Pyramid of Khafra 144 m (472 ft)
Pyramid of Menkaura 68 m (218 ft)

Modern-day comparisons
St Paul's Cathedral 110 m (360 ft)
Statue of Liberty 92 m (300 ft)
Arc de Triomphe 49.5 m (165 ft)

PYRAMIDS WORLDWIDE

- The Mayas and Aztecs of Mexico and Central America built flat-topped towers in steep receding blocks and often used them as temples. Mayan pyramids in Mexico were crowned with ritual chambers.

Aztec temples in Mexico

- The Romans also built pyramidal tombs. The most famous example was the Pyramid of Cestius (62–12 B.C.), a high-ranking official in Rome. The pyramid was built with cement, covered with marble, and had an interior tomb vault 35 m (116 ft) high.

- The Chinese architect I.M. Pei added a large glass pyramid to the entrance of the Louvre Museum in Paris, in 1989. Stainless-steel tubes form the 21 m (69 ft) high frame.

THE FIRST PYRAMID

The Step Pyramid at Saqqara was the first step pyramid ever built. Thought to be designed for King Djoser by the great architect Imhotep around 2680 B.C., it rose to a height of 60 m (198 ft). The pyramid is a series of six mastabas (tombs) built one on top of another. The base is 121 m (398 ft) long and 109 m (358 ft) wide.

The pyramid complex is surrounded by an outer wall, 1,645 m (5,397 ft) wide and 10.5 m (34 ft) high. Its white limestone façade was designed to imitate other palace façades. The wall had 14 entrances, but only one was real.

The Step Pyramid was built entirely of stone.

GRAVE-ROBBERS

- After 4,000 years of looting, not one Egyptian pyramid has survived intact.

- Threatening inscriptions carved on the walls of burial chambers warned grave-robbers against stealing furnishings and offerings. Some described an evil serpent that would blind or poison the intruder.

- Builders tried to fool thieves by building passageways, and sealing them with stones.

- In the New Kingdom (1550–1086 B.C.), tombs were cut into valley rockfaces to hide them from grave-robbers.

- Papyrus records of grave-robber trials contain detailed descriptions of how the gangs operated, which tombs they robbed, how much they stole, and how they were punished.

- Even some Egyptian kings stole from the tombs of their ancestors. Amenemhat I (1985–1955 B.C.), the founder of the 12th Dynasty, used stone from the 4th-dynasty temples of Cheops (Khufu, 2587–2564 B.C.). The crime was easily detected because the stones from Cheops's temples were marked with his name.

CREATION MYTHS

IN THE BEGINNING

- The ancient Egyptians had many creation myths. In fact, every major temple had its own version.

- They thought that a number of their gods were responsible for creating the world, including Amun-Ra, Aten, Atum, Khnum, Neith, Ptah, Ra, Sobek, and Thoth.

- Three basic myths emerged. All agreed that before the beginning of the world there was a dark watery chaos, ruled by the god Nun.

THE MYTH FROM MEMPHIS

- This creation myth dates from the New Kingdom (1550–1086 B.C.) and tells how the creator god Ptah shaped the world like a master craftsman.

- Ptah created all the gods, people, and animals by his thoughts and words. They emerged when he pronounced their names.

- This story is recorded in hieroglyphs on a 25th-dynasty slab of volcanic rock found in Memphis.

THE MYTH OF THE ENNEAD FROM HELIOPOLIS

- Arising from the temple of the sun god at Heliopolis, this creation myth dates from at least the Old Kingdom (2686–2160 B.C.).

- The sun god Atum was said to have created himself out of Nun's watery depths, through some form of magic.

- By spitting and sneezing, Atum produced new life and split it into two elements: air (the god Shu), and moisture (the goddess Tefnut).

- Shu and Tefnut gave birth to Nut, the goddess of heaven, and Geb, the god of earth. They were in love and

had two sons, Osiris and Seth, and two daughters, Isis and Nephthys. In some versions, Horus is their fifth child.

- The linking of heaven and earth in Nut and Geb became the model for kingship – the king was considered to be a living god on earth.

- According to legend, Osiris was the first pharaoh of Egypt, and together with Isis, his sister-wife, he ruled over a peaceful and prosperous kingdom.

- Together these gods shaped and created the world, and afterwards protected it, ensuring that good prevailed over evil.

THE MYTH FROM HERMOPOLIS MAGNA

- Dating from the Middle Kingdom (2040–1750 B.C.), a well-known creation myth from Hermopolis describes how four pairs of gods called the Ogdoad (*khmun*) emerged to shape the universe.

- The Ogdoad symbolized different aspects of the chaos before creation.

- They appeared as frog gods and snake goddesses. Each frog god was paired off with a snake goddess.

- These four pairs created the "primeval hill", the main symbol of creation. On it they placed the egg of the sun god, from which the creator, Atum or Thoth, was born.

- Another creation myth from Hermopolis described a lotus flower that opened its petals, chasing away the darkness. The light of the sun was then able to shine on the earth for the first time.

The cartouche of Rameses II, which included the name of the sun god Ra.

CREATION VERSUS CHAOS

The sun god Ra travelled across the sky daily dispensing heat and light.

All myths seem to agree that, when life was created, destructive forces came into being at the same time. These took the form of chaos monsters such as Apophis, who tried to destroy the work of the creator. Every night and at the change of each season, the forces of creation battled against the forces of chaos to keep the world safe. The sun god Ra's appearance at sunrise, his journey across the sky, and his disappearance below the horizon every evening represented this constant struggle.

157

THE INDIVIDUAL SOUL

THE FIVE ELEMENTS OF THE PERSONALITY

- Ancient Egyptians believed that a person's body housed the personality. It was made up of five essential elements – the *Akh*, the *Ba*, the *Ka*, the Name, and the Shadow.

- When a person died, the five elements were released and separated. However, they still remained closely linked to the body.

- For the elements to live on in the afterlife, a physical representation of the body was needed. The body was replaced by a statue or other image of the dead person, or by a mummy.

Guardian statues, such as this one found in Tutankhamun's tomb, protected the mummy and allowed the elements to survive in the afterlife.

THE BODY

The Egyptians believed that the five elements of the personality left the body at death, but were reunited once the body was buried. The process of mummification was therefore very important. Preserving the body provided a home for the elements in the afterlife and ensured eternal life for the deceased.

THE NAME

- This element was vital to the identity of a person, and had to be given at birth. Names were chosen by what was in fashion at the time.

- The Name was a powerful part of the personality. After death, as long as the name was still spoken or written, the person's spirit continued to live.

- The removal of people's names from monuments was thought to harm their spirits in the afterlife because it destroyed their memory and existence.

THE BA

- This element was sometimes represented as a bird with a human head and arms.

- The *Ba* was released from the body on death and kept the same qualities it had when it lived in the body.

- After death, the job of the *Ba* was to journey from the tomb to rejoin the *Ka*, so that the person could be transformed into an *Akh*.

- The *Ba* moved freely between heaven and earth, journeying to and from the land of the living.

- It was closely linked to the physical body and needed food.

THE KA

- This element of the personality was represented as a pair of outstretched arms that warded off evil. It was the life force of the individual.

- The *Ka* came into being when a person was born, but had its own personality and led an independent existence during that person's life.

- After death, the *Ka* lived on. Like the *Ba*, it needed food in order to fulfil its role. Offerings of food and drink were left in tombs to feed it.

- When the *Ba* and the *Ka* were reunited after death, they transformed the person into an *Akh*.

THE AKH

- This element was represented as a crested ibis, a type of bird that helped the dead reach the stars on their journey to the afterlife.

- The *Akh*, a "transfigured being", achieved an ideal state after death if the deceased had a good burial, and if provisions were made for the *Ba*, *Ka*, Name, and Shadow.

- The *Akh* also represented spirits and demons, which acted as mediums between humans and the gods.

THE SHADOW

- This element (*shwt*) was represented as a feather, or palm fan. It helped protect a person from harm in life and in death.

- The Shadow was powerful and able to move at great speeds. It was black, had the same outline and appearance as the living person, and could not be separated from its owner.

- It was associated with restfulness, well-being, good health, happiness, and long life.

ANCIENT TOURISTS

EARLY VISITORS

We know a great deal about Egypt through the writings of ancient travellers and historians.

- The Greeks traded extensively with Egypt from about 700 B.C. Many Greeks visited and lived in Egypt. They left records of their travels in papyrus scrolls and books.

- The Greek writer Plutarch (c.A.D. 46–126), author of *Parallel Lives of Famous Greeks and Romans*, travelled widely in Egypt. He wrote about Horus, Seth, and Osiris.

- According to legend, Menelaus the Greek king visited Egypt on his way back to Greece with Helen of Troy.

HERODOTUS – THE FIRST TRAVEL WRITER

- The Greek traveller and historian Herodotus (c.484–420 B.C.) wrote nine books of *Histories*, including one on Egypt.

- He travelled through Egypt in about 450 B.C., and talked to priests about the pyramids, festivals, and mummification. His description of the method of embalming bodies is one of the most detailed of this time.

- He visited the pyramid complex of Amenemhat III (1854–1808 B.C.) at Hawara, and described its 3,000 rooms connected by winding passages. Many of the monuments he wrote about have since disappeared, but his works have helped archaeologists relocate a number of sites.

- His descriptions of Hawara made it a top tourist spot for Greek and Roman travellers of the time. Hawara was first identified by the German Egyptologist Karl Lepsius in 1843, and the English archaeologist Flinders Petrie excavated there in 1888 and 1911.

- Herodotus was a keen observer of customs, and wrote about almost every aspect of Egyptian life.

- He recorded that priests shaved their heads and had no body hair. They washed twice a day and twice at night in cold water. Although they could marry, they were allowed to have only one wife, and they were not allowed to have children while they were in office as priests.

STRABO – THE ANCIENT GEOGRAPHER

- The Greek historian and geographer Strabo (c. 63 B.C.–A.D. 21) was also a famous cartographer, and made surprisingly accurate maps of the known world around the Mediterranean Sea.

- He spent several years in Alexandria and wrote about Egypt in his eighth book of *Geography*.

- Strabo visited Lower Egypt and the Theban monuments, including the Colossi of Memnon, which he noted made a whistling sound.

- He visited the First Cataract on the Nile in about 25 B.C. and saw the Nilometer at Elephantine.

- He also visited the Serapeum at Saqqara. Centuries later, Auguste Mariette (1821–1881), a French Egyptologist, dug it up using Strabo's account as a guide.

DIODORUS SICULUS

- The Sicilian-born historian Diodorus Siculus (c.90–21 B.C.) travelled extensively through Egypt, gathering material for Book I of his *Bibliotheca Historica*.

- He provided a valuable insight into the geography, history, and customs of ancient Egypt, including the processes and rituals of mummification.

- He was a keen food critic, and enjoyed Egyptian beer – he said it was almost as good as wine.

- He also observed, perhaps not accurately, that in times of famine Egyptians preferred to eat each other than their sacred animals.

Sphinx with the face of Ramses II, who built the famous Ramesseum, visited by Siculus

- Siculus is also responsible for incorrectly labelling Ramses II's tomb as the "tomb of Ozymandias".

CLEOPATRA

THE LAST QUEEN OF EGYPT

One of the most fascinating figures in history, Cleopatra has inspired many artists, sculptors, and writers in the 2,000 years since her death.

- Cleopatra VII Philopator (51–30 B.C.) was descended from Alexander the Great, and was the last ruler of the Ptolemaic dynasty.

- She became queen at the age of seventeen, and ruled Egypt during one of the most chaotic periods in the country's long history.

- She broke with centuries of Ptolemaic tradition by learning to speak Egyptian and worshipping the traditional gods.

- Historical sources such as Plutarch describe Cleopatra as extremely intelligent, well educated, and cultured. As well as having an interest in the sciences, she spoke Egyptian, Greek, Arabic, and Hebrew.

- She is famous for her relationships with two of the most powerful men of her day, Julius Caesar (100–44 B.C.) and Mark Antony (c.83–30 B.C.)

CLEOPATRA'S CARPET TRICK

To gain access to Caesar, Cleopatra had herself rolled up in a carpet and carried into his presence. According to the Greek writer Plutarch (c.A.D. 46–120) in his *Life of Caesar*, the Roman leader "was captivated by her conversation and grace". She became his mistress and secured the Egyptian throne for herself.

A relief showing Cleopatra and Caesarion, her son by Caesar, making an offering to Hathor.

TUMULTUOUS TIMES

- Cleopatra came to the throne at a time of civil war and unrest. Egypt was torn apart by famine, rebellion, and an unstable economy.

- Forced to flee Alexandria by her scheming brother-husband, Ptolemy XIII, Cleopatra set about regaining power on her own.

- Rome, also torn apart by warring factions, saw this as an opportunity to make Egypt a part of its empire. Rome needed Egypt's gold and wheat.

- Caesar's rise to power in Rome meant that Egypt and Cleopatra's fates were now in his hands.

Julius Caesar

- After meeting Cleopatra, Caesar confirmed her as queen of Egypt. She had maintained her country's independence, and ruled with Caesar's support.

- Caesar's assassination in 44 B.C. threw Rome back into political turmoil. Caesar's heir, Octavian (63 B.C.–A.D. 14), fought Mark Antony for the control of Rome and Egypt.

- Mark Antony set sail for Alexandria. On meeting Cleopatra, he too fell in love, and confirmed her as queen of Egypt. Together they dreamed of ruling an empire.

THE END OF PHARAONIC EGYPT

- Octavian's decisive victory over Antony and Cleopatra at the Battle of Actium in 31 B.C. gave him sole control over the Mediterranean and the Roman world.

- Cleopatra and Mark Antony managed to escape unhurt to Alexandria. However, as Octavian approached Alexandria, Mark Antony committed suicide by falling on his sword.

- Cleopatra, on learning of Mark Antony's death, and unable to tolerate her country being ruled by Rome, also committed suicide. Legend has it that she was bitten by an asp (cobra), which was hidden in a basket of figs.

- Cleopatra's death marked the end of pharaonic Egypt, and heralded its inclusion into the Roman empire.

FAMOUS EGYPTOLOGISTS & THEIR DISCOVERIES

JEAN-FRANÇOIS CHAMPOLLION

- This French Egyptologist (1790–1832) deciphered the hieroglyphic inscriptions on the Rosetta Stone in 1822. This meant that Egyptian texts could be understood for the first time. The Rosetta Stone is now in the British Museum, London.

- He excavated at Karnak in 1828, moved on to Nubia in 1829, then returned to Luxor where he read, translated, and recorded a wide range of hieroglyphic texts.

- He bought more than 100 works for the Louvre Museum, in Paris.

KARL RICHARD LEPSIUS

- This German archaeologist (1810–1884) was considered to be one of the fathers of Egyptology. He was particularly interested in funerary papyri, and coined the term *The Book of the Dead* for the scrolls placed in coffins to protect the dead.

- He discovered the *Canopus Decree*, a document that helped to decipher demotic (everyday) script.

AUGUSTE MARIETTE

- In 1851, this French Egyptologist (1821–1881) found the famous Serapeum, the huge burial site of the sacred Apis bulls at Saqqara. The Apis bull represented the god Ptah.

- He also found 134 sphinxes, and an underground passageway with 28 chambers, including an intact burial chamber from the reign of Ramses II (1279–1213 B.C.).

CHRISTIANE DESROCHES-NOBLECOURT

- This French Egyptologist (born 1913) was in charge of the Egyptian collection of the Louvre Museum, in Paris, during World War II. She organized the relocation of the treasures to protect them from bombing.

- She was appointed by the international organisation UNESCO to save the temples of Nubia that were threatened by the construction of the Aswan Dam.

- Her international appeal for help resulted in 14 of the most important temples being moved to avoid being flooded by Lake Nasser.

HOWARD CARTER

This English archaeologist (1874–1939) discovered the tomb of Tutankhamun in 1922, significant because the tomb had not been spoiled by grave-robbers. When 17 people associated with the discovery died unexpectedly within a few years, there was speculation that a curse had guarded the tomb.

During Carter's lifetime, there was a craze for all things Egyptian. This mummy was unwrapped at the Cairo Museum in 1891.

EMILE BRUGSCH

- In 1881, this German archaeologist (1842–1930) found the sarcophagi and mummies of the greatest pharaohs of the New Kingdom (1550–1086 B.C.) at Deir el-Bahri. These included Ahmose I, Amenhotep I, Thutmose I and III, Ramses I, II, III, IX, Sety I, Hatshepsut, and Nefertari.

- The mummies were put there by priests in about 1000 B.C. to keep them safe from grave-robbers, who, after looting the tombs, had discarded them.

- They remained undiscovered until Brugsch found them, with the help of a former grave-robber, Mohammed Abd-el Rassul.

FLINDERS PETRIE

- This English archaeologist (1853–1942) discovered over 3,000 tombs from the Predynastic era (5500–3100 B.C.) at Naqada, 16 km (10 miles) north of Thebes, in 1894.

- This was the first Predynastic discovery and provided evidence for the origins of pharaonic culture.

- By studying the pottery pieces he had excavated, he developed his "Sequence Dating" theory, which dated pottery by the progression of its style. It enabled him to create a chronology of the Predynastic era, even though there were no ancient texts from this period.

REFERENCE SECTION

167

MAPS
OF EGYPT

MOST OF Egypt's monuments
are easily accessible from
Cairo in the north and
Luxor in the south.
Temples are generally on
the east bank of the Nile.
Tombs are on the west.
The pyramids of Old
Kingdom pharaohs are
south of Cairo, and the
rock-cut tombs of the New
Kingdom lie across the
river from Luxor.

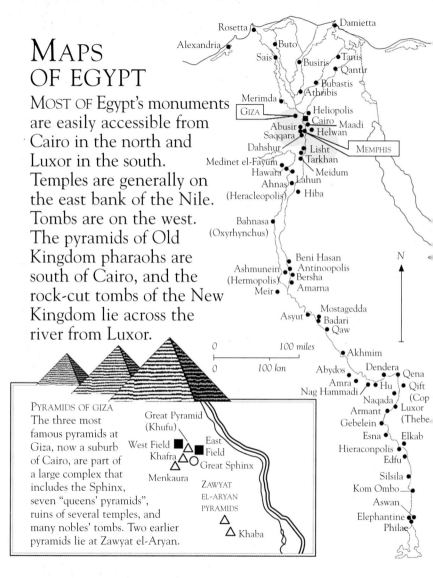

PYRAMIDS OF GIZA
The three most
famous pyramids at
Giza, now a suburb
of Cairo, are part of
a large complex that
includes the Sphinx,
seven "queens' pyramids",
ruins of several temples, and
many nobles' tombs. Two earlier
pyramids lie at Zawyat el-Aryan.

Great Pyramid
(Khufu)
West Field — East Field
Khafra — Great Sphinx
Menkaura
ZAWYAT
EL-ARYAN
PYRAMIDS
Khaba

N

0   100 miles
0   100 km

Rosetta · Damietta
Alexandria · Buto
Sais · Busiris · Tanis
· Qantir
· Bubastis
Merimda · Athribis
GIZA · Heliopolis
Abusir · Cairo · Maadi
Saqqara · Helwan
Dahshur · Lisht · MEMPHIS
Medinet el-Fayum · Tarkhan
Hawara · Meidum
Ahnas · Lahun
(Heracleopolis) · Hiba
Bahnasa ·
(Oxyrhynchus)
Beni Hasan
Ashmunein · Antinoopolis
(Hermopolis) · Bersha
Meir · Amarna
Mostagedda
Asyut · Badari
· Qaw
· Akhmim
Abydos · Dendera
Amra · Hu · Qena
Nag Hammadi · Qift
Naqada · (Cop
Armant · Luxor
Gebelein · (Thebe
Esna · Elkab
Hieraconpolis ·
· Edfu
Silsila
Kom Ombo
Aswan
Elephantine
Philae

168

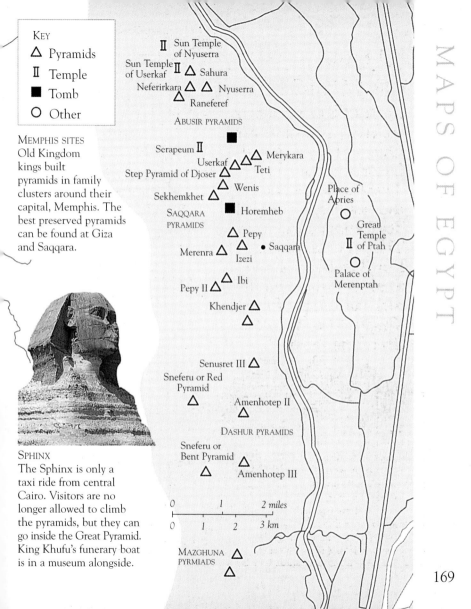

KEY
△ Pyramids
Ⅱ Temple
■ Tomb
○ Other

MEMPHIS SITES
Old Kingdom kings built pyramids in family clusters around their capital, Memphis. The best preserved pyramids can be found at Giza and Saqqara.

Ⅱ Sun Temple of Nyuserra

Sun Temple of Userkaf Ⅱ

Ⅱ △ Sahura

Neferirkara △ △ Nyuserra

△ Raneferef

ABUSIR PYRAMIDS

Serapeum Ⅱ

△ △ Merykara

Userkaf △ △

Step Pyramid of Djoser △ Teti

△ Wenis

Sekhemkhet △

SAQQARA PYRAMIDS

■ Horemheb

△ Pepy

Merenra △ △ • Saqqara

Izezi

△ Ibi

Pepy II △

Khendjer △

△

Place of Apries ○

Great Temple of Ptah Ⅱ

Palace of Merenptah ○

Senusret III △

Sneferu or Red Pyramid

△ Amenhotep II △

DASHUR PYRAMIDS

Sneferu or Bent Pyramid △

△ Amenhotep III

0   1   2 miles
0   1   2   3 km

MAZGHUNA PYRMIADS △

△

SPHINX
The Sphinx is only a taxi ride from central Cairo. Visitors are no longer allowed to climb the pyramids, but they can go inside the Great Pyramid. King Khufu's funerary boat is in a museum alongside.

REFERENCE

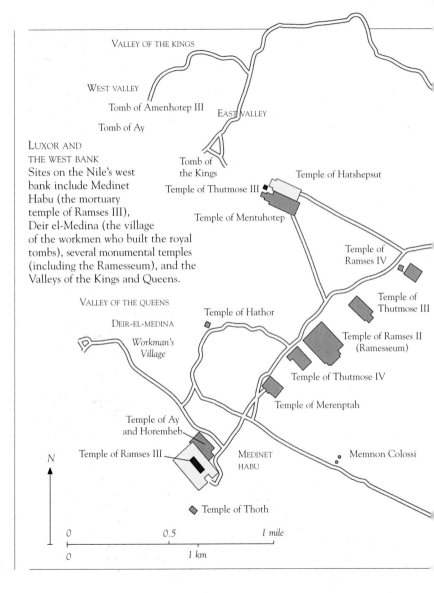

VALLEY OF THE KINGS

WEST VALLEY

Tomb of Amenhotep III

EAST VALLEY

Tomb of Ay

Tomb of the Kings

Temple of Thutmose III

Temple of Hatshepsut

LUXOR AND THE WEST BANK

Sites on the Nile's west bank include Medinet Habu (the mortuary temple of Ramses III), Deir el-Medina (the village of the workmen who built the royal tombs), several monumental temples (including the Ramesseum), and the Valleys of the Kings and Queens.

Temple of Mentuhotep

Temple of Ramses IV

Temple of Thutmose III

VALLEY OF THE QUEENS

DEIR-EL-MEDINA

Workman's Village

Temple of Hathor

Temple of Ramses II (Ramesseum)

Temple of Thutmose IV

Temple of Merenptah

Temple of Ay and Horemheb

Temple of Ramses III

MEDINET HABU

Memnon Colossi

N

Temple of Thoth

0   0.5   1 mile

0   1 km

VALLEY OF THE KINGS
The many rock-cut tombs in this desolate valley include those of Tutankhamun (whose mummy has been returned to his burial chamber), Ramses VI (which has brightly painted walls), and Sety I (one of the deepest).

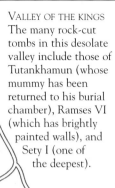

Temple of Sety I

COLOSSI OF MEMNON
A short ferry trip across the Nile from Luxor takes visitors to the West Bank. One of the first sights is nearly all that remains of Amenhotep III's mortuary temple – the massive Colossi of Memnon.

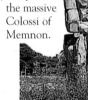

THE WEST BANK SITES

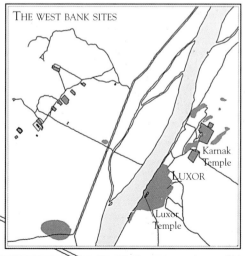

Karnak Temple

LUXOR

Luxor Temple

LUXOR
This modern city lies near the site of Thebes, the New Kingdom capital. In ancient times, the great temples of Karnak and Luxor were linked by an avenue of ram-headed sphinxes. Luxor Museum has a fine collection of antiquities.

KINGDOMS AND DYNASTIES

THE PHARAOHS ruled Egypt
for more than 3,000 years.
Historians usually divide
this vast stretch of time
into 31 dynasties. All
the dates given in these
tables are approximate.

DJOSER

**EARLY DYNASTIC PERIOD
3100–2613 B.C.**
FIRST DYNASTY
  (3100–2690 B.C.)
Narmer
Aha
Djer
Djet
Den
Anedjib
Semerkhet
Qaa

SECOND DYNASTY
  (2890–2686 B.C.)
Hotepsekhemwy
Nebra
Nynetjer
Peribsen
Khasekhem

**OLD KINGDOM
2686–2160 B.C.**
THIRD DYNASTY
  (2686–2613 B.C.)
Sanakht
Djoser
Sekhemkhet
Khaba
Huni

FOURTH DYNASTY
  (2613–2494 B.C.)
Sneferu
Khufu (Cheops)
Djedefra
Khafra (Chephren)
Menkaura (Mycerinus)
Shepseskaf

FIFTH DYNASTY
  (2494–2345 B.C.)
Userkaf
Sahura
Neferirkara
Shepseskara
Neferefra
Nyuserra
Menkauhor
Djedkara
Unas

SIXTH DYNASTY
  (2345–2181 B.C.)
Teti
Userkara
Pepy I
Merenra
Pepy II

SEVENTH/EIGHTH DYNASTIES
  (2181–2125 B.C.)

**FIRST INTERMEDIATE
PERIOD 2160–2040 B.C.**
NINTH DYNASTY
  (2160–2130 B.C.)
TENTH DYNASTY
  (2125–2025 B.C.)
Meryibra Khety
Wahkara Khety
Merykara

ELEVENTH DYNASTY (THEBES)
  (2125–1985 B.C.)
Mentuhotep I
Intef I
Intef II
Intef III

**MIDDLE KINGDOM
2040–1750 B.C.**
ELEVENTH DYNASTY (Continued)
Mentuhotep II   2055–2004 B.C.

TWELFTH DYNASTY
  (1985–1795 B.C.)
Amenemhat I   1985–1955 B.C.
Senusret I   1965–1920 B.C.
Amenemhat II   1922–1878 B.C.
Senusret II   1880–1874 B.C.
Senusret III   1874–1855 B.C.
Amenemhat III   1854–1808 B.C.
Amenemhat IV   1808–1799 B.C.
Sobekkara Sobekneferu
                 1799–1795 B.C.

**SECOND INTERMEDIATE
PERIOD
1750–1650 B.C.**
THIRTEENTH DYNASTY
  (1795–1650 B.C.)
Sobekhotep III
Sobekhotep IV
Neferhotep I

FOURTEENTH DYNASTY
  (1750–1650 B.C.)

FIFTEENTH DYNASTY
  (1650–1550 B.C.)
Khyan
Apepi

SIXTEENTH DYNASTY
(1650–1550 B.C.)

SEVENTEENTH DYNASTY
(1650–1550 B.C.)
Intef V
Taa I
Kamose

NEW KINGDOM
1550–1086 B.C.
EIGHTEENTH DYNASTY
(1550–1295 B.C.)
Ahmose I	1550–1525 B.C.
Amenhotep I	1525–1504 B.C.
Thutmose I	1504–1492 B.C.
Thutmose II	1492–1479 B.C.
Hatshepsut	1479–1457 B.C.
Thutmose III	1479–1425 B.C.
Amenhotep II	1427–1400 B.C.
Thutmose IV	1400–1390 B.C.
Amenhotep III	1390–1352 B.C.
Amenhotep IV	
(Akhenaten)	1352–1336 B.C.
Tutankhamun	1336–1327 B.C.
Ay	1327–1323 B.C.
Horemheb	1323–1295 B.C.

NINETEENTH DYNASTY
(1295–1186 B.C.)
Ramses I	1295–1294 B.C.
Sety I	1294–1279 B.C.
Ramses II	1279–1213 B.C.
Merenptah	1213–1203 B.C.
Sety II	1200–1194 B.C.
Saptah	1194–1188 B.C.
Tausret	1188–1186 B.C.

TWENTIETH DYNASTY
(1186–1069 B.C.)
Setnakht	1186–1184 B.C.
Ramses III	1184–1153 B.C.
Ramses IV	1153–1147 B.C.
Ramses V	1147–1143 B.C.
Ramses VI	1143–1136 B.C.
Ramses VII	1136–1129 B.C.
Ramses VIII	1129–1126 B.C.
Ramses IX	1126–1108 B.C.
Ramses X	1108–1099 B.C.
Ramses XI	1099–1069 B.C.

THIRD INTERMEDIATE
PERIOD
1086–661 B.C.
TWENTY-FIRST DYNASTY
(1069–945 B.C.)
Smendes	1069–1043 B.C.
Psusennes I	1039–991 B.C.
Amenemope	993–984 B.C.
Saamun	978–959 B.C.
Psusennes II	959–945 B.C.

TWENTY-SECOND DYNASTY
(945–715 B.C.)
Sheshonq I	945–924 B.C.
Osorkon I	924–889 B.C.
Takelot I	889–874 B.C.
Osorkon II	874–850 B.C.
Takelot II	850–825 B.C.
Sheshonq III	825–773 B.C.
Pimay	773–767 B.C.
Sheshonq V	767–730 B.C.

TWENTY-THIRD DYNASTY
(818–715 B.C.)
Padibast I	818–793 B.C.
Osorkon III	777–749 B.C.

TWENTY-FOURTH DYNASTY
(727–715 B.C.)
Tefnakht

TWENTY-FIFTH DYNASTY
(NUBIAN KINGS)
(747–656 B.C.)
Piy	747–716 B.C.
Shabako	716–702 B.C.
Shabitko	702–690 B.C.
Taharqo	690–664 B.C.
Tanutamani	664–656 B.C.

LATE PERIOD
661–332 B.C.
TWENTY-SIXTH DYNASTY
(664–525 B.C.)
Psamtek I	664–610 B.C.
Nekau II	610–595 B.C.
Psamtek II	595–589 B.C.
Apries	589–570 B.C.
Amasis	570–526 B.C.
Psamtek III	526–525 B.C.

TWENTY-SEVENTH DYNASTY
(PERSIAN KINGS)
(525–404 B.C.)
Cambyses	525–522 B.C.
Darius I	522–486 B.C.
Xerxes	486–465 B.C.
Artaxerxes I	465–424 B.C.
Darius II	424–405 B.C.
Artaxerxes II	405–359 B.C.

TWENTY-EIGHTH DYNASTY
(404–399 B.C.)
Amyrtaeus	404–399 B.C.

TWENTY-NINTH DYNASTY
(399–380 B.C.)
Nepherites I	399–393 B.C.
Achoris	392–380 B.C.

THIRTIETH DYNASTY
(380–343 B.C.)
Nectanebo I	380–362 B.C.
Teos	362–360 B.C.
Nectanebo II	360–343 B.C.

THIRTY-FIRST DYNASTY
(PERSIAN KINGS)
(343–332 B.C.)
Artaxerxes III	343–338 B.C.
Arses	338–336 B.C.
Darius III	336–332 B.C.

GREEK PERIOD
332–30 B.C.
Alexander	
the Great	332–323 B.C.
Philip Arrhidaeus	323–317 B.C.
Alexander IV	317–305 B.C.
Ptolemy I	305–282 B.C.
Ptolemy II	284–246 B.C.
Ptolemy III	246–222 B.C.
Ptolemy IV	222–205 B.C.
Ptolemy V	205–180 B.C.
Ptolemy VI	180–145 B.C.
Ptolemy VII	145 B.C.
Ptolemy VIII	170–116 B.C.
Ptolemy IX	116–107 B.C.
Ptolemy X	107–88 B.C.
Ptolemy XI	80 B.C.
Ptolemy XII	80–51 B.C.
Cleopatra VII	51–30 B.C.

FAMOUS PHARAOHS

THE NAMES of over one hundred pharaohs are known from inscriptions. But little is known about most of them. Much more is known about a few famous kings, like Ramses II, who covered temple walls with detailed accounts of his exploits. Royal mummies have also revealed many fascinating details.

DJOSER (REIGNED C.2650 B.C.)
The earliest known reference to the sun god Ra is on a relief celebrating Djoser's name. This powerful king led expeditions to Sinai in search of turquoise. He built the first pyramid, the Step Pyramid at Saqqara, and was buried inside.

KHUFU (CHEOPS) (2587–2564 B.C.)
Khufu built the Great Pyramid at Giza. This monumental feat must have used nearly all of Egypt's workforce for about 20 years.
Its treasures were robbed long ago. But in 1925, gilded furniture from the burial of Khufu's mother was discovered.

KHAFRA (CHEPHREN) (2556–2530 B.C.)
This pharaoh was the builder of the second pyramid at Giza, which is only 4 m (13 ft) shorter than Great Pyramid. Khafra succeeded Khufu and may well have been his younger brother. Khafra's pyramid is part of a complex of buildings, which includes a well-preserved valley temple, made from massive slabs of granite. The temple housed 23 life-size statues of the king. Amongst these was the famous seated statue of Khafra, the falcon god Horus perched on the back of his throne. Carved  from diorite, it is now in Cairo Museum. The Great Sphinx, which crouches in front of the Giza complex, is thought to be a portrait of Khafra.

MENKAURA (MYCERINUS) (2526–2506 B.C.)

He built Giza's third pyramid (the smallest). The earliest known statue of a king and queen is Menkaura arm in arm with his favourite wife.

MENTUHOTEP II (2055–2004 B.C.)

He was a Theban prince and energetic warrior. In c.2040 B.C. he became founder of the Middle Kingdom when he conquered the north and re-united Egypt. He ruled for 51 years and was buried in a great rock tomb in the cliffs at Deir el-Bahri.

SENUSRET III (1874–1855 B.C.)

This Middle Kingdom pharaoh extended royal control over Egypt's many *nomes* (districts). He also conquered part of Nubia and developed the chain of massive mud-brick forts protecting Egypt's southern border.

HATSHEPSUT (1479–1457 B.C.)

Hatshepsut was the first woman pharaoh. She married her half-brother, Thutmose II, and ruled alongside him, holding most of the power. When he died, her step-son Thutmose III took the throne. But he was still a child, so Hatshepsut ruled Egypt until her death. She pursued peaceful policies, building up the economy instead of fighting her neighbours. She opened new turquoise mines, sent a trading expedition to Punt, and erected two obelisks at Karnak. On the walls of her temple at Deir el-Bahri, she had herself portrayed as a man, with a false beard and all the other symbols of kingship.

THUTMOSE III (1479–1425 B.C.)

After his step-mother's death, Thutmose III became a powerful warrior king, extending Egyptian power deep into Asia. He added to the great temple to Amun at Karnak and erected obelisks, including *Cleopatra's Needle* – now in London.

AMENHOTEP III
(1390–1352 B.C.)
This pharaoh ruled a huge empire at the height of its wealth. He built the Colossi of Memnon and Luxor temple. He also added to Karnak temple. His new palace at Malkata was next to the world's first known chariot racetrack.

AKHENATEN (1352–1336 B.C.)

Crowned Amenhotep IV, the "heretic pharaoh" took a great interest in the sun god Aten. After six years as king, he changed his name to Akhenaten in the god's honour. His new religion was the first in history to worship a single god. He created a new city, Akhetaten, at Amarna. Here, art flourished in new, original styles, and lavish offerings were made to Aten. The pharaoh closed the traditional temples, depriving many priests of their power. He also ignored affairs of state, and the normally efficient Egyptian government was in chaos. When he died, his city was abandoned and his statues defaced. His wife Nefertiti may have ruled on alone.

TUTANKHAMUN
(1336–1327 B.C.)
The old gods were restored under Akhenaten's successor, the boy-king Tutankhamun. His father was probably Akhenaten. Another wife, Kiya, is more likely to have been his mother than Nefertiti. For most of the pharaoh's nine-year reign, power lay with an army general (Horemheb) and an elderly official (Ay). Both went on to rule Egypt after Tutankhamun died at age 18 or 19. His mummy shows skull damage, and some experts think he may have been murdered by Ay. He would barely have been remembered at all had his intact tomb full of glittering treasures not been found in 1922.

HOREMHEB (1323–1295 B.C.)
This king was a successful army general, who took the throne after the death of Tutankhamun's elderly successor Ay. He banned the Aten religion and set about erasing the names of "heretics" Akhenaten and Tutankhamun (born Tutankh*aten*).

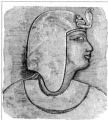

SETY I (1294–1279 B.C.)
Great war leader Sety I revived Egypt's expansion policy in the East by marching into Syria and driving back the Hittites. In 1817, his splendid Theban tomb was discovered. His well-preserved mummy is in Cairo Museum.

TAHARQO (690–664 B.C.)
The most famous Nubian king of Egypt, Taharqo is mentioned in the Bible. He revived classic traditions in art and followed Egyptian gods. Ousted by Assyrian invaders, he was buried in a pyramid in Nubia (Sudan).

RAMSES II (1279–1213 B.C.)
Known as Ramses the Great, this king fought an indecisive battle with the Hittites, then signed the world's first official peace treaty. In the 60 peaceful years that followed, he built many monuments to celebrate his "victory". Ramses II had more than 100 children. His mummy shows that he was very tall.

RAMSES III (1184–1153 B.C.)
He saved Egypt from a series of foreign invasions and fought against corruption. Court members, including one of his wives, tried to poison him. They were tried and forced to kill themselves. A second plot may have succeeded; he died a year later.

CLEOPATRA VII (51–30 B.C.)
The last Ptolemaic pharaoh and the only one to speak Egyptian, Cleopatra tried to prevent Rome taking over Egypt. She had an affair with the Roman general Julius Caesar, and they had a son. After Caesar's death, she fell in love with another Roman general, Mark Antony. They had three children and planned to rule a mighty kingdom together. But they were defeated by Octavian, Antony's political rival. Octavian pursued them to Egypt, where Antony killed himself after receiving a false report of Cleopatra's death. She surrendered to Octavian. But when she could not win him over, she committed suicide – legend says, by clasping a poisonous asp (cobra) to her breast.

GODS OF ANCIENT EGYPT

DIFFERENT GODS AND GODDESSES were popular at different times, and most changed their character over the centuries. Here are a few of ancient Egypt's most important deities.

KHNUM
Creator god Khnum was worshipped as a ram or a ram-headed man. He was said to mould children on a potter's wheel, then plant them in their mother's body.

GEB
One myth tells that the earth god Geb and his wife, sky goddess Nut, created the sun, which is reborn each day. Geb is shown with a goose, the hieroglyph for his name.

PTAH
The centre of worship for this god was Memphis. The city priests maintained that Ptah was the supreme god, who created all the other gods by speaking their names.

ANUBIS
Jackal-headed Anubis was god of the dead and mummification. He watched over the mummy and supervised many funerary rites.

NEPHTHYS
This goddess was the sister of Isis, and she helped Isis resurrect the mutilated body of Osiris. The two sisters are usually shown together. They protected coffins and canopic jars, often in the form of a pair of hawks.

SOBEK
This crocodile god was ruler of the water, and the Nile was said to be his sweat. The main centres of worship were places where the danger of crocodile attacks was high.

ABYDOS TRIAD

Triads were small families of gods worshipped in a particular area. The family consisted of a husband, wife, and son. The Abydos triad was Osiris, his wife Isis, and their son, the sky god Horus.

HORUS · ISIS · OSIRIS

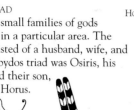

KHONS · MUT · AMUN

THEBAN TRIAD

The chief god worshipped at the temples of Karnak and Luxor was the creator god Amun. His wife Mut was a war goddess, sometimes shown as a vulture or a lioness. Their son was Khons, a moon god, often depicted as a mummy.

FORMS OF MAAT

Many gods took various forms in different times or settings. Here are three representations of the goddess Maat, who stood for justice, truth, and order. In each of these forms, she is wearing the *Feather of Truth* on her head.

HATHOR

This goddess of the sky and of love was associated with the cow. She was often shown with horns that held the sun.

THOTH

A patron of scribes and the god of wisdom and writing, Thoth was also a moon god. He was depicted as an ibis or a baboon.

HIEROGLYPHS

EGYPTIAN picture-writing is called hieroglyphs, which means "sacred symbols" in Greek. The symbols could have various meanings.

The alphabet

Symbol is used for these sounds

Every word was written exactly as it was pronounced, although only in consonants. Vowels were omitted. The alphabet consisted of 24 hieroglyphs, each representing different sounds.

Owl faces right, so read right to left

This is a weak consonant, not a vowel

READING THE RIGHT WAY

A hieroglyphic text could be read from left to right, right to left, or top to bottom. The symbols of animals or people tell you which way to read – always read towards the faces.

W MOON UNDER WICK QUAIL CHICK	**TH** THREE COW'S BELLY	**Y,I** YOUNG INK KITE REED LEAF
J JUNK GIN SNAKE	**T** LOAF OF BREAD	**B** LEG
G GAP POT STAND	**P** MAT	**TH** THAT UNKNOWN
N WATER	**D** HAND	**M** OWL
F,V HORNED VIPER	**K** HILL	**H** TWISTED FLAX
H REED HUT	**L,R** MOUTH	**A** MAY ARM
A,E,O VULTURE	**Z** DOOR BOLT	**CH** CHIP TETHERING ROPE
S FOLDED CLOTH	**SH** POND	**K** BASKET

GROUP SIGNS

To save time, many hieroglyphs represent not one, but two or even three sounds together. For example, instead of spelling "sa" with two hieroglyphs, one for each of the separate sounds, it could be spelt with one symbol, a duck.

DUCK
= S+A = SA

BEETLE
= KH+P+R= KHEPER

HOUSE
= P+R = PER

TABLE WITH BREAD
= H+T+P = HOTEP

ARRANGING SYMBOLS

Symbols that made up a word did not have to be in a line; they could be fitted together in several ways, to please the eye.

TWO WAYS
TO WRITE
"QUEEN"

DETERMINATIVES

Some symbols are like clues. These are determinatives. They were added to the text to make the meaning clear, but they were not read as sounds.

PERSON   WALK, RUN   SEE   PLURAL

CLUE

Here is an example of a determinative. A scribe's pallete had two meanings. Next to a figure of a man it read "scribe", but next to a roll of papyrus it meant "to write".

FIGHTING EVIL

Egyptians thought symbols had power for good or evil. Scribes sometimes cut the heads off snakes or drew hawks with no claws to protect themselves from any harm.

GOOD LUCK
Symbols like the *Wadjet* Eye were thrown in for good luck.

EGYPTIAN NUMERALS

1 STROKE	**I**	The Egyptian counting system was based on the number 10, with
10 CATTLE HOBBLE	**∩**	different symbols for 1, 10, 100, etc.
100 COIL OF ROPE	**ℓ**	Adding
1,000 LOTUS PLANT	**Ⱡ**	up the
10,000 FINGER	**ℓ**	symbols gives
100,000 TADPOLE		the total.
1,000,000 GOD SUPPORTING SKY		

(9)

(27)

(1,200)

(54,700)

ARCHITECTURE

THE SURVIVING buildings of
ancient Egypt are mostly
religious, either temples
or tombs. Their
forms symbolize
natural cycles
and beliefs.

COLONNADE
Long colonnades were a
feature of many temples.
This one with palm-tree
capitals is from Philae.

ARTISTIC LICENCE
Some of the highly elaborate
architectural forms depicted
in tomb paintings were
obviously exaggerated.

PLANT FORMS
These Old Kingdom
columns are shaped like
papyrus stems (left)
and a palm tree (right).

Opening bud

Decorated with images of gods

CAPITAL
FROM THE
TEMPLE
OF ESNA

CARVED
Square pillars were
sculpted with figures
of gods and men, some
massive, in relief or
even in the round.
This is the god Osiris.

COLUMN
Temple columns could
be fluted or smooth. But
most were sculpted, often
with elaborate reliefs
that were then painted.

HIGH GATEWAY (MEDINET HABU)
Ramses III's mortuary temple and palace are enclosed within massive, 10 m (33 ft) thick walls. This ruined gateway was the main entrance to this Theban complex.

Window

KING'S HAREM
Some of rooms in the three-storey gateway were used as a harem. Walls show scenes of Ramses III being attended by young women.

Detail from the painted pavement at Akhenaten's palace

FLOOR FRESCOES
The walls and floors of palaces and villas were plastered and painted with bright frescoes of patterns or nature scenes. These are from Akhenaten's palace.

AKHENATEN'S PALACE AT AMARNA
Nothing but ruined foundations of this palace remain. But it can be imagined from paintings in the tomb of high priest Meryre. This reconstructed storage area was just a small part of the vast palace complex, which was set amongst landscaped gardens with many trees and shady pools.

Glossary

AMULET
A lucky charm, worn or carried to ward off evil.

ANKH
A kind of amulet, it was the symbol of life. Only gods and kings are shown holding the ankh.

BA
A person's spirit or soul, thought to live on after death. The *Ba* is often depicted as a human-headed bird.

BOOK OF THE DEAD
A collection of up to 200 spells, placed with the mummy to help the deceased reach the other world safely.

CANOPIC JARS
Four jars used to hold the embalmed stomach, liver, lungs, and intestines.

CARNELIAN
A red semi-precious gemstone.

CARTOUCHE
A hieroglyphic symbol representing an oval-shaped loop. A pharaoh's name was written inside the cartouche.

CATARACT
A stretch of rapids that interrupt the Nile's flow.

CAUSEWAY
A raised road or path.

COLOSSUS
A larger than life-size statue, usually of a king. They are often found outside temples.

DELTA
The flat area at the mouth of a river, where the mainstream splits into marshy branches.

DEMOTIC
Developed from hieratic writing, this cursive form is found on Egyptian monuments and papyri.

DYNASTY
A succession of rulers from related families. Egypt's pharaohs formed 31 dynasties.

FAIENCE
A glazed earthenware.

FALSE DOOR
A symbolic gateway carved or painted on tombs and coffins, through which a dead person's spirit was thought to pass.

HIERATIC
A form of writing adapted from hieroglyphs. It was written on papyrus using an ink and brush.

KOHL
Black eye make-up worn by Egyptian men, women, and children.

LOWER EGYPT
The northern part of Egypt around the Nile Delta.

MUMMY
When an Egyptian died, the body was turned into a mummy. To do this, it was dried, preserved, and wrapped in linen.

MUMMY CASE
A coffin containing the mummified remains of an ancient Egyptian.

NATRON
A salt that occurs naturally in Egypt. It was used to purify and dry out the body when it was being mummified.

NECROPOLIS
A Greek word that means "city of the dead". It is used to describe Egyptian cemeteries.

NOME
A province of ancient Egypt – it was divided into areas to make government easier.

OBELISK
A tapering four-sided pillar made of stone.

OSTRACON
A flake of limestone or broken pottery that was used for writing or making rough sketches on.

PAPYRUS
A water reed used to make a kind of paper. It was the main writing material used in Egypt.

PECTORAL
A piece of jewellery that was worn on the chest.

PHARAOH
An Egyptian king. The word means "The Great House", the royal palace.

PUNT
A semi-mythical land that Egyptian texts refer to as a source for trade. Its exact location is still unclear, but it was south of Egypt, perhaps in Somalia.

PYLON
The monumental entrance wall of a temple.

PYRAMID
A huge tomb with a square base and four sloping sides, built to house a pharaoh when he died.

PYRAMID TEXTS
Religious writings carved on the walls inside a pyramid. They are an early version of the *Book of the Dead*, a collection of spells to help the dead pharaoh reach the next world.

RELIEF
A carved or moulded sculpture that stands out from its background.

SARCOPHAGUS
A stone coffin that is either rectangular or human-shaped. The word means "flesh-eater" in Greek.

SCARAB
An Egyptian dung-beetle, symbol of rebirth.

SHABTI
From an Egyptian word meaning "to answer", this mummy-shaped figurine was placed in the tomb with a mummy. When the dead were called upon to work in the next life, they would call their *shabtis*, who they believed would answer and do the work instead.

SPHINX
A statue in the shape of a lion with the head of a man or ram. A sphinx was a symbol of royal power.

STELA
A slab of stone (or sometimes wood) with text and pictures, set up in a tomb or temple.

UPPER EGYPT
The southern part of ancient Egypt. The main city was Thebes.

URAEUS
The royal cobra, worn by the pharaoh on his brow. It was thought to spit fire at the pharaoh's enemies.

VALLEY OF THE KINGS
A desolate valley on the west bank of the Nile near Luxor, which contains the tombs of many of the New Kingdom pharaohs.

VIZIER
The chief minister. He looked after government departments responsible for running the country and reported to the pharaoh every day.

INDEX

Acknowledgments

Dorling Kindersley would like to thank:
Hilary Bird for the index; Joanne Little
for design assistance; Sarah Goulding for
editorial assistance; James Putnam for
consulting on additional material; James
Anderson and Yak El-Droubie for cartography;
The British Museum for supplying references
for the Dynasties, pages 172/173; and The
Metropolitan Museum New York for supplying
references for the hieroglyphs, pages 180/182.

Photographs by:
Peter Anderson, Geoff Brightling,
Christi Graham, Peter Hayman,
Alan Hills, Dave King, Nick Nicholls,
Kim Sayer, Ivor Kerslake, Karl Shone.

Illustrations by:
Peter Anderson, Russell Barnett,
Stephen Conlin, Peter Dennis,
Dave Donkin, Simone End, Eugene Fleury,
Will Giles, Thomas Keenes, Sandra Pond,
Sarah Ponder, Peter Visscher,
J. G. Wilkinson, John Woodcock.

Picture Credits
t top; *c* centre; *a* above; *b* below; *l* left; *r* right.

The Publisher would like to thank the
following for their kind permission to
reproduce their photographs:

Ashmolean Museum, Oxford 43cra,cr,crb,
58tr;/The Griffith Institute 123tl,ca,cr; Bolton
Museum, 2br, 3tr, 12br, 23tr, 27tl, 28b, 86/7,
99br, 105tr, 111cr, 117c; Bridgeman Art
Library 61br, 72/3br;/Louvre, Paris 54bl;/The
British Library 66cr; The British Library/
Laurence Pordes 14cr; The British Museum 1c,
2tl, tr, bl, 3l, br, 5t, 7br, 11r, 12bl, 13cb, 14b,
15tl,cl, 16tr,c,bl, 17b, 20tr, 20/21b, 21br, 27tc,
29tl,tr,cr, 30tr,b, 31tl,c,br, 32cl,clb, 34bl,
35br,tc, 37bc,tl, 38/39tc, 44/45b, 44tl,cr,
45tr,c,tl, 46/47bl, 47tl, 49bc, 50br, 54cr, 55c,
56bl, 57r,c,cl, 58cb, bl,tl, 59tl,r,bl,bc, 60br, 61tl,
62/3c, 68tl, c,br, 69tr,cla,br, 71t, 74tl,bl,
75tl,c,br, 78cr, 79br,bl, 80c, 81t,ca, 82c,cl,cr,
83tr,bl,crb,cr, 91tr, 92tl, 93br, 94tr, 95cl,c,
96/97, 98bl,r, 99tl, 101l,tr,, 102tl, 103tr, 104tr,
105bc, br,tc,cl, 107tr, 108/9tc, 108bl,br, 109bl,
110l, 112tl,cl,br,bl, 113tl,cr,bc,br,tr, 114tr,b,
115cr, 116tr,bl,cl, 117b,tl, 118cl, 119tl,ca,tr,bl,
126/7b, 127tl,tr, 129tl, 130l,cr,bc; Cairo Museum
18bl,br; Lester Cheeseman 22cr, 129r; Peter
Clayton 55br, 123bc; Robert Harding Picture
Library 100bl; Michael Holford 100cl, 103c;
The Manchester Museum (jacket), 17tl,tc,tr,
22bl, 29b, 35cr,tl, 53tr, 54bc, 55tl,tr, 66/67bc,
67cr, 78tl,cl,bl, 79ca, 82tl, 90tr,cl,cr, 91cl, cr,br,
99cl, 100tr, 103tc, 104bl,bc, 106tr,cra,bl,
106/107bc, 107br, 109br, 110cr, 111tl,
115tl,tr,br, 116br, 118br,l, 129c, 131tl, tr;
Metropolitan Museum New York 88/89bc;
John G. Ross 8/9, 12tr, 13tl, 14tl, 18c, 19tc,br,
20cl, 21tl, 23b, 26tl, 27r, 33tr,br, 35bc, 36br,
37cl, 38br, 39cla,br, 43b, 64/5, 72br, 83tl,
88c,tr, 92br, 93c, 94bl, cr, 95br,tr, 102br, 109tr,
110/1b, 120cr, 121tl,tr,cr, 120/1b, 122,cr,b,
123tr, 124/5, 128bl;/Rapho 32cr, 36clb; The
Science Museum 51br; Lin White 10tr,cr, 11tl,
23tl, 36tl, 37r, 39bc, 76/77, 88bl, 103br, 107tl,
111tr, 120cl, 126c, 128cr, 129bl, 131bl,
171tr,cr.

Every effort has been made to trace the
copyright holders and we apologise in
advance for any unintentional omissions.
We would be pleased to insert the
appropriate acknowledgment in any
subsequent edition of this publication.

PENGUIN POPULAR CLASSICS

THE PICTURE OF DORIAN GRAY

OSCAR WILDE

PENGUIN BOOKS

PENGUIN BOOKS

Published by the Penguin Group

Penguin Books Ltd, 80 Strand, London WC2R 0RL, England

Penguin Putnam Inc., 375 Hudson Street, New York, New York 10014, USA

Penguin Books Australia Ltd, Ringwood, Victoria, Australia

Penguin Books Canada Ltd, 10 Alcorn Avenue, Toronto, Ontario, Canada M4V 3B2

Penguin Books India (P) Ltd, 11 Community Centre, Panchsheel Park,
New Delhi — 110 017, India

Penguin Books (NZ) Ltd, Cnr Rosedale and Airborne Roads, Albany, Auckland,
New Zealand

Penguin Books (South Africa) (Pty) Ltd, 24 Sturdee Avenue, Rosebank 2196
South Africa

Penguin Books Ltd, Registered Offices: 80 Strand, London WC2R 0RL, England

www.penguin.com

First published 1891
Published in Penguin Popular Classics 1994

38

Printed and bound in Great Britain by Bookmarque Ltd, Croydon

THE PREFACE

THE artist is the creator of beautiful things.

To reveal art and conceal the artist is art's aim.

The critic is he who can translate into another manner or a new material his impression of beautiful things.

The highest, as the lowest, form of criticism is a mode of autobiography.

Those who find ugly meanings in beautiful things are corrupt without being charming. This is a fault.

Those who find beautiful meanings in beautiful things are the cultivated. For these there is hope.

They are the elect to whom beautiful things mean only Beauty.

There is no such thing as a moral or an immoral book. Books are well written, or badly written. That is all.

The nineteenth century dislike of Realism is the rage of Caliban seeing his own face in a glass.

The nineteenth century dislike of Romanticism is the rage of Caliban not seeing his own face in a glass.

The moral life of man forms part of the subject-matter of the artist, but the morality of art consists in the perfect use of an imperfect medium. No artist desires to prove anything. Even things that are true can be proved.

No artist has ethical sympathies. An ethical sympathy in an artist is an unpardonable mannerism of style.

No artist is ever morbid. The artist can express everything.

Thought and language are to the artist instruments of an art.

Vice and virtue are to the artist materials for an art.

From the point of view of form, the type of all the arts is the art of the musician. From the point of view of feeling, the actor's craft is the type.

All art is at once surface and symbol.

Those who go beneath the surface do so at their peril.

Those who read the symbol do so at their peril.

It is the spectator, and not life, that art really mirrors.

Diversity of opinion about a work of art shows that the work is new, complex, and vital.

When critics disagree the artist is in accord with himself.

We can forgive a man for making a useful thing as long as he does not admire it. The only excuse for making a useless thing is that one admires it intensely.

All art is quite useless.

OSCAR WILDE

THE PICTURE
OF DORIAN GRAY

CHAPTER I

THE studio was filled with the rich odour of roses, and when the light summer wind stirred amidst the trees of the garden, there came through the open door the heavy scent of the lilac, or the more delicate perfume of the pink-flowering thorn.

From the corner of the divan of Persian saddle-bags on which he was lying, smoking, as was his custom, innumerable cigarettes, Lord Henry Wotton could just catch the gleam of the honey-sweet and honey-coloured blossoms of a laburnum, whose tremulous branches seemed hardly able to bear the burden of a beauty so flame-like as theirs; and now and then the fantastic shadows of birds in flight flitted across the long tussore-silk curtains that were stretched in front of the huge window, producing a kind of momentary Japanese effect, and making him think of those pallid jade-faced painters of Tokio who, through the medium of an art that is necessarily immobile, seek to convey the sense of swiftness and motion. The sullen murmur of the bees shouldering their way through the long unmown grass, or circling with monotonous insistence round the dusty gilt horns of the straggling woodbine, seemed to make the stillness more oppressive. The dim roar of London was like the bourdon note of a distant organ.

In the centre of the room, clamped to an upright easel, stood the full-length portrait of a young man of extraordinary personal beauty, and in front of it, some little distance away, was sitting the artist himself, Basil Hallward, whose sudden disappearance some years ago caused, at the time, such public excitement, and gave rise to so many strange conjectures.

As the painter looked at the gracious and comely form he had so skilfully mirrored in his art, a smile of pleasure passed across his face, and seemed about to linger there. But he suddenly started up, and, closing his eyes, placed his fingers upon the lids, as though he sought to imprison within his brain some curious dream from which he feared he might awake.

'It is your best work, Basil, the best thing you have ever done,' said Lord Henry, languidly. 'You must certainly send it next year to the Grosvenor. The Academy is too large and too vulgar. Whenever I have gone there, there have been either so many people that I have not been able to see the pictures, which was dreadful, or so many pictures that I have not been able to see the people, which was worse. The Grosvenor is really the only place.'

'I don't think I shall send it anywhere,' he answered, tossing his head back in that odd way that used to make his friends laugh at him at Oxford. 'No: I won't send it anywhere.'

Lord Henry elevated his eyebrows, and looked at him in amazement through the thin blue wreaths of smoke that curled up in such fanciful whorls from his heavy opium-tainted cigarette. 'Not send it anywhere? My dear fellow, why? Have you any reason? What odd chaps you painters are! You do anything in the world to gain a reputation. As soon as you have one, you seem to want to throw it away. It is silly of you, for there is only one thing in the world worse than being talked about, and that is not being talked about. A portrait like this would set you far above all the young men in England, and make the old men quite jealous, if old men are ever capable of any emotion.'

'I know you will laugh at me,' he replied, 'but I really can't exhibit it. I have put too much of myself into it.'

Lord Henry stretched himself out on the divan and laughed. 'Yes, I knew you would; but it is quite true, all the same.'

'Too much of yourself in it! Upon my word, Basil, I didn't know you were so vain; and I really can't see any resemblance between you, with your rugged strong face and your coal-black hair, and this young Adonis, who looks as if he was made out of ivory and rose-leaves. Why, my dear Basil, he is a Narcissus, and you—well, of course you have an intellectual expression, and all that. But beauty, real beauty, ends where an intellectual expression begins. Intellect is in itself a mode of exaggeration, and destroys the harmony of any face. The moment one sits down to think, one becomes all nose, or all forehead, or something horrid. Look at the successful men in any of the learned professions. How perfectly hideous they are! Except, of course, in the Church. But then in the Church they don't think. A bishop keeps on saying at the age of eighty what he was told to say when he was a boy of eighteen, and as a natural consequence he always looks absolutely delightful. Your mysterious young friend, whose name you have never told me, but whose picture really fascinates me, never thinks. I feel quite sure of that. He is some brainless, beautiful creature, who should be always here in winter when we have no flowers to look at, and always here in summer when we want something to chill our intelligence. Don't flatter yourself, Basil: you are not in the least like him.'

'You don't understand me, Harry,' answered the artist. 'Of course I am not like him. I know that perfectly well. Indeed, I should be sorry to look like him. You shrug your shoulders? I am telling you the truth. There is a fatality about all physical and intellectual distinction, the sort of fatality that seems to dog through history the faltering

9

steps of kings. It is better not to be different from one's fellows. The ugly and the stupid have the best of it in this world. They can sit at their ease and gape at the play. If they know nothing of victory, they are at least spared the knowledge of defeat. They live as we all should live, undisturbed, indifferent, and without disquiet. They neither bring ruin upon others, nor ever receive it from alien hands. Your rank and wealth, Harry; my brains, such as they are— my art, whatever it may be worth; Dorian Gray's good looks—we shall all suffer for what the gods have given us, suffer terribly.'

'Dorian Gray? Is that his name?' asked Lord Henry, walking across the studio towards Basil Hallward.

'Yes, that is his name. I didn't intend to tell it to you.'

'But why not?'

'Oh, I can't explain. When I like people immensely I never tell their names to anyone. It is like surrendering a part of them. I have grown to love secrecy. It seems to be the one thing that can make modern life mysterious or marvellous to us. The commonest thing is delightful if one only hides it. When I leave town now I never tell my people where I am going. If I did, I should lose all my pleasure. It is a silly habit, I daresay, but somehow it seems to bring a great deal of romance into one's life. I suppose you think me awfully foolish about it?'

'Not at all,' answered Lord Henry, 'not at all, my dear Basil. You seem to forget that I am married, and the one charm of marriage is that it makes a life of deception absolutely necessary for both parties. I never know where my wife is, and my wife never knows what I am doing. When we meet—we do meet occasionally, when we dine out together, or go down to the Duke's—we tell each other the most absurd stories with the most serious faces. My wife is very good at it—much better, in fact, than I am.

She never gets confused over her dates, and I always do. But when she does find me out, she makes no row at all. I sometimes wish she would; but she merely laughs at me.'

'I hate the way you talk about your married life, Harry,' said Basil Hallward, strolling towards the door that led into the garden. 'I believe that you are really a very good husband, but that you are thoroughly ashamed of your own virtues. You are an extraordinary fellow. You never say a moral thing, and you never do a wrong thing. Your cynicism is simply a pose.'

'Being natural is simply a pose, and the most irritating pose I know,' cried Lord Henry, laughing; and the two young men went out into the garden together, and ensconced themselves on a long bamboo seat that stood in the shade of a tall laurel bush. The sunlight slipped over the polished leaves. In the grass, white daisies were tremulous.

After a pause, Lord Henry pulled out his watch. 'I am afraid I must be going, Basil,' he murmured, 'and before I go, I insist on your answering a question I put to you some time ago.'

'What is that?' said the painter, keeping his eyes fixed on the ground.

'You know quite well.'

'I do not, Harry.'

'Well, I will tell you what it is. I want you to explain to me why you won't exhibit Dorian Gray's picture. I want the real reason.'

'I told you the real reason.'

'No, you did not. You said it was because there was too much of yourself in it. Now, that is childish.'

'Harry,' said Basil Hallward, looking him straight in the face, 'every portrait that is painted with feeling is a portrait of the artist, not of the sitter. The sitter is merely the accident, the occasion. It is not he who is revealed by the painter; it is rather the painter who, on the coloured canvas, reveals himself. The reason I will not exhibit this picture is that I am afraid that I have shown in it the secret of my own soul.'

Lord Henry laughed. 'And what is that?' he asked.

'I will tell you,' said Hallward; but an expression of perplexity came over his face.

'I am all expectation, Basil,' continued his companion, glancing at him.

'Oh, there is really very little to tell, Harry,' answered the painter; 'and I am afraid you will hardly understand it. Perhaps you will hardly believe it.'

Lord Henry smiled, and, leaning down, plucked a pink-petalled daisy from the grass, and examined it. "I am quite sure I shall understand it,' he replied, gazing intently at the little golden white-feathered disk, 'and as for believing things, I can believe anything, provided that it is quite incredible.'

The wind shook some blossoms from the trees, and the heavy lilac-blooms, with their clustering stars, moved to and fro in the languid air. A grasshopper began to chirrup by the wall, and like a blue thread a long thin dragon-fly floated past on its brown gauze wings. Lord Henry felt as if he could hear Basil Hallward's heart beating, and wondered what was coming.

'The story is simply this,' said the painter after some time. 'Two months ago I went to a crush at Lady Brandon's. You know we poor artists have to show ourselves in society from time to time, just to remind the public that we are not savages. With an evening coat and a white tie, as you told me once, anybody, even a stockbroker, can gain a reputation for being civilised. Well, after I had been in the room about ten minutes, talking to huge, overdressed dowagers and tedious Academicians, I suddenly became conscious that someone was looking at me. I turned halfway round, and saw Dorian Gray for the first time. When our eyes met, I felt that I was growing pale. A curious sensation of terror came over me. I knew that I had come face to face with someone whose mere personality was so fascinating that, if I allowed it to do so, it would absorb my whole nature, my whole soul, my very art itself. I did not want any external influence in my life. You know yourself, Harry, how independent I am by nature. I have always been my own master; had at least always been so, till I met Dorian Gray. Then—— but I don't know how to explain it to you. Something seemed to tell me that I was on the verge of a terrible crisis in my life. I had a strange feeling that Fate had in store for me exquisite joys and exquisite sorrows. I grew afraid, and turned to quit the room. It was not conscience that made me do so; it was a sort of cowardice. I take no credit to myself for trying to escape.'

'Conscience and cowardice are really the same things, Basil. Conscience is the trade-name of the firm. That is all.'

'I don't believe that, Harry, and I don't believe you do either. However, whatever was my motive—and it may have been pride, for I used to be very proud—I certainly struggled to the door. There, of course, I stumbled against Lady Brandon. "You are not going to run away so soon, Mr. Hallward?" she screamed out. You know her curiously shrill voice?'

'Yes; she is a peacock in everything but beauty,' said Lord Henry, pulling the daisy to bits with his long, nervous fingers.

'I could not get rid of her. She brought me up to Royalties, and people with Stars and Garters, and elderly ladies with gigantic tiaras and parrot noses. She spoke of me as her dearest friend. I had only met her once before, but she took it into her head to lionise me. I believe some picture of mine had made a great success at the time, at least had been chattered about in the penny newspapers, which is the nineteenth-century standard of immortality. Suddenly I found myself face to face with the young man whose personality had so strangely stirred me. We were quite close, almost touching. Our eyes met again. It was reckless of me, but I asked Lady Brandon to introduce me to him. Perhaps it was not so reckless, after all. It was simply inevitable. We would have spoken to each other without any introduction. I am sure of that. Dorian told me so afterwards. He, too, felt that we were destined to know each other.'

'And how did Lady Brandon describe this wonderful young man?' asked his companion. 'I know she goes in for giving a rapid *précis* of all her guests. I remember her bringing me up to a truculent and red-faced old gentleman covered all over with orders and ribbons, and hissing into my ear, in a tragic whisper which must have been perfectly audible to everybody in the room, the most astounding details. I simply fled. I like to find out people for myself. But Lady Brandon treats her guests exactly as an auctioneer treats his goods. She either explains them entirely away, or tells one everything about them except what one wants to know.'

'Poor Lady Brandon! You are hard on her, Harry!' said Hallward listlessly.

'My dear fellow, she tried to found a *salon*, and only succeeded in opening a restaurant. How could I admire her? But tell me, what did she say about Mr. Dorian Gray?'

'Oh, something like, "Charming boy—poor dear mother and I absolutely inseparable. Quite forget what he does—afraid he—doesn't do anything—oh, yes, plays the piano

—or is it the violin, dear Mr. Gray?" Neither of us could help laughing, and we became friends at once.'

'Laughter is not at all a bad beginning for a friendship, and it is far the best ending for one,' said the young lord, plucking another daisy.

Hallward shook his head. 'You don't understand what friendship is, Harry,' he murmured—'or what enmity is, for that matter. You like everyone; that is to say, you are indifferent to everyone.'

'How horribly unjust of you!' cried Lord Henry, tilting his hat back, and looking up at the little clouds that, like ravelled skeins of glossy white silk, were drifting across the hollowed turquoise of the summer sky. 'Yes; horribly unjust of you. I make a great difference between people. I choose my friends for their good looks, my acquaintances for their good characters, and my enemies for their good intellects. A man cannot be too careful in the choice of his enemies. I have not got one who is a fool. They are all men of some intellectual power, and consequently they all appreciate me. Is that very vain of me? I think it is rather vain.'

'I should think it was, Harry. But according to your category I must be merely an acquaintance.'

'My dear old Basil, you are much more than an acquaintance.'

'And much less than a friend. A sort of brother, I suppose?'

'Oh, brothers! I don't care for brothers. My elder brother won't die, and my younger brothers seem never to do anything else.'

'Harry!' exclaimed Hallward, frowning.

'My dear fellow, I am not quite serious. But I can't help detesting my relations. I suppose it comes from the fact that none of us can stand other people having the same faults as ourselves. I quite sympathise with the rage of the English democracy against what they call the vices of the upper orders. The masses feel that drunkenness, stupidity, and immorality should be their own special property, and that if anyone of us makes an ass of himself he is poaching on their preserves. When poor Southwark got into the Divorce Court, their indignation was quite magnificent. And yet I don't suppose that ten per cent of the proletariat live correctly.'

'I don't agree with a single word that you have said, and, what is more, Harry, I feel sure you don't either.'

Lord Henry stroked his pointed brown beard, and tapped the toe of his patent-leather boot with a tasselled ebony cane. 'How English you are, Basil! That is the second time you have made that observation. If one puts forward an idea to a true Englishman—always a rash thing to do—he never dreams of considering whether the idea is right or wrong. The only thing he considers of any importance is whether one believes it oneself. Now, the value of an idea has nothing whatsoever to do with the sincerity of the man who expresses it. Indeed, the probabilities are that the more insincere the man is, the more purely intellectual will the idea be, as in that case it will not be coloured by either his wants, his desires, or his prejudices. However, I don't propose to discuss politics, sociology, or metaphysics with you. I like persons better than principles, and I like persons with no principles better than anything else in the world. Tell me more about Mr. Dorian Gray. How often do you see him?'

'Every day. I couldn't be happy if I didn't see him every day. He is absolutely necessary to me.'

'How extraordinary! I thought you would never care for anything but your art.'

'He is all my art to me now,' said the painter, gravely. 'I sometimes think, Harry, that there are only two eras of any importance in the world's history. The first is the appearance of a new medium for art, and the second is the appearance of a new personality for art also. What the invention of oil-painting was to the Venetians, the face of Antinoüs was to late Greek sculpture, and the face of Dorian Gray will some day be to me. It is not merely that I paint from him, draw from him, sketch from him. Of course I have done all that. But he is much more to me than a model or a sitter. I won't tell you that I am dissatisfied with what I have done of him, or that his beauty is such that Art cannot express it. There is nothing that Art cannot express, and I know that the work I have done, since I met Dorian Gray, is good work, is the best work of my life. But in some curious way—I wonder will you understand me?—his personality has suggested to me an entirely new manner in art, an entirely new mode of style. I see things differently, I think of them differently. I can now recreate life in a way that was hidden from me before. "A dream of form in days of thought:"—who is it who says that? I forget; but it is what Dorian Gray has been to me. The merely visible presence of this lad—for he seems to me little more than a lad, though he is really over twenty—his merely visible presence—ah! I wonder can you realise all that that means? Unconsciously he defines for me the lines of a fresh school, a school that is to have in it all the passion of the romantic spirit, all the perfection of the spirit that is Greek. The harmony of soul and body—how much that is! We in our madness have separated the two, and have invented a realism that is vulgar, an ideality that is void. Harry! if you only knew what Dorian Gray is to me! You remember that landscape of mine, for which Agnew offered me such a huge price, but which I would not part with? It is one of the best things I have ever done. And why is it so? Because, while I was painting it, Dorian Gray sat beside me. Some subtle influence passed from him to me, and for the first time in my life I saw in the plain woodland the wonder I had always looked for, and always missed.'

'Basil, this is extraordinary! I must see Dorian Gray.'

Hallward got up from the seat, and walked up and down the garden. After some time he came back. 'Harry,' he said, 'Dorian Gray is to me simply a motive in art. You might see nothing in him. I see everything in him. He is never more present in my work than when no image of him is there. He is a suggestion, as I have said, of a new manner. I find him in the curves of certain lines, in the loveliness and subtleties of certain colours. That is all.'

'Then why won't you exhibit his portrait?' asked Lord Henry.

'Because, without intending it, I have put into it some expression of all this curious artistic idolatry, of which, of course, I have never cared to speak to him. He knows nothing about it. He shall never know anything about it. But the world might guess it; and I will not bare my soul to their shallow prying eyes. My heart shall never be put under their microscope. There is too much of myself in the thing, Harry—too much of myself!'

'Poets are not so scrupulous as you are. They know how useful passion is for publication. Nowadays a broken heart will run to many editions.'

'I hate them for it,' cried Hallward. 'An artist should create beautiful things, but should put nothing of his own life into them. We live in an age when men treat art as if it were meant to be a form of autobiography. We have lost the abstract sense of beauty. Some day I will show the world what it is; and for that reason the world shall never see my portrait of Dorian Gray.'

'I think you are wrong, Basil, but I won't argue with you. It is only the intellectually lost who ever argue. Tell me, is Dorian Gray very fond of you?'

The painter considered for a few moments. 'He likes me,' he answered, after a pause; 'I know he likes me. Of course I flatter him dreadfully. I find a strange pleasure in saying things to him that I know I shall be sorry for having said. As a rule, he is charming to me, and we sit in the studio and talk of a thousand things. Now and then, however, he is horribly thoughtless, and seems to take a real delight in giving me pain. Then I feel, Harry, that I have given away my whole soul to someone who treats it as if it were a flower to put in his coat, a bit of decoration to charm his vanity, an ornament for a summer's day.'

'Days in summer, Basil, are apt to linger,' murmured Lord Henry. 'Perhaps you will tire sooner than he will. It is a sad thing to think of, but there is no doubt that Genius lasts longer than Beauty. That accounts for the fact that we all take such pains to over-educate ourselves. In the wild struggle for existence, we want to have something that endures, and so we fill our minds with rubbish and facts, in the silly hope of keeping our place. The thoroughly well-informed man—that is the modern ideal. And the mind of the thoroughly well-informed man is a dreadful thing. It is like a bric-à-brac shop, all monsters and dust, with everything priced above its proper value. I think you will tire first, all the same. Some day you will look at your friend, and he will seem to you to be a little out of drawing, or you won't like his tone of colour, or something. You will bitterly reproach him in your own heart, and seriously think that he has behaved very badly to you. The next time he calls, you will be perfectly cold and indifferent. It will be a great pity, for it will alter you. What you have told me is quite a romance, a romance of art one might call it, and the worst of having a romance of any kind is that it leaves one so unromantic.'

'Harry, don't talk like that. As long as I live, the

personality of Dorian Gray will dominate me. You can't feel what I feel. You change too often.'

'Ah, my dear Basil, that is exactly why I can feel it. Those who are faithful know only the trivial side of love: it is the faithless who know love's tragedies.' And Lord Henry struck a light on a dainty silver case, and began to smoke a cigarette with a self-conscious and satisfied air, as if he had summed up the world in a phrase. There was a rustle of chirruping sparrows in the green lacquer leaves of the ivy, and the blue cloud-shadows chased themselves across the grass like swallows. How pleasant it was in the garden! And how delightful other people's emotions were!—much more delightful than their ideas, it seemed to him. One's own soul, and the passions of one's friends—those were the fascinating things in life. He pictured to himself with silent amusement the tedious luncheon that he had missed by staying so long with Basil Hallward. Had he gone to his aunt's he would have been sure to have met Lord Goodbody there, and the whole conversation would have been about the feeding of the poor, and the necessity for model lodging-houses. Each class would have preached the importance of those virtues, for whose exercise there was no necessity in their own lives. The rich would have spoken on the value of thrift, and the idle grown eloquent over the dignity of labour. It was charming to have escaped all that! As he thought of his aunt, an idea seemed to strike him. He turned to Hallward, and said, 'My dear fellow, I have just remembered.'

'Remembered what, Harry?'

'Where I heard the name of Dorian Gray.'

'Where was it?' asked Hallward, with a slight frown.

'Don't look so angry, Basil. It was at my aunt, Lady Agatha's. She told me she had discovered a wonderful young man, who was going to help her in the East End, and that his name was Dorian Gray. I am bound to state that she never told me he was good-looking. Women have no appreciation of good looks; at least, good women have not. She said that he was very earnest, and had a beautiful nature. I at once pictured to myself a creature with spectacles and lank hair, horribly freckled, and tramping about on huge feet. I wish I had known it was your friend.'

'I am very glad· you didn't, Harry.'

'Why?'

'I don't want you to meet him.'

'You don't want me to meet him?'

'No.'

'Mr. Dorian Gray is in the studio, sir,' said the butler, coming into the garden.

'You must introduce me now,' cried Lord Henry, laughing.

The painter turned to his servant, who stood blinking in the sunlight. 'Ask Mr. Gray to wait, Parker: I shall be in in a few moments.' The man bowed, and went up the walk. Then he looked at Lord Henry. 'Dorian Gray is my dearest friend,' he said. 'He has a simple and a beautiful nature. Your aunt was quite right in what she said of him. Don't spoil him. Don't try to influence him. Your influence would be· bad. The world is wide, and has many marvellous people in it. Don't take away from me the one person who gives to my art whatever charm it possesses; my life as an artist depends on him. Mind, Harry, I trust you.' He spoke very slowly, and the words seemed wrung out of him almost against his will.

'What nonsense you talk!' said Lord Henry, smiling, and, taking Hallward by the arm, he almost led him into the house.

CHAPTER II

As they entered they saw Dorian Gray. He was seated at the piano, with his back to them, turning over the pages of a volume of Schumann's 'Forest Scenes.' 'You must lend me these, Basil,' he cried. 'I want to learn them. They are perfectly charming.'

'That entirely depends on how you sit to-day, Dorian.'

'Oh, I am tired of sitting, and I don't want a life-sized portrait of myself,' answered the lad, swinging round on the music-stool, in a wilful, petulant manner. When he caught sight of Lord Henry, a faint blush coloured his cheeks for a moment, and he started up. 'I beg your pardon, Basil, but I didn't know you had anyone with you.'

'This is Lord Henry Wotton, Dorian, an old Oxford friend of mine. I have just been telling him what a capital sitter you were, and now you have spoiled everything.'

'You have not spoiled my pleasure in meeting you, Mr. Gray,' said Lord Henry, stepping forward and extending his hand. 'My aunt has often spoken to me about you. You are one of her favourites, and, I am afraid, one of her victims also.'

'I am in Lady Agatha's black books at present,' answered Dorian, with a funny look of penitence. 'I promised to go to a club in Whitechapel with her last Tuesday, and I really forgot all about it. We were to have played a duet together—three duets, I believe. I don't know what she will say to me. I am far too frightened to call.'

'Oh, I will make your peace with my aunt. She is quite devoted to you. And I don't think it really matters about your not being there. The audience probably thought it was a

22

duet. When Aunt Agatha sits down to the piano she makes quite enough noise for two people.'

'That is very horrid to her, and not very nice to me,' answered Dorian, laughing.

Lord Henry looked at him. Yes, he was certainly wonderfully handsome, with his finely-curved scarlet lips, his frank blue eyes, his crisp gold hair. There was something in his face that made one trust him at once. All the candour of youth was there, as well as all youth's passionate purity. One felt that he had kept himself unspotted from the world. No wonder Basil Hallward worshipped him.

'You are too charming to go in for philanthropy, Mr. Gray—far too charming.' And Lord Henry flung himself down on the divan, and opened his cigarette-case.

The painter had been busy mixing his colours and getting his brushes ready. He was looking worried, and when he heard Lord Henry's last remark he glanced at him, hesitated for a moment, and then said, 'Harry, I want to finish this picture to-day. Would you think it awfully rude of me if I asked you to go away?'

Lord Henry smiled, and looked at Dorian Gray. 'Am I to go, Mr. Gray?' he asked.

'Oh, please don't, Lord Henry. I see that Basil is in one of his sulky moods; and I can't bear him when he sulks. Besides, I want you to tell me why I should not go in for philanthropy.'

'I don't know that I shall tell you that, Mr. Gray. It is so tedious a subject that one would have to talk seriously about it. But I certainly shall not run away, now that you have asked me to stop. You don't really mind, Basil, do you? You have often told me that you liked your sitters to have someone to chat to.'

Hallward bit his lip. 'If Dorian wishes it, of course you must stay. Dorian's whims are laws to everybody, except himself.'

Lord Henry took up his hat and gloves. 'You are very pressing, Basil, but I am afraid I must go. I have promised to meet a man at the Orleans. Good-bye, Mr. Gray. Come and see me some afternoon in Curzon Street. I am nearly always at home at five o'clock. Write to me when you are coming. I should be sorry to miss you.'

'Basil,' cried Dorian Gray, 'if Lord Henry Wotton goes I shall go too. You never open your lips while you are painting, and it is horribly dull standing on a platform and trying to look pleasant. Ask him to stay. I insist upon it.'

'Stay, Harry, to oblige Dorian, and to oblige me,' said Hallward, gazing intently at his picture. 'It is quite true, I never talk when I am working, and never listen either, and it must be dreadfully tedious for my unfortunate sitters. I beg you to stay.'

'But what about my man at the Orleans?'

The painter laughed. 'I don't think there will be any difficulty about that. Sit down again, Harry. And now, Dorian, get up on the platform, and don't move about too much, or pay any attention to what Lord Henry says. He has a very bad influence over all his friends, with the single exception of myself.'

Dorian Gray stepped up on the dais, with the air of a young Greek martyr, and made a little *moue* of discontent to Lord Henry, to whom he had rather taken a fancy. He was so unlike Basil. They made a delightful contrast. And he had such a beautiful voice. After a few moments he said to him, 'Have you really a very bad influence, Lord Henry? As bad as Basil says?'

'There is no such thing as a good influence, Mr. Gray. All influence is immoral—immoral from the scientific point of view.'

'Why?'

'Because to influence a person is to give him one's own

soul. He does not think his natural thoughts, or burn with his natural passions. His virtues are not real to him. His sins, if there are such things as sins, are borrowed. He becomes an echo of someone else's music, an actor of a part that has not been written for him. The aim of life is self-development. To realise one's nature perfectly—that is what each of us is here for. People are afraid of themselves, nowadays. They have forgotten the highest of all duties, the duty that one owes to one's self. Of course they are charitable. They feed the hungry, and clothe the beggar. But their own souls starve, and are naked. Courage has gone out of our race. Perhaps we never really had it. The terror of society, which is the basis of morals, the terror of God, which is the secret of religion—these are the two things that govern us. And yet——'

'Just turn your head a little more to the right, Dorian, like a good boy,' said the painter, deep in his work, and conscious only that a look had come into the lad's face that he had never seen there before.

'And yet,' continued Lord Henry, in his low, musical voice, and with that graceful wave of the hand that was always so characteristic of him, and that he had even in his Eton days, ' I believe that if one man were to live out his life fully and completely, were to give form to every feeling, expression to every thought, reality to every dream—I believe that the world would gain such a fresh impulse of joy that we would forget all the maladies of mediævalism, and return to the Hellenic ideal—to something finer, richer, than the Hellenic ideal, it may be. But the bravest man amongst us is afraid of himself. The mutilation of the savage has its tragic survival in the self-denial that mars our lives. We are punished for our refusals. Every impulse that we strive to strangle broods in the mind, and poisons us. The body sins once, and has done with its sin, for action is a mode of purification. Nothing remains then but the recollection of a pleasure, or the luxury of a regret. The only way to get rid of a temptation is to yield to it. Resist it, and your soul grows sick with longing for the things it has forbidden to itself, with desire for what its monstrous laws have made monstrous and unlawful. It has been said that the great events of the world take place in the brain. It is in the brain, and the brain only, that the great sins of the world take place also. You, Mr. Gray, you yourself, with your rose-red youth and your rose-white boyhood, you have had passions that have made you afraid, thoughts that have filled you with terror, day-dreams and sleeping dreams whose mere memory might stain your cheek with shame——'

'Stop!' faltered Dorian Gray, 'stop! you bewilder me. I don't know what to say. There is some answer to you, but I cannot find it. Don't speak. Let me think. Or, rather, let me try not to think.'

For nearly ten minutes he stood there, motionless, with parted lips, and eyes strangely bright. He was dimly conscious that entirely fresh influences were at work within him. Yet they seemed to him to have come really from himself. The few words that Basil's friend had said to him—words spoken by chance, no doubt, and with wilful paradox in them—had touched some secret chord that had never been touched before, but that he felt was now vibrating and throbbing to curious pulses.

Music had stirred him like that. Music had troubled him many times. But music was not articulate, It was not a new world, but rather another chaos, that it created in us. Words! Mere words! How terrible they were! How clear, and vivid and cruel! One could not escape from them. And yet what a subtle magic there was in them! They seemed to be able to give a plastic form to formless things, and to have a music of their own as sweet as that of viola or of lute. Mere words! Was there anything so real as words?

Yes; there had been things in his boyhood that he had not understood. He understood them now. Life suddenly became fiery-coloured to him. It seemed to him that he had been walking in fire. Why had he not known it?

With his subtle smile, Lord Henry watched him. He knew the precise psychological moment when to say nothing. He felt intensely interested. He was amazed at the sudden impression that his words had produced, and, remembering a book that he had read when he was sixteen, a book which had revealed to him much that he had not known before, he wondered whether Dorian Gray was passing through a similar experience. He had merely shot an arrow into the air. Had it hit the mark? How fascinating the lad was!

Hallward painted away with that marvellous bold touch of his, that had the true refinement and perfect delicacy that in art, at any rate, comes only from strength. He was unconscious of the silence.

'Basil, I am tired of standing,' cried Dorian Gray, suddenly. 'I must go out and sit in the garden. The air is stifling here.'

'My dear fellow, I am so sorry. When I am painting, I can't think of anything else. But you never sat better. You were perfectly still. And I have caught the effect I wanted— the half-parted lips, and the bright look in the eyes. I don't know what Harry has been saying to you, but he has certainly made you have the most wonderful expression. I suppose he has been paying you compliments. You mustn't believe a word that he says.'

'He has certainly not been paying me compliments. Perhaps that is the reason that I don't believe anything he has told me.'

'You know you believe it all,' said Lord Henry, looking at him with his dreamy, languorous eyes. 'I will go out to the garden with you. It is horribly hot in the studio. Basil, let us have something iced to drink, something with strawberries in it.'

'Certainly, Harry. Just touch the bell, and when Parker comes I will tell him what you want. I have got to work up this background, so I will join you later on. Don't keep Dorian too long. I have never been in better form for painting than I am to-day. This is going to be my masterpiece. It is my masterpiece as it stands.'

Lord Henry went out to the garden, and found Dorian Gray burying his face in the great cool lilac-blossoms, feverishly drinking in their perfume as if it had been wine. He came close to him, and put his hand upon his shoulder. 'You are quite right to do that,' he murmured. 'Nothing can cure the soul but the senses, just as nothing can cure the senses but the soul.'

The lad started and drew back. He was bare-headed, and the leaves had tossed his rebellious curls and tangled all their gilded threads. There was a look of fear in his eyes, such as people have when they are suddenly awakened. His finely-chiselled nostrils quivered, and some hidden nerve shook the scarlet of his lips and left them trembling.

'Yes,' continued Lord Henry, 'that is one of the great secrets of life—to cure the soul by means of the senses, and the senses by means of the soul. You are a wonderful creation. You know more than you think you know, just as you know less than you want to know.'

Dorian Gray frowned and turned his head away. He could not help liking the tall, graceful young man who was standing by him. His romantic olive-coloured face and worn expression interested him. There was something in his low, languid voice that was absolutely fascinating. His cool, white, flower-like hands, even, had a curious charm. They moved, as he spoke, like music, and seemed to have a language of their own. But he felt afraid of him, and ashamed of being afraid. Why had it been left for a stranger to reveal him to himself? He had known Basil Hallward for months, but the friendship between them had never altered him. Suddenly there had come someone across his life who seemed to have disclosed to him life's mystery. And, yet, what was there to be afraid of? He was not a schoolboy or a girl. It was absurd to be frightened.

'Let us go and sit in the shade,' said Lord Henry. 'Parker has brought out the drinks, and if you stay any longer in this glare you will be quite spoiled, and Basil will never paint you again. You really must not allow yourself to become sunburnt. It would be unbecoming.'

'What can it matter?' cried Dorian Gray, laughing, as he sat down on the seat at the end of the garden.

'It should matter everything to you, Mr. Gray.'

'Why?'

'Because you have the most marvellous youth, and youth is the one thing worth having.'

'I don't feel that, Lord Henry.'

'No, you don't feel it now. Some day, when you are old and wrinkled and ugly, when thought has seared your forehead with its lines, and passion branded your lips with its hideous fires, you will feel it, you will feel it terribly. Now, wherever you go, you charm the world. Will it always be so? . . . You have a wonderfully beautiful face, Mr. Gray. Don't frown. You have. And Beauty is a form of Genius—is higher, indeed, than Genius, as it needs no explanation. It is of the great facts of the world, like sunlight, or spring-time, or the reflection in dark waters of that silver shell we call the moon. It cannot be questioned. It has its divine right of sovereignty. It makes princes of those who have it. You smile? Ah! when you have lost it you won't smile. . . . People say sometimes that Beauty is only superficial. That may be so. But at least it is not so superficial as Thought is. To me, Beauty is the wonder of wonders. It is only shallow people who do not judge by appearances. The true mystery of the world is the visible, not the invisible. . . . Yes, Mr. Gray, the gods have been good to you. But what the gods give they quickly take away. You have only a few years in which to live really, perfectly, and fully. When your youth goes, your beauty will go with it, and then you will suddenly discover that there are no triumphs left for you, or have to content yourself with those mean triumphs that the memory of your past will make more bitter than defeats. Every month as it wanes brings you nearer to something dreadful. Time is jealous of you, and wars against your lilies and your roses. You will become sallow, and hollow-cheeked, and dull-eyed. You will suffer horribly. . . . Ah! realise your youth while you have it. Don't squander the gold of your days, listening to the tedious, trying to improve the hopeless failure, or giving away your life to the ignorant, the common, and the vulgar. These are the sickly aims, the false ideals, of our age. Live! Live the wonderful life that is in you! Let nothing be lost upon you. Be always searching for new sensations. Be afraid of nothing. . . . A new Hedonism—that is what our century wants. You might be its visible symbol. With your personality there is nothing you could not do. The world belongs to you for a season. . . . The moment I met you I saw that you were quite unconscious of what you really are, of what you really might be. There was so much in you that charmed me that I felt I must tell you something about yourself. I thought how tragic it would be if you were wasted. For there is such a little time that your youth will last—such a little time. The common hill-flowers wither, but they blossom again. The laburnum will be as yellow next June as it is now. In a month there will be purple stars on the clematis, and year after year the green night of its leaves will hold its purple stars. But we never get back our youth. The pulse of joy that beats in us at twenty, becomes sluggish. Our limbs fail, our senses rot. We degenerate into hideous puppets, haunted by the memory of the passions of which we were too much afraid, and the exquisite temptations that we had not the courage to yield to. Youth! Youth! There is absolutely nothing in the world but youth!'

Dorian Gray listened, open-eyed and wondering. The spray of lilac fell from his hand upon the gravel. A furry bee came and buzzed round it for a moment. Then it began to scramble all over the oval stellated globe of the tiny blossoms. He watched it with that strange interest in trivial things that we try to develop when things of high import make us afraid, or when we are stirred by some new emotion for which we cannot find expression, or when some thought that terrifies us lays sudden siege to the brain and calls on us to yield. After a time the bee flew away. He saw it creeping into the stained trumpet of a Tyrian convolvulus. The flower seemed to quiver, and then swayed gently to and fro.

Suddenly the painter appeared at the door of the studio, and made staccato signs for them to come in. They turned to each other, and smiled.

'I am waiting,' he cried. 'Do come in. The light is quite perfect and you can bring your drinks.'

They rose up, and sauntered down the walk together. Two green-and-white butterflies fluttered past them, and in the pear-tree at the corner of the garden a thrush began to sing.

'You are glad you have met me, Mr. Gray,' said Lord Henry, looking at him.

'Yes, I am glad now. I wonder shall I always be glad?'

'Always! That is a dreadful word. It makes me shudder when I hear it. Women are so fond of using it. They spoil every romance by trying to make it last for ever. It is a mean-ingless word, too. The only difference between a caprice and a life-long passion is that the caprice lasts a little longer.'

As they entered the studio, Dorian Gray put his hand upon Lord Henry's arm. 'In that case, let our friendship be a caprice,' he murmured, flushing at his own boldness, then stepped up on the platform and resumed his pose.

Lord Henry flung himself into a large wicker arm-chair, and watched him. The sweep and dash of the brush on the canvas made the only sound that broke the stillness, except when, now and then, Hallward stepped back to look at his work from a distance. In the slanting beams that streamed through the open doorway the dust danced and was golden. The heavy scent of the roses seemed to brood over every-thing.

After about a quarter of an hour Hallward stopped painting, looked for a long time at Dorian Gray, and then for a long time at the picture, biting the end of one of his huge brushes, and frowning. 'It is quite finished,' he cried at last, and stooping down he wrote his name in long vermilion letters on the left-hand corner of the canvas.

Lord Henry came over and examined the picture. It was certainly a wonderful work of art, and a wonderful likeness as well.

'My dear fellow, I congratulate you most warmly,' he said. 'It is the finest portrait of modern times. Mr. Gray, come over and look at yourself.'

The lad started, as if awakened from some dream. 'Is it really finished?' he murmured, stepping down from the platform.

'Quite finished,' said the painter. 'And you have sat splendidly to-day. I am awfully obliged to you.'

'That is entirely due to me,' broke in Lord Henry. 'Isn't it, Mr. Gray?'

Dorian made no answer, but passed listlessly in front of his picture, and turned towards it. When he saw it he drew back, and his cheeks flushed for a moment with pleasure. A look of joy came into his eyes, as if he had recognised himself for the first time. He stood there motionless and in wonder, dimly conscious that Hallward was speaking to him, but not catching the meaning of his words. The sense of his own beauty came on him like a revelation. He had never felt it before. Basil Hallward's compliments had seemed to him to be merely the charming exaggerations of friendship. He had listened to them, laughed at them, forgotten them. They had not influenced his nature. Then had come Lord Henry Wotton with his strange panegyric on youth, his terrible warning of its brevity. That had stirred him at the time, and now, as he stood gazing at the shadow of his own loveliness, the full reality of the description flashed across him. Yes, there would be a day when his face would be wrinkled and wizen, his eyes dim and colourless, the grace of his figure broken and deformed. The scarlet would pass away from his lips, and the gold steal from his hair. The life that was to make his soul would mar his body. He would become dreadful, hideous and uncouth.

As he thought of it, a sharp pang of pain struck through him like a knife, and made each delicate fibre of his nature quiver. His eyes deepened into amethyst, and across them came a mist of tears. He felt as if a hand of ice had been laid upon his heart.

'Don't you like it?' cried Hallward at last, stung a little by the lad's silence, not understanding what it meant.

'Of course he likes it,' said Lord Henry. 'Who wouldn't like it? It is one of the greatest things in modern art. I will give you anything you like to ask for it. I must have it.'

'It is not my property, Harry.'

'Whose property is it?'

'Dorian's, of course,' answered the painter.

'He is a very lucky fellow.'

'How sad it is!' murmured Dorian Gray, with his eyes still fixed upon his own portrait. 'How sad it is! I shall grow old, and horrible, and dreadful. But this picture will remain always young. It will never be older than this particular day of June. . . . If it were only the other way! If it were I who was to be always young, and the picture that was to grow old! For that—for that—I would give everything! Yes, there is nothing in the whole world I would not give! I would give my soul for that!'

'You would hardly care for such an arrangement, Basil,' cried Lord Henry, laughing. 'It would be rather hard lines on your work.'

'I should object very strongly, Harry,' said Hallward.

Dorian Gray turned and looked at him. 'I believe you would, Basil. You like your art better than your friends. I am no more to you than a green bronze figure. Hardly as much, I dare say.'

The painter stared in amazement. It was so unlike Dorian to speak like that. What had happened? He seemed quite angry. His face was flushed and his cheeks burning.

'Yes,' he continued, 'I am less to you than your ivory Hermes or your silver Faun. You will like them always. How long will you like me? Till I have my first wrinkle, I suppose. I know, now, that when one loses one's good looks, whatever they may be, one loses everything. Your picture has taught me that. Lord Henry Wotton is perfectly right. Youth is the only thing worth having. When I find that I am growing old, I shall kill myself.'

Hallward turned pale, and caught his hand. 'Dorian! Dorian!' he cried, 'don't talk like that. I have never had such a friend as you, and I shall never have such another. You are

34

not jealous of material things, are you—you who are finer than any of them!'

'I am jealous of everything whose beauty does not die. I am jealous of the portrait you have painted of me. Why should it keep what I must lose? Every moment that passes takes something from me, and gives something to it. Oh, if it were only the other way! If the picture could change, and I could be always what I am now! Why did you paint it? It will mock me some day—mock me horribly!' The hot tears welled into his eyes; he tore his hand away, and, flinging himself on the divan, he buried his face in the cushions, as though he was praying.

'This is your doing, Harry,' said the painter, bitterly.

Lord Henry shrugged his shoulders. 'It is the real Dorian Gray—that is all.'

'It is not.'

'If it is not, what have I to do with it?'

'You should have gone away when I asked you,' he muttered.

'I stayed when you asked me,' was Lord Henry's answer.

'Harry, I can't quarrel with my two best friends at once, but between you both you have made me hate the finest piece of work I have ever done, and I will destroy it. What is it but canvas and colour? I will not let it come across our three lives and mar them.'

Dorian Gray lifted his golden head from the pillow, and with pallid face and tear-stained eyes looked at him, as he walked over to the deal painting-table that was set beneath the high-curtained window. What was he doing there? His fingers were straying about among the litter of tin tubes and dry brushes, seeking for something. Yes, it was for the long palette-knife, with its thin blade of lithe steel. He had found it at last. He was going to rip up the canvas.

With a stifled sob the lad leaped from the couch, and,

rushing over to Hallward, tore the knife out of his hand, and flung it to the end of the studio. 'Don't, Basil, don't!' he cried. 'It would be murder!'

'I am glad you appreciate my work at last, Dorian,' said the painter, coldly, when he had recovered from his surprise. 'I never thought you would.'

'Appreciate it? I am in love with it, Basil. It is part of myself. I feel that.'

'Well, as soon as you are dry, you shall be varnished, and framed, and sent home. Then you can do what you like with yourself.' And he walked across the room and rang the bell for tea. 'You will have tea, of course, Dorian? And so will you, Harry? Or do you object to such simple pleasures?'

'I adore simple pleasures,' said Lord Henry. 'They are the last refuge of the complex. But I don't like scenes, except on the stage. What absurd fellows you are, both of you! I wonder who it was defined man as a rational animal. It was the most premature definition ever given. Man is many things, but he is not rational. I am glad he is not, after all: though I wish you chaps would not squabble over the picture. You had much better let me have it, Basil. This silly boy doesn't really want it, and I really do.'

'If you let anyone have it but me, Basil, I shall never forgive you!' cried Dorian Gray; 'and I don't allow people to call me a silly boy.'

'You know the picture is yours, Dorian. I gave it to you before it existed.'

'And you know you have been a little silly, Mr. Gray, and that you don't really object to being reminded that you are extremely young.'

'I should have objected very strongly this morning, Lord Henry.'

'Ah! this morning! You have lived since then.'

There came a knock at the door, and the butler entered with a laden tea-tray and set it down upon a small Japanese table. There was a rattle of cups and saucers and the hissing of a fluted Georgian urn. Two globe-shaped china dishes were brought in by a page. Dorian Gray went over and poured out the tea. The two men sauntered languidly to the table, and examined what was under the covers.

'Let us go to the theatre to-night,' said Lord Henry. 'There is sure to be something on, somewhere. I have promised to dine at White's, but it is only with an old friend, so I can send him a wire to say that I am ill, or that I am prevented from coming in consequence of a subsequent engagement. I think that would be a rather nice excuse: it would have all the surprise of candour.'

'It is such a bore putting on one's dress-clothes,' muttered Hallward. 'And, when one has them on, they are so horrid.'

'Yes,' answered Lord Henry, dreamily, 'the costume of the nineteenth century is detestable. It is so sombre, so depressing. Sin is the only real colour-element left in modern life.'

'You really must not say things like that before Dorian, Harry.'

'Before which Dorian? The one who is pouring out tea for us, or the one in the picture?'

'Before either.'

'I should like to come to the theatre with you, Lord Henry,' said the lad.

'Then you shall come; and you will come too, Basil, won't you?'

'I can't really. I would sooner not. I have a lot of work to do.'

'Well, then, you and I will go alone, Mr. Gray.'

'I should like that awfully.'

The painter bit his lip and walked over, cup in hand, to the picture. 'I shall stay with the real Dorian,' he said, sadly.

'Is it the real Dorian?' cried the original of the portrait, strolling across to him. 'Am I really like that?'

'Yes; you are just like that.'

'How wonderful, Basil!'

'At least you are like it in appearance. But it will never alter,' sighed Hallward. 'That is something.'

'What a fuss people make about fidelity!' exclaimed Lord Henry. 'Why, even in love it is purely a question for physiology. It has nothing to do with our own will. Young men want to be faithful, and are not; old men want to be faithless, and cannot: that is all one can say.'

'Don't go to the theatre to-night, Dorian,' said Hallward. 'Stop and dine with me.'

'I can't, Basil.'

'Why?'

'Because I have promised Lord Henry Wotton to go with him.'

'He won't like you the better for keeping your promises. He always breaks his own. I beg you not to go.'

Dorian Gray laughed and shook his head.

'I entreat you.'

The lad hesitated, and looked over at Lord Henry, who was watching them from the tea-table with an amused smile.

'I must go, Basil,' he answered.

'Very well,' said Hallward; and he went over and laid down his cup on the tray. 'It is rather late, and, as you have to dress, you had better lose no time. Good-bye, Harry. Good-bye, Dorian. Come and see me soon. Come to-morrow.'

'Certainly.'

'You won't forget?'

'No, of course not,' cried Dorian.

'And . . . Harry!'

'Yes, Basil?'

'Remember what I asked you, when we were in the garden this morning.'

'I have forgotten it.'

'I trust you.'

'I wish I could trust myself,' said Lord Henry, laughing. 'Come, Mr. Gray, my hansom is outside, and I can drop you at your own place. Good-bye, Basil. It has been a most interesting afternoon.'

As the door closed behind them, the painter flung himself down on a sofa, and a look of pain came into his face.

CHAPTER III

AT half-past twelve next day Lord Henry Wotton strolled from Curzon Street over to the Albany to call on his uncle, Lord Fermor, a genial if somewhat rough-mannered old bachelor, whom the outside world called selfish because it derived no particular benefit from him, but who was considered generous by Society as he fed the people who amused him. His father had been our ambassador at Madrid when Isabella was young, and Prim unthought of, but had retired from the Diplomatic Service in a capricious moment of annoyance at not being offered the Embassy at Paris, a post to which he considered that he was fully entitled by reason of his birth, his indolence, the good English of his despatches, and his inordinate passion for pleasure. The son, who had been his father's secretary, had resigned along with his chief, somewhat foolishly as was thought at the time, and on succeeding some months later to the title, had set himself to the serious study of the great aristocratic art of doing absolutely nothing. He had two large town houses, but preferred to live in chambers, as it was less trouble, and took most of his meals at his club. He paid some attention to the management of his collieries in the Midland counties, excusing himself for this taint of industry on the ground that the one advantage of having coal was that it enabled a gentleman to afford the decency of burning wood on his own hearth. In politics he was a Tory, except when the Tories were in office, during which period he roundly abused them for being a pack of Radicals. He was a hero to his valet, who bullied him, and a terror to most of his relations, whom he bullied in turn. Only England could have produced him, and he always said that the country was going to the dogs. His principles were out of date, but there was a good deal to be said for his prejudices.

When Lord Henry entered the room, he found his uncle sitting in a rough shooting coat, smoking a cheroot, and grumbling over *The Times*. 'Well, Harry,' said the old gentleman, 'what brings you out so early? I thought you dandies never got up till two, and were not visible till five.'

'Pure family affection, I assure you, Uncle George. I want to get something out of you.'

'Money, I suppose,' said Lord Fermor, making a wry face. 'Well, sit down and tell me all about it. Young people, nowadays, imagine that money is everything.'

'Yes,' murmured Lord Henry, settling his button-hole in his coat; 'and when they grow older they know it. But I don't want money. It is only people who pay their bills who want that, Uncle George, and I never pay mine. Credit is the capital of a younger son, and one lives charmingly upon it. Besides, I always deal with Dartmoor's tradesmen, and consequently they never bother me. What I want is information; not useful information, of course; useless information.'

'Well, I can tell you anything that is in an English Blue-book, Harry, although those fellows nowadays write a lot of nonsense. When I was in the Diplomatic, things were much better. But I hear they let them in now by examination. What can you expect? Examinations, sir, are pure humbug from beginning to end. If a man is a gentleman, he knows quite enough, and if he is not a gentleman, whatever he knows is bad for him.'

'Mr. Dorian Gray does not belong to Blue-books, Uncle George,' said Lord Henry languidly.

'Mr. Dorian Gray? Who is he?' asked Lord Fermor, knitting his bushy white eyebrows.

'That is what I have come to learn, Uncle George. Or rather, I know who he is. He is the last Lord Kelso's grandson. His mother was a Devereux; Lady Margaret Devereux. I want you to tell me about his mother. What was she like? Whom did she marry? You have known nearly everybody in your time, so you might have known her. I am very much interested in Mr. Gray at present. I have only just met him.'

'Kelso's grandson!' echoed the old gentleman. 'Kelso's grandson! . . . Of course. . . . I knew his mother intimately. I believe I was at her christening. She was an extraordinarily beautiful girl, Margaret Devereux; and made all the men frantic by running away with a penniless young fellow; a mere nobody, sir, a subaltern in a foot regiment, or something of that kind. Certainly. I remember the whole thing as if it happened yesterday. The poor chap was killed in a duel at Spa, a few months after the marriage. There was an ugly story about it. They said Kelso got some rascally adventurer, some Belgian brute, to insult his son-in-law in public; paid him, sir, to do it, paid him; and that the fellow spitted his man as if he had been a pigeon. The thing was hushed up, but, egad, Kelso ate his chop alone at the club for some time afterwards. He brought his daughter back with him, I was told, and she never spoke to him again. Oh, yes; it was a bad business. The girl died too; died within a year. So she left a son, did she? I had forgotten that. What sort of boy is he? If he is like his mother he must be a good-looking chap.'

'He is very good-looking,' assented Lord Henry.

'I hope he will fall into proper hands,' continued the old man. 'He should have a pot of money waiting for him if Kelso did the right thing by him. His mother had money too. All the Selby property came to her through her grandfather. Her grandfather hated Kelso, thought him a mean dog. He was, too. Came to Madrid once when I was there. Egad, I was ashamed of him. The Queen used to ask me about the English noble who was always quarrelling with the cabmen about their fares. They made quite a story of it. I didn't dare to show my face at Court for a month. I hope he treated his grandson better than he did the jarvies.'

'I don't know,' answered Lord Henry. 'I fancy that the boy will be well off. He is not of age yet. He has Selby, I know. He told me so. And . . . his mother was very beautiful?'

'Margaret Devereux was one of the loveliest creatures I ever saw, Harry. What on earth induced her to behave as she did, I never could understand. She could have married anybody she chose. Carlington was mad after her. She was romantic, though. All the women of that family were. The men were a poor lot, but, egad! the women were wonderful. Carlington went on his knees to her. Told me so himself. She laughed at him, and there wasn't a girl in London at the time who wasn't after him. And by the way, Harry, talking about silly marriages, what is this humbug your father tells me about Dartmoor wanting to marry an American? Ain't English girls good enough for him?'

'It is rather fashionable to marry Americans just now, Uncle George.'

'I'll back English women against the world, Harry,' said Lord Fermor, striking the table with his fist.

'The betting is on the Americans.'

'They don't last, I am told,' muttered his uncle.

'A long engagement exhausts them, but they are capital at a steeplechase. They take things flying. I don't think Dartmoor has a chance.'

'Who are her people?' grumbled the old gentleman. 'Has she got any?'

Lord Henry shook his head. 'American girls are as clever at concealing their parents as English women are at concealing their past,' he said, rising to go.

'They are pork-packers, I suppose?'

'I hope so, Uncle George, for Dartmoor's sake. I am told that pork-packing is the most lucrative profession in America, after politics.'

'Is she pretty?'

'She behaves as if she was beautiful. Most American women do. It is the secret of their charm.'

'Why can't these American women stay in their own country? They are always telling us that it is the Paradise for women.'

'It is. That is the reason why, like Eve, they are so excessively anxious to get out of it,' said Lord Henry. 'Good-bye, Uncle George. I shall be late for lunch, if I stop any longer. Thanks for giving me the information I wanted. I always like to know everything about my new friends, and nothing about my old ones.''

'Where are you lunching, Harry?'

'At Aunt Agatha's. I have asked myself and Mr. Gray. He is her latest *protégé*.'

'Humph! Tell your Aunt Agatha, Harry, not to bother me any more with her charity appeals. I am sick of them. Why, the good woman thinks that I have nothing to do but to write cheques for her silly fads.'

'All right, Uncle George, I'll tell her, but it won't have any effect. Philanthropic people lose all sense of humanity. It is their distinguishing characteristic.'

The old gentleman growled approvingly, and rang the bell for his servant. Lord Henry passed up the low arcade into Burlington Street, and turned his steps in the direction of Berkeley Square.

So that was the story of Dorian Gray's parentage. Crudely

as it had been told to him, it had yet stirred him by its suggestion of a strange, almost modern romance. A beautiful woman risking everything for a mad passion. A few wild weeks of happiness cut short by a hideous, treacherous crime. Months of voiceless agony, and then a child born in pain. The mother snatched away by death, the boy left to solitude and the tyranny of an old and loveless man. Yes; it was an interesting background. It posed the lad, made him more perfect as it were. Behind every exquisite thing that existed, there was something tragic. Worlds had to be in travail, that the meanest flower might blow.*. . . And how charming he had been at dinner the night before, as, with startled eyes and lips parted in frightened pleasure, he had sat opposite to him at the club, the red candleshades staining to a richer rose the wakening wonder of his face. Talking to him was like playing upon an exquisite violin. He answered to every touch and thrill of the bow. . . . There was something terribly enthralling in the exercise of influence. No other activity was like it. To project one's soul into some gracious form, and let it tarry there for a moment; to hear one's own intellectual views echoed back to one with all the added music of passion and youth; to convey one's temperament into another as though it were a subtle fluid or a strange perfume; there was a real joy in that—perhaps the most satisfying joy left to us in an age so limited and vulgar as our own, an age grossly carnal in its pleasures, and grossly common in its aims. . . . He was a marvellous type, too, this lad, whom by so curious a chance he had met in Basil's studio; or could be fashioned into a marvellous type, at any rate. Grace was his, and the white purity of boyhood, and beauty such as old Greek marbles kept for us. There was nothing that one could not do with him. He could be made a Titan or a toy. What a pity it was that such beauty was destined to fade! . . . And Basil? From

45

a psychological point of view, how interesting he was! The new manner in art, the fresh mode of looking at life, suggested so strangely by the merely visible presence of one who was unconscious of it all; the silent spirit that dwelt in dim woodland, and walked unseen in open field, suddenly showing herself, Dryad-like and not afraid, because in his soul who sought for her there had been wakened that wonderful vision to which alone are wonderful things revealed; the mere shapes and patterns of things becoming, as it were, refined, and gaining a kind of symbolical value, as though they were themselves patterns of some other and more perfect form whose shadow they made real: how strange it all was! He remembered something like it in history. Was it not Plato, that artist in thought, who had first analysed it? Was it not Buonarroti who had carved it in the coloured marbles of a sonnet-sequence? But in our own century it was strange. . . . Yes; he would try to be to Dorian Gray what, without knowing it, the lad was to the painter who had fashioned the wonderful portrait. He would seek to dominate him—had already, indeed, half done so. He would make that wonderful spirit his own. There was something fascinating in this son of Love and Death.

Suddenly he stopped, and glanced up at the houses. He found that he had passed his aunt's some distance, and, smiling to himself, turned back. When he entered the somewhat sombre hall the butler told him that they had gone in to lunch. He gave one of the footmen his hat and stick, and passed into the dining-room.

'Late as usual, Harry,' cried his aunt, shaking her head at him.

He invented a facile excuse, and having taken the vacant seat next to her, looked round to see who was there. Dorian bowed to him shyly from the end of the table, a flush of pleasure stealing into his cheek. Opposite was the Duchess of Harley; a lady of admirable good-nature and good temper, much liked by everyone who knew her, and of those ample architectural proportions that in women who are not Duchesses are described by contemporary historians as stoutness. Next to her sat, on her right, Sir Thomas Burdon, a Radical member of Parliament, who followed his leader in public life, and in private life followed the best cooks, dining with the Tories, and thinking with the Liberals, in accordance with a wise and well-known rule. The post on her left was occupied by Mr. Erskine of Treadley, an old gentleman of considerable charm and culture, who had fallen, however, into bad habits of silence, having, as he explained once to Lady Agatha, said everything that he had to say before he was thirty. His own neighbour was Mrs. Vandeleur, one of his aunt's oldest friends, a perfect saint amongst women, but so dreadfully dowdy, that she reminded one of a badly bound hymn-book. Fortunately for him she had on the other side Lord Faudel, a most intelligent middle-aged mediocrity, as bald as a Ministerial statement in the House of Commons, with whom she was conversing in that intensely earnest manner which is the one unpardonable error, as he remarked once himself, that all really good people fall into, and from which none of them ever quite escape.

'We are talking about poor Dartmoor, Lord Henry,' cried the Duchess, nodding pleasantly to him across the table. 'Do you think he will really marry this fascinating young person?'

'I believe she has made up her mind to propose to him, Duchess.'

'How dreadful!' exclaimed Lady Agatha. 'Really, someone should interfere.'

'I am told, on excellent authority, that her father keeps

an American dry-goods store,' said Sir Thomas Burdon, looking supercilious.

'My uncle has already suggested pork-packing, Sir Thomas.'

'Dry-goods! What are American dry-goods?' asked the Duchess, raising her large hands in wonder, and accentuating the verb.

'American novels,' answered Lord Henry, helping himself to some quail.

The Duchess looked puzzled.

'Don't mind him, my dear,' whispered Lady Agatha. 'He never means anything that he says.'

'When America was discovered,' said the Radical member and he began to give some wearisome facts. Like all people who try to exhaust a subject, he exhausted his listeners. The Duchess sighed, and exercised her privilege of interruption. 'I wish to goodness it never had been discovered at all!' she exclaimed. 'Really, our girls have no chance nowadays. It is most unfair.'

'Perhaps, after all, America never has been discovered,' said Mr. Erskine. 'I myself would say that it had merely been detected.'

'Oh! but I have seen specimens of the inhabitants,' answered the Duchess, vaguely. 'I must confess that most of them are extremely pretty. And they dress well, too. They get all their dresses in Paris. I wish I could afford to do the same.'

'They say that when good Americans die they go to Paris,' chuckled Sir Thomas, who had a large wardrobe of Humour's cast-off clothes.

'Really! And where do bad Americans go to when they die?' inquired the Duchess.

'They go to America,' murmured Lord Henry.

Sir Thomas frowned. 'I am afraid that your nephew is

prejudiced against that great country,' he said to Lady Agatha. 'I have travelled all over it, in cars provided by the directors, who, in such matters, are extremely civil. I assure you that it is an education to visit it.'

'But must we really see Chicago in order to be educated?' asked Mr. Erskine, plaintively. 'I don't feel up to the journey.'

Sir Thomas waved his hand. 'Mr. Erskine of Treadley has the world on his shelves. We practical men like to see things not to read about them. The Americans are an extremely interesting people. They are absolutely reasonable. I think that is their distinguishing characteristic. Yes, Mr. Erskine, an absolutely reasonable people. I assure you there is no nonsense about the Americans.'

'How dreadful!' cried Lord Henry. 'I can stand brute force, but brute reason is quite unbearable. There is something unfair about its use. It is hitting below the intellect.'

'I do not understand you,' said Sir Thomas, growing rather red.

'I do, Lord Henry,' murmured Mr. Erskine, with a smile.

'Paradoxes are all very well in their way . . .' rejoined the Baronet.

'Was that a paradox?' asked Mr. Erskine. 'I did not think so. Perhaps it was. Well, the way of paradoxes is the way of truth. To test Reality we must see it on the tight-rope. When the Verities become acrobats we can judge them.'

'Dear me!' said Lady Agatha, 'how you men argue! I am sure I never can make out what you are talking about. Oh! Harry, I am quite vexed with you. Why do you try to persuade our nice Mr. Dorian Gray to give up the East End? I assure you he would be quite invaluable. They would love his playing.'

'I want him to play to me,' cried Lord Henry, smiling, and he looked down the table and caught a bright answering glance.

'But they are so unhappy in Whitechapel,' continued Lady Agatha.

'I can sympathise with everything, except suffering,' said Lord Henry, shrugging his shoulders. 'I cannot sympathise with that. It is too ugly, too horrible, too distressing. There is something terribly morbid in the modern sympathy with pain. One should sympathise with the colour, the beauty, the joy of life. The less said about life's sores the better.'

'Still, the East End is a very important problem,' remarked Sir Thomas, with a grave shake of the head.

'Quite so,' answered the young lord. 'It is the problem of slavery, and we try to solve it by amusing the slaves.'

The politician looked at him keenly. 'What change do you propose, then?' he asked.

Lord Henry laughed. 'I don't desire to change anything in England except the weather,' he answered. 'I am quite content with philosophic contemplation. But, as the nineteenth century has gone bankrupt through an over-expenditure of sympathy, I would suggest that we should appeal to Science to put us straight. The advantage of the emotions is that they lead us astray, and the advantage of Science is that it is not emotional.'

'But we have such grave responsibilities,' ventured Mrs. Vandeleur, timidly.

'Terribly grave,' echoed Lady Agatha.

Lord Henry looked over at Mr. Erskine. 'Humanity takes itself too seriously. It is the world's original sin. If the caveman had known how to laugh, History would have been different.'

'You are really very comforting,' warbled the Duchess. 'I have always felt rather guilty when I came to see your dear aunt, for I take no interest at all in the East End. For the future I shall be able to look her in the face without a blush.'

'A blush is very becoming, Duchess,' remarked Lord Henry.

'Only when one is young,' she answered. 'When an old woman like myself blushes, it is a very bad sign. Ah! Lord Henry, I wish you would tell me how to become young again.'

He thought for a moment. 'Can you remember any great error that you committed in your early days, Duchess?' he asked, looking at her across the table.

'A great many, I fear,' she cried.

'Then commit them over again,' he said, gravely. 'To get back one's youth, one has merely to repeat one's follies.'

'A delightful theory!' she exclaimed. 'I must put it into practice.'

'A dangerous theory!' came from Sir Thomas's tight lips. Lady Agatha shook her head, but could not help being amused. Mr. Erskine listened.

'Yes,' he continued, 'that is one of the great secrets of life. Nowadays most people die of a sort of creeping common sense, and discover when it is too late that the only things one never regrets are one's mistakes.'

A laugh ran round the table.

He played with the idea, and grew wilful; tossed it into the air and transformed it; let it escape and recaptured it; made it iridescent with fancy, and winged it with paradox. The praise of folly, as he went on, soared into a philosophy, and Philosophy herself became young, and catching the mad music of Pleasure, wearing, one might fancy, her wine-stained robe and wreath of ivy, danced like a Bacchante over the hills of life, and mocked the slow Silenus for being sober. Facts fled before her like frightened forest things. Her white feet trod the huge press at which wise Omar sits, till the seething grape-juice rose round her bare limbs in waves of purple bubbles, or crawled in red foam over the vat's black, dripping, sloping sides. It was an extraordinary improvisation. He felt that the eyes of Dorian Gray were fixed on him, and the consciousness that amongst his audience there was one whose temperament he wished to fascinate, seemed to give his wit keenness, and to lend colour to his imagination. He was brilliant, fantastic, irresponsible. He charmed his listeners out of themselves, and they followed his pipe laughing. Dorian Gray never took his gaze off him, but sat like one under a spell, smiles chasing each other over his lips, and wonder growing grave in his darkening eyes.

At last, liveried in the costume of the age, Reality entered the room in the shape of a servant to tell the Duchess that her carriage was waiting. She wrung her hands in mock despair. 'How annoying!' she cried. 'I must go. I have to call for my husband at the club, to take him to some absurd meeting at Willis's Rooms, where he is going to be in the chair. If I am late, he is sure to be furious, and I couldn't have a scene in this bonnet. It is far too fragile. A harsh word would ruin it. No, I must go, dear Agatha. Good-bye, Lord Henry, you are quite delightful, and dreadfully demoralising. I am sure I don't know what to say about your views. You must come and dine with us some night. Tuesday? Are you disengaged Tuesday?'

'For you I would throw over anybody, Duchess,' said Lord Henry, with a bow.

'Ah! that is very nice, and very wrong of you,' she cried; 'so mind you come;' and she swept out of the room, followed by Lady Agatha and the other ladies.

When Lord Henry had sat down again, Mr. Erskine moved round, and taking a chair close to him, placed his hand upon his arm.

'You talk books away,' he said; 'why don't you write one?'

'I am too fond of reading books to care to write them,

Mr. Erskine. I should like to write a novel certainly; a novel that would be as lovely as a Persian carpet, and as unreal. But there is no literary public in England for anything except newspapers, primers, and encyclopædias. Of all people in the world the English have the least sense of the beauty of literature.'

'I fear you are right,' answered Mr. Erskine. 'I myself used to have literary ambitions, but I gave them up long ago. And now, my dear young friend, if you will allow me to call you so, may I ask if you really meant all that you said to us at lunch?'

'I quite forget what I said,' smiled Lord Henry. 'Was it all very bad?'

'Very bad indeed. In fact I consider you extremely dangerous, and if anything happens to our good Duchess we shall all look on you as being primarily responsible. But I should like to talk to you about life. The generation into which I was born was tedious. Some day, when you are tired of London, come down to Treadley, and expound to me your philosophy of pleasure over some admirable Burgundy I am fortunate enough to possess.'

'I shall be charmed. A visit to Treadley would be a great privilege. It has a perfect host, and a perfect library.'

'You will complete it,' answered the old gentleman, with a courteous bow. 'And now I must bid good-bye to your excellent aunt. I am due at the Athenæum. It is the hour when we sleep there.'

'All of you, Mr. Erskine?'

'Forty of us, in forty arm-chairs. We are practising for an English Academy of Letters.'

Lord Henry laughed, and rose. 'I am going to the Park,' he cried.

As he was passing out of the door Dorian Gray touched him on the arm. 'Let me come with you,' he murmured.

'But I thought you had promised Basil Hallward to go and see him,' answered Lord Henry.

'I would sooner come with you; yes, I feel I must come with you. Do let me. And you will promise to talk to me all the time? No one talks so wonderfully as you do.'

'Ah! I have talked quite enough for to-day,' said Lord Henry, smiling. 'All I want now is to look at life. You may come and look at it with me, if you care to.'

CHAPTER IV

ONE afternoon, a month later, Dorian Gray was reclining in a luxurious arm-chair, in the little library of Lord Henry's house in Mayfair. It was, in its way, a very charming room, with its high-panelled wainscoting of olive-stained oak, its cream-coloured frieze and ceiling of raised plaster-work, and its brickdust felt carpet strewn with silk long-fringed Persian rugs. On a tiny satinwood table stood a statuette by Clodion, and beside it lay a copy of *Les Cent Nouvelles*, bound for Margaret of Valois by Clovis Eve, and powdered with the gilt daisies that Queen had selected for her device. Some large blue china jars and parrot-tulips were ranged on the mantelshelf, and through the small leaded panels of the window streamed the apricot-coloured light of a summer day in London.

Lord Henry had not yet come in. He was always late on principle, his principle being that punctuality is the thief of time. So the lad was looking rather sulky, as with listless fingers he turned over the pages of an elaborately-illustrated edition of *Manon Lescaut* that he had found in one of the bookcases. The formal monotonous ticking of the Louis Quatorze clock annoyed him. Once or twice he thought of going away.

At last he heard a step outside, and the door opened. 'How late you are, Harry!' he murmured.

'I am afraid it is not Harry, Mr. Gray,' answered a shrill voice.

He glanced quickly round, and rose to his feet. 'I beg your pardon. I thought——'

'You thought it was my husband. It is only his wife.

You must let me introduce myself. I know you quite well by your photographs. I think my husband has got seventeen of them.'

'Not seventeen, Lady Henry?'

'Well, eighteen, then. And I saw you with him the other night at the Opera.' She laughed nervously as she spoke, and watched him with her vague forget-me-not eyes. She was a curious woman, whose dresses always looked as if they had been designed in a rage and put on in a tempest. She was usually in love with somebody, and, as her passion was never returned, she had kept all her illusions. She tried to look picturesque, but only succeeded in being untidy. Her name was Victoria, and she had a perfect mania for going to church.

'That was at "Lohengrin," Lady Henry, I think?'

'Yes; it was at dear "Lohengrin." I like Wagner's music better than anybody's. It is so loud that one can talk the whole time without other people hearing what one says. That is a great advantage: don't you think so, Mr. Gray?'

The same nervous staccato laugh broke from her thin lips, and her fingers began to play with a long tortoise-shell paper-knife.

Dorian smiled, and shook his head: 'I am afraid I don't think so, Lady Henry. I never talk during music, at least, during good music. If one hears bad music, it is one's duty to drown it in conversation.'

'Ah! that is one of Harry's views, isn't it, Mr. Gray? I always hear Harry's views from his friends. It is the only way I get to know of them. But you must not think I don't like good music. I adore it, but I am afraid of it. It makes me too romantic. I have simply worshipped pianists—two at a time, sometimes, Harry tells me. I don't know what it is about them. Perhaps it is that they are foreigners. They all are, ain't they? Even those that are born in England become foreigners after a time, don't they? It is so clever of them, and such a compliment to art. Makes it quite cosmopolitan, doesn't it? You have never been to any of my parties, have you, Mr. Gray? You must come. I can't afford orchids, but I spare no expense in foreigners. They make one's rooms look so picturesque. But here is Harry!—Harry, I came in to look for you, to ask you something—I forget what it was—and I found Mr. Gray here. We have had such a pleasant chat about music. We have quite the same ideas. No; I think our ideas are quite different. But he has been most pleasant. I am so glad I've seen him.'

'I am charmed, my love, quite charmed,' said Lord Henry, elevating his dark crescent-shaped eyebrows and looking at them both with an amused smile. 'So sorry I am late, Dorian. I went to look after a piece of old brocade in Wardour Street, and had to bargain for hours for it. Nowadays people know the price of everything, and the value of nothing.'

'I am afraid I must be going,' exclaimed Lady Henry, breaking an awkward silence with her silly sudden laugh. 'I have promised to drive with the Duchess. Good-bye, Mr. Gray. Good-bye, Harry. You are dining out, I suppose? So am I. Perhaps I shall see you at Lady Thornbury's.'

'I dare say, my dear,' said Lord Henry, shutting the door behind her, as, looking like a bird of paradise that had been out all night in the rain, she flitted out of the room, leaving a faint odour of frangipanni. Then he lit a cigarette and flung himself down on the sofa.

'Never marry a woman with straw-coloured hair, Dorian,' he said, after a few puffs.

'Why, Harry?'

'Because they are so sentimental.'

'But I like sentimental people.'

'Never marry at all, Dorian. Men marry because they

are tired; women, because they are curious; both are disappointed.'

'I don't think I am likely to marry, Henry. I am too much in love. That is one of your aphorisms. I am putting it into practice, as I do everything that you say.'

'Who are you in love with?' asked Lord Henry, after a pause.

'With an actress,' said Dorian Gray, blushing.

Lord Henry shrugged his shoulders. 'That is a rather commonplace *début*.'

'You would not say so if you saw her, Harry.'

'Who is she?'

'Her name is Sibyl Vane.'

'Never heard of her.'

'No one has. People will some day, however. She is a genius.'

'My dear boy, no woman is a genius. Women are a decorative sex. They never have anything to say, but they say it charmingly. Women represent the triumph of matter over mind, just as men represent the triumph of mind over morals.'

'Harry, how can you?'

'My dear Dorian, it is quite true. I am analysing women at the present, so I ought to know. The subject is not so abstruse as I thought it was. I find that, ultimately, there are only two kinds of women, the plain and the coloured. The plain women are very useful. If you want to gain a reputation for respectability, you have merely to take them down to supper. The other women are very charming. They commit one mistake, however. They paint in order to try and look young. Our grandmothers painted in order to try and talk brilliantly. *Rouge* and *esprit* used to go together. That is all over now. As long as a woman can look ten years younger than her own daughter, she is perfectly satisfied. As for conversation, there are only five women in London worth talking to, and two of these can't be admitted into decent society. However, tell me about your genius. How long have you known her?'

'Ah! Harry, your views terrify me.'

'Never mind that. How long have you known her?'

'About three weeks.'

'And where did you come across her?'

'I will tell you, Harry; but you mustn't be unsympathetic about it. After all, it never would have happened if I had not met you. You filled me with a wild desire to know everything about life. For days after I met you, something seemed to throb in my veins. As I lounged in the Park, or strolled down Piccadilly, I used to look at every one who passed me, and wonder, with a mad curiosity, what sort of lives they led. Some of them fascinated me. Others filled me with terror. There was an exquisite poison in the air. I had a passion for sensations. . . . Well, one evening about seven o'clock, I determined to go out in search of some adventure. I felt that this grey, monstrous London of ours, with its myriads of people, its sordid sinners, and its splendid sins, as you once phrased it, must have something in store for me. I fancied a thousand things. The mere danger gave me a sense of delight. I remembered what you had said to me on that wonderful evening when we first dined together, about the search for beauty being the real secret of life. I don't know what I expected, but I went out and wandered eastward, soon losing my way in a labyrinth of grimy streets and black, grassless squares. About half-past eight I passed by an absurd little theatre, with great flaring gas-jets and gaudy play-bills. A hideous Jew, in the most amazing waistcoat I ever beheld in my life, was standing at the entrance smoking a vile cigar. He had greasy ringlets, and an enormous diamond glazed in the centre of a soiled shirt. 'Have a box, my Lord?' he said, when he saw me, and he took off his hat with an air of gorgeous servility. There was something about him, Harry, that amused me. He was such a monster. You will laugh at me, I know, but I really went in and paid a whole guinea for the stage-box. To the present day I can't make out why I did so; and yet if I hadn't—my dear Harry, if I hadn't, I should have missed the greatest romance of my life. I see you are laughing. It is horrid of you!'

'I am not laughing, Dorian; at least I am not laughing at you. But you should not say the greatest romance of your life. You should say the first romance of your life. You will always be loved, and you will always be in love with love. A *grande passion* is the privilege of people who have nothing to do. That is the one use of the idle classes of a country. Don't be afraid. There are exquisite things in store for you. This is merely the beginning.'

'Do you think my nature so shallow?' cried Dorian Gray, angrily.

'No; I think your nature so deep.'

'How do you mean?'

'My dear boy, the people who love only once in their lives are really the shallow people. What they call their loyalty, and their fidelity, I call either the lethargy of custom or their lack of imagination. Faithfulness is to the emotional life what consistency is to the life of the intellect—simply a confession of failures. Faithfulness! I must analyse it some day. The passion for property is in it. There are many things that we would throw away if we were not afraid that others might pick them up. But I don't want to interrupt you. Go on with your story.'

'Well, I found myself seated in a horrid little private box, with a vulgar drop-scene staring me in the face. I looked out from behind the curtain, and surveyed the house. It was a tawdry affair, all Cupids and cornucopias, like a third-rate wedding cake. The gallery and pit were fairly full, but the two rows of dingy stalls were quite empty, and there was hardly a person in what I suppose they called the dress-circle. Women went about with oranges and ginger-beer, and there was a terrible consumption of nuts going on.'

'It must have been just like the palmy days of the British Drama.'

'Just like, I should fancy, and very depressing. I began to wonder what on earth I should do, when I caught sight of the play-bill. What do you think the play was, Harry?'

'I should think "The Idiot Boy, or Dumb but Innocent." Our fathers used to like that sort of piece, I believe. The longer I live, Dorian, the more keenly I feel that whatever was good enough for our fathers is not good enough for us. In art, as in politics, *les grand-pères ont toujours tort.*'

'This play was good enough for us, Harry. It was "Romeo and Juliet." I must admit that I was rather annoyed at the idea of seeing Shakespeare done in such a wretched hole of a place. Still, I felt interested, in a sort of way. At any rate, I determined to wait for the first act. There was a dreadful orchestra, presided over by a young Hebrew who sat at a cracked piano, that nearly drove me away, but at last the drop-scene was drawn up, and the play began. Romeo was a stout elderly gentleman, with corked eyebrows, a husky tragedy voice, and a figure like a beer-barrel. Mercutio was almost as bad. He was played by the low-comedian, who had introduced gags of his own and was on most friendly terms with the pit. They were both as grotesque as the scenery, and that looked as if it had come out of a country-booth. But Juliet! Harry, imagine a girl, hardly seventeen years of age, with a little flower-like face, a small Greek head with plaited coils of dark-brown hair, eyes that were violet wells of passion, lips that were like the petals of a

61

rose. She was the loveliest thing I had ever seen in my life. You said to me once that pathos left you unmoved, but that beauty, mere beauty, could fill your eyes with tears. I tell you, Harry, I could hardly see this girl for the mist of tears that came across me. And her voice—I never heard such a voice. It was very low at first, with deep mellow notes, that seemed to fall singly upon one's ear. Then it became a little louder, and sounded like a flute or a distant hautbois. In the garden-scene it had all the tremulous ecstasy that one hears just before dawn when nightingales are singing. There were moments, later on, when it had the wild passion of violins. You know how a voice can stir one. Your voice and the voice of Sibyl Vane are two things that I shall never forget. When I close my eyes, I hear them, and each of them says something different. I don't know which to follow. Why should I not love her? Harry, I do love her. She is everything to me in life. Night after night I go to see her play. One evening she is Rosalind, and the next evening she is Imogen. I have seen her die in the gloom of an Italian tomb, sucking the poison from her lover's lips. I have watched her wandering through the forest of Arden, disguised as a pretty boy in hose and doublet and dainty cap. She has been mad, and has come into the presence of a guilty king, and given him rue to wear, and bitter herbs to taste of. She has been innocent, and the black hands of jealousy have crushed her reed-like throat. I have seen her in every age and in every costume. Ordinary women never appeal to one's imagination. They are limited to their century. No glamour ever transfigures them. One knows their minds as easily as one knows their bonnets. One can always find them. There is no mystery in any of them. They ride in the Park in the morning, and chatter at tea-parties in the afternoon. They have their stereotyped smile, and their fashionable manner. They are quite obvious. But an actress!

How different an actress is! Harry! why didn't you tell me that the only thing worth loving is an actress?'

'Because I have loved so many of them, Dorian.'

'Oh, yes, horrid people with dyed hair and painted faces.'

'Don't run down dyed hair and painted faces. There is an extraordinary charm in them, sometimes,' said Lord Henry.

'I wish now I had not told you about Sibyl Vane.'

'You could not have helped telling me, Dorian. All through your life you will tell me everything you do.'

'Yes, Harry, I believe that is true. I cannot help telling you things. You have a curious influence over me. If I ever did a crime, I would come and confess it to you. You would understand me.'

'People like you—the wilful sunbeams of life—don't commit crimes, Dorian. But I am much obliged for the compliment, all the same. And now tell me—reach me the matches, like a good boy: thanks—what are your actual relations with Sibyl Vane?'

Dorian Gray leaped to his feet, with flushed cheeks and burning eyes. 'Harry! Sibyl Vane is sacred!'

'It is only the sacred things that are worth touching, Dorian,' said Lord Henry, with a strange touch of pathos in his voice. 'But why should you be annoyed? I suppose she will belong to you some day. When one is in love, one always begins by deceiving one's self, and one always ends by deceiving others. That is what the world calls a romance. You know her, at any rate, I suppose?'

'Of course I know her. On the first night I was at the theatre, the horrid old Jew came round to the box after the performance was over, and offered to take me behind the scenes and introduce me to her. I was furious with him, and told him that Juliet had been dead for hundreds of years, and that her body was lying in a marble tomb in Verona. I think, from his blank look of amazement, that he was under the impression that I had taken too much champagne, or something.'

'I am not surprised.'

'Then he asked me if I wrote for any of the newspapers. I told him I never even read them. He seemed terribly disappointed at that, and confided to me that all the dramatic critics were in a conspiracy against him, and that they were every one of them to be bought.'

'I should not wonder if he was quite right there. But, on the other hand, judging from their appearance, most of them cannot be at all expensive.'

'Well, he seemed to think they were beyond his means,' laughed Dorian. 'By this time, however, the lights were being put out in the theatre, and I had to go. He wanted me to try some cigars that he strongly recommended. I declined. The next night, of course, I arrived at the place again. When he saw me he made me a low bow, and assured me that I was a munificent patron of art. He was a most offensive brute, though he had an extraordinary passion for Shakespeare. He told me once, with an air of pride, that his five bankruptcies were entirely due to "The Bard," as he insisted on calling him. He seemed to think it a distinction.'

'It was a distinction, my dear Dorian—a great distinction. Most people become bankrupt through having invested too heavily in the prose of life. To have ruined one's self over poetry is an honour. But when did you first speak to Miss Sibyl Vane?'

'The third night. She had been playing Rosalind. I could not help going round. I had thrown her some flowers, and she had looked at me; at least I fancied that she had. The old Jew was persistent. He seemed determined to take me behind, so I consented. It was curious my not wanting to know her, wasn't it?'

'No; I don't think so.'

'My dear Harry, why?'

'I will tell you some other time. Now I want to know about the girl.'

'Sibyl? Oh, she was so shy, and so gentle. There is something of a child about her. Her eyes opened wide in exquisite wonder when I told her what I thought of her performance, and she seemed quite unconscious of her power. I think we were both rather nervous. The old Jew stood grinning at the doorway of the dusty greenroom, making elaborate speeches about us both, while we stood looking at each other like children. He would insist on calling me "My Lord," so I had to assure Sibyl that I was not anything of the kind. She said quite simply to me, "You look more like a prince. I must call you Prince Charming."'

'Upon my word, Dorian, Miss Sibyl knows how to pay compliments.'

'You don't understand her, Harry. She regarded me merely as a person in a play. She knows nothing of life. She lives with her mother, a faded, tired woman who played Lady Capulet in a sort of magenta dressing-wrapper on the first night, and looks as if she had seen better days.'

'I know that look. It depresses me,' murmured Lord Henry, examining his rings.

'The Jew wanted to tell me her history, but I said it did not interest me.'

'You were quite right. There is always something infinitely mean about other people's tragedies.'

'Sibyl is the only thing I care about. What is it to me where she came from? From her little head to her little feet, she is absolutely and entirely divine. Every night of my life I go to see her act, and every night she is more marvellous.'

'That is the reason, I suppose, that you never dine with

me now. I thought you must have some curious romance on hand. You have; but it is not quite what I expected.'

'My dear Harry, we either lunch or sup together every day, and I have been to the Opera with you several times,' said Dorian, opening his blue eyes in wonder.

'You always come dreadfully late.'

'Well, I can't help going to see Sibyl play,' he cried, 'even if it is only for a single act. I get hungry for her presence; and when I think of the wonderful soul that is hidden away in that little ivory body, I am filled with awe.'

'You can dine with me to-night, Dorian, can't you?'

He shook his head. 'To-night she is Imogen,' he answered. 'and to-morrow night she will be Juliet.'

'When is she Sibyl Vane?'

'Never.'

'I congratulate you.'

'How horried you are! She is all the great heroines of the world in one. She is more than an individual. You laugh, but I tell you she has genius. I love her, and I must make her love me. You, who know all the secrets of life, tell me how to charm Sibyl Vane to love me! I want to make Romeo jealous. I want the dead lovers of the world to hear our laughter, and grow sad. I want a breath of our passion to stir their dust into consciousness, to wake their ashes into pain. My God, Harry, how I worship her!' He was walking up and down the room as he spoke. Hectic spots of red burned on his cheeks. He was terribly excited.

Lord Henry watched him with a subtle sense of pleasure. How different he was now from the shy, frightened boy he had met in Basil Hallward's studio! His nature had developed like a flower, had borne blossoms of scarlet flame. Out of its secret hiding-place had crept his Soul, and Desire had come to meet it on the way.

'And what do you propose to do?' said Lord Henry, at last.

'I want you and Basil to come with me some night and see her act. I have not the slightest fear of the result. You are certain to acknowledge her genius. Then we must get her out of the Jew's hands. She is bound to him for three years—at least for two years and eight months—from the present time. I shall have to pay him something, of course. When all that is settled, I shall take a West End theatre and bring her out properly. She will make the world as mad as she has made me.'

'That would be impossible, my dear boy?'

'Yes, she will. She has not merely art, consummate art-instinct, in her, but she has personality also; and you have often told me that it is personalities, not principles, that move the age.'

'Well, what night shall we go?'

'Let me see. To-day is Tuesday. Let us fix to-morrow. She plays Juliet to-morrow.'

'All right. The Bristol at eight o'clock; and I will get Basil.'

'Not eight, Harry, please. Half-past six. We must be there before the curtain rises. You must see her in the first act, where she meets Romeo.'

'Half-past six! What an hour! It will be like having a meat-tea, or reading an English novel. It must be seven. No gentleman dines before seven. Shall you see Basil between this and then? Or shall I write to him?'

'Dear Basil! I have not laid eyes on him for a week. It is rather horrid of me, as he has sent me my portrait in the most wonderful frame, specially designed by himself, and, though I am a little jealous of the picture for being a whole month younger than I am, I must admit that I delight in it. Perhaps you had better write to him. I don't want to see him alone. He says things that annoy me. He gives me good advice.'

Lord Henry smiled. 'People are very fond of giving away what they need most themselves. It is what I call the depth of generosity.'

'Oh, Basil is the best of fellows, but he seems to me to be just a bit of a Philistine. Since I have known you, Harry, I have discovered that.'

'Basil, my dear boy, puts everything that is charming in him into his work. The consequence is that he has nothing left for life but his prejudices, his principles, and his common-sense. The only artists I have ever known, who are personally delightful, are bad artists. Good artists exist simply in what they make, and consequently are perfectly uninteresting in what they are. A great poet, a really great poet, is the most unpoetical of all creatures. But inferior poets are absolutely fascinating. The worse their rhymes are, the more picturesque they look. The mere fact of having published a book of second-rate sonnets makes a man quite irresistible. He lives the poetry that he cannot write. The others write the poetry that they dare not realise.'

'I wonder is that really so, Harry?' said Dorian Gray, putting some perfume on his handkerchief out of a large gold-topped bottle that stood on the table. 'It must be, if you say it. And now I am off. Imogen is waiting for me. Don't forget about to-morrow. Good-bye.'

As he left the room, Lord Henry's heavy eyelids drooped, and he began to think. Certainly few people had ever interested him so much as Dorian Gray, and yet the lad's mad adoration of some one else caused him not the slightest pang of annoyance or jealousy. He was pleased by it. It made him a more interesting study. He had been always enthralled by the methods of natural science, but the ordinary subject-matter of that science had seemed to him trivial and of no import. And so he had begun by vivisecting himself, as he had ended by vivisecting others. Human life—that appeared to him the one thing worth investigating. Compared to it there was nothing else of any value. It was true that as one watched life in its curious crucible of pain and pleasure, one could not wear over one's face a mask of glass, nor keep the sulphurous fumes from troubling the brain, and making the imagination turbid with monstrous fancies and misshapen dreams. There were poisons so subtle that to know their properties one had to sicken of them. There were maladies so strange that one had to pass through them if one sought to understand their nature. And, yet, what a great reward one received! How wonderful the whole world became to one! To note the curious hard logic of passion, and the emotional coloured life of the intellect—to observe where they met, and where they separated, at what point they were in unison, and at what point they were at discord—there was a delight in that! What matter what the cost was? One could never pay too high a price for any sensation.

He was conscious—and the thought brought a gleam of pleasure into his brown agate eyes—that it was through certain words of his, musical words said with musical utterance, that Dorian Gray's soul had turned to this white girl and bowed in worship before her. To a large extent the lad was his own creation. He had made him premature. That was something. Ordinary people waited till life disclosed to them its secrets, but to the few, to the elect, the mysteries of life were revealed before the veil was drawn away. Sometimes this was the effect of art, and chiefly of the art of literature, which dealt immediately with the passions and the intellect. But now and then a complex personality took the place and assumed the office of art; was indeed, in its way, a real work of art, Life having its elaborate master-pieces, just as poetry has, or sculpture, or painting.

Yes, the lad was premature. He was gathering his harvest while it was yet spring. The pulse and passion of youth were in him, but he was becoming self-conscious. It was delightful to watch him. With his beautiful face, and his beautiful soul, he was a thing to wonder at. It was no matter how it all ended, or was destined to end. He was like one of those gracious figures in a pageant or a play, whose joys seem to be remote from one, but whose sorrows stir one's sense of beauty, and whose wounds are like red roses.

Soul and body, body and soul—how mysterious they were! There was animalism in the soul, and the body had its moments of spirituality. The senses could refine, and the intellect could degrade. Who could say where the fleshly impulse ceased, or the physical impulse began? How shallow were the arbitrary definitions of ordinary psychologists! And yet how difficult to decide between the claims of the various schools! Was the soul a shadow seated in the house of sin? Or was the body really in the soul, as Giordano Bruno thought? The separation of spirit from matter was a mystery, and the union of spirit with matter was a mystery also.

He began to wonder whether we could ever make psychology so absolute a science that each little spring of life would be revealed to us. As it was, we always misunderstood ourselves, and rarely understood others. Experience was of no ethical value. It was merely the name men gave to their mistakes. Moralists had, as a rule, regarded it as a mode of warning, had claimed for it a certain ethical efficacy in the formation of character, had praised it as something that taught us what to follow and showed us what to avoid. But there was no motive power in experience. It was as little of an active cause as conscience itself. All that it really demonstrated was that our future would be the same as our past, and that the sin we had done once, and with loathing, we would do many times, and with joy.

It was clear to him that the experimental method was the only method by which one could arrive at any scientific analysis of the passions; and certainly Dorian Gray was a subject made to his hand, and seemed to promise rich and fruitful results. His sudden mad love for Sibyl Vane was a psychological phenomenon of no small interest. There was no doubt that curiosity had much to do with it, curiosity and the desire for new experiences; yet it was not a simple but rather a very complex passion. What there was in it of the purely sensuous instinct of boyhood had been transformed by the workings of the imagination, changed into something that seemed to the lad himself to be remote from sense, and was for that very reason all the more dangerous. It was the passions about whose origin we deceived ourselves that tyrannised most strongly over us. Our weakest motives were those of whose nature we were conscious. If often happened that when we thought we were experimenting on others we were really experimenting on ourselves.

While Lord Henry sat dreaming on these things, a knock came to the door, and his valet entered, and reminded him it was time to dress for dinner. He got up and looked out into the street. The sunset had smitten into scarlet gold the upper windows of the houses opposite. The panes glowed like plates of heated metal. The sky above was like a faded rose. He thought of his friend's young fiery-coloured life, and wondered how it was all going to end.

When he arrived home, about half-past twelve o'clock, he saw a telegram lying on the hall table. He opened it, and found it was from Dorian Gray. It was to tell him that he was engaged to be married to Sibyl Vane.

CHAPTER V

'MOTHER, mother, I am so happy!' whispered the girl, burying her face in the lap of the faded, tired-looking woman who, with back turned to the shrill intrusive light, was sitting in the one arm-chair that their dingy sitting-room contained. 'I am so happy!' she repeated, 'and you must be happy too!'

Mrs. Vane winced, and put her thin bismuth-whitened hands on her daughter's head. 'Happy!' she echoed, 'I am only happy, Sibyl, when I see you act. You must not think of anything but your acting. Mr. Isaacs has been very good to us, and we owe him money.'

The girl looked up and pouted. 'Money, mother?' she cried, 'what does money matter? Love is more than money.'

'Mr. Isaacs has advanced us fifty pounds to pay off our debts, and to get a proper outfit for James. You must not forget that, Sibyl. Fifty pounds is a very large sum. Mr. Isaacs has been most considerate.'

'He is not a gentleman, mother, and I hate the way he talks to me,' said the girl, rising to her feet, and going over to the window.

'I don't know how we could manage without him,' answered the elder woman, querulously.

Sibyl Vane tossed her head and laughed. 'We don't want him any more, mother. Prince Charming rules life for us now.' Then she paused. A rose shook in her blood, and shadowed her cheeks. Quick breath parted the petals of her lips. They trembled. Some southern wind of passion swept over her, and stirred the dainty folds of her dress. 'I love him,' she said, simply.

72

'Foolish child! foolish child!' was the parrot-phrase flung in answer. The waving of crooked, false-jewelled fingers gave grotesqueness to the words.

The girl laughed again. The joy of a caged bird was in her voice. Her eyes caught the melody, and echoed it in radiance; then closed for a moment, as though to hide their secret. When they opened, the mist of a dream had passed across them.

Thin-lipped wisdom spoke at her from the worn chair, hinted at prudence, quoted from that book of cowardice whose author apes the name of common sense. She did not listen. She was free in her prison of passion. Her prince, Prince Charming, was with her. She had called on Memory to remake him. She had sent her soul to search for him, and it had brought him back. His kiss burned again upon her mouth. Her eyelids were warm with his breath.

Then Wisdom altered its method and spoke of espial and discovery. This young man might be rich. If so, marriage should be thought of. Against the shell of her ear broke the waves of worldly cunning. The arrows of craft shot by her. She saw the thin lips moving, and smiled.

Suddenly she felt the need to speak. The wordy silence troubled her. 'Mother, mother,' she cried, 'why does he love me so much? I know why I love him. I love him because he is like what Love himself should be. But what does he see in me? I am not worthy of him. And yet—why, I cannot tell—though I feel so much beneath him, I don't feel humble. I feel proud, terribly proud. Mother, did you love my father as I love Prince Charming?'

The elder woman grew pale beneath the coarse powder that daubed her cheeks, and her dry lips twitched with a spasm of pain. Sibyl rushed to her, flung her arms round her neck, and kissed her. 'Forgive me, mother. I know it pains you to talk about our father. But it only pains you because you loved him so much. Don't look so sad. I am as happy to-day as you were twenty years ago. Ah! let me be happy for ever!'

'My child, you are far too young to think of falling in love. Besides, what do you know of this young man? You don't even know his name. The whole thing is most inconvenient, and really, when James is going away to Australia, and I have so much to think of, I must say that you should have shown more consideration. However, as I said before, if he is rich . . .'

'Ah! Mother, mother, let me be happy!'

Mrs. Vane glanced at her, and with one of those false theatrical gestures that so often become a mode of second nature to a stage-player, clasped her in her arms. At this moment the door opened, and a young lad with rough brown hair came into the room. He was thick-set of figure, and his hands and feet were large, and somewhat clumsy in movement. He was not so finely bred as his sister. One would hardly have guessed the close relationship that existed between them. Mrs. Vane fixed her eyes on him, and intensified the smile. She mentally elevated her son to the dignity of an audience. She felt sure that the *tableau* was interesting.

'You might keep some of your kisses for me, Sibyl, I think,' said the lad, with a good-natured grumble.

'Ah! but you don't like being kissed, Jim,' she cried. 'You are a dreadful old bear.' And she ran across the room and hugged him.

James Vane looked into his sister's face with tenderness. 'I want you to come out with me for a walk, Sibyl. I don't suppose I shall ever see this horrid London again. I am sure I don't want to.'

'My son, don't say such dreadful things,' murmured Mrs. Vane, taking up a tawdry theatrical dress, with a sigh, and beginning to patch it. She felt a little disappointed that he had not joined the group. It would have increased the theatrical picturesqueness of the situation.

'Why not, mother? I mean it.'

'You pain me, my son. I trust you will return from Australia in a position of affluence. I believe there is no society of any kind in the Colonies, nothing that I would call society; so when you have made your fortune you must come back and assert yourself in London.'

'Society!' muttered the lad. 'I don't want to know anything about that. I should like to make some money to take you and Sibyl off the stage. I hate it.'

'Oh, Jim!' said Sibyl, laughing, 'how unkind of you! But are you really going for a walk with me? That will be nice! I was afraid you were going to say good-bye to some of your friends—to Tom Hardy, who gave you that hideous pipe, or Ned Langton, who makes fun of you for smoking it. It is very sweet of you to let me have your last afternoon. Where shall we go? Let us go to the Park.'

'I am too shabby,' he answered, frowning. 'Only swell people go to the Park.'

'Nonsense, Jim,' she whispered, stroking the sleeve of his coat.

He hesitated for a moment. 'Very well,' he said at last, 'but don't be too long dressing.' She danced out of the door. One could hear her singing as she ran upstairs. Her little feet pattered overhead.

He walked up and down the room two or three times. Then he turned to the still figure in the chair. 'Mother, are my things ready?' he asked.

'Quite ready, James,' she answered, keeping her eyes on her work. For some months past she had felt ill at ease when she was alone with this rough, stern son of hers. Her shallow secret nature was troubled when their eyes met. She used to wonder if he suspected anything. The silence, for he made no other observation, became intolerable to her. She began to complain. Women defend themselves by attacking, just as they attack by sudden and strange surrenders. 'I hope you will be contented, James, with your sea-faring life,' she said. 'You must remember that it is your own choice. You might have entered a solicitor's office. Solicitors are a very respectable class, and in the country often dine with the best families.'

'I hate offices, and I hate clerks,' he replied. 'But you are quite right. I have chosen my own life. All I say is, watch over Sibyl. Don't let her come to any harm. Mother, you must watch over her.'

'James, you really talk very strangely. Of course I watch over Sibyl.'

'I hear a gentleman comes every night to the theatre, and goes behind to talk to her. Is that right? What about that?'

'You are speaking about things you don't understand, James. In the profession we are accustomed to receive a great deal of most gratifying attention. I myself used to receive many bouquets at one time. That was when acting was really understood. As for Sibyl, I do not know at present whether her attachment is serious or not. But there is no doubt that the young man in question is a perfect gentleman. He is always most polite to me. Besides, he has the appearance of being rich, and the flowers he sends are lovely.'

'You don't know his name, though,' said the lad, harshly.

'No,' answered his mother, with a placid expression in her face. 'He has not yet revealed his real name. I think it is quite romantic of him. He is probably a member of the aristocracy.'

James Vane bit his lip. 'Watch over Sibyl, mother,' he cried, 'watch over her.'

'My son, you distress me very much. Sibyl is always under my special care. Of course, if this gentleman is wealthy, there is no reason why she should not contract an alliance with him. I trust he is one of the aristocracy. He has all the appearance of it, I must say. It might be a most brilliant marriage for Sibyl. They would make a charming couple. His good looks are really quite remarkable; everybody notices them.'

The lad muttered something to himself and drummed on the window-pane with his coarse fingers. He had just turned round to say something, when the door opened, and Sibyl ran in.

'How serious you both are!' she cried. 'What is the matter?'

'Nothing,' he answered, 'I suppose one must be serious sometimes. Good-bye, mother; I will have my dinner at five o'clock. Everything is packed, except my shirts, so you need not trouble.'

'Good-bye, my son,' she answered, with a bow of strained stateliness.

She was extremely annoyed at the tone he had adopted with her, and there was something in his look that had made her feel afraid.

'Kiss me, mother,' said the girl. Her flower-like lips touched the withered cheek, and warmed its frost.

'My child! my child!' cried Mrs. Vane, looking up to the ceiling in search of an imaginary gallery.

'Come, Sibyl,' said her brother, impatiently. He hated his mother's affectations.

They went out into the flickering wind-blown sunlight, and strolled down the dreary Euston Road. The passers-by glanced in wonder at the sullen, heavy youth, who, in coarse, ill-fitting clothes, was in the company of such a graceful, refined-looking girl. He was like a common gardener walking with a rose.

Jim frowned from time to time when he caught the

inquisitive glance of some stranger. He had that dislike of being stared at which comes on geniuses late in life, and never leaves the commonplace. Sibyl, however, was quite unconscious of the effect she was producing. Her love was trembling in laughter on her lips. She was thinking of Prince Charming, and, that she might think of him all the more, she did not talk of him but prattled on about the ship in which Jim was going to sail, about the gold he was certain to find, about the wonderful heiress whose life he was to save from the wicked, red-shirted bushrangers. For he was not to remain a sailor, or a super-cargo, or whatever he was going to be. Oh, no! A sailor's existence was dreadful. Fancy being cooped up in a horrid ship, with the hoarse, hump-backed waves trying to get in, and a black wind blowing the masts down, and tearing the sails into long screaming ribands! He was to leave the vessel at Melbourne, bid a polite good-bye to the captain, and go off at once to the gold-fields. Before a week was over he was to come across a large nugget of pure gold, the largest nugget that had ever been discovered, and bring it down to the coast in a waggon guarded by six mounted policemen. The bushrangers were to attack them three times, and be defeated with immense slaughter. Or, no. He was not to go to the gold-fields at all. They were horrid places, where men got intoxicated, and shot each other in bar-rooms, and used bad language. He was to be a nice sheep-farmer, and one evening, as he was riding home, he was to see the beautiful heiress being carried off by a robber on a black horse, and give chase, and rescue her. Of course she would fall in love with him, and he with her, and they would get married, and come home, and live in an immense house in London. Yes, there were delightful things in store for him. But he must be very good, and not lose his temper, or spend his money foolishly. She was only a year older than he was, but she knew so much more of life. He must be sure, also, to write to her by every mail, and to say his prayers each night before he went to sleep. God was very good, and would watch over him. She would pray for him, too, and in a few years he would come back quite rich and happy.

The lad listened sulkily to her, and made no answer. He was heart-sick at leaving home.

Yet it was not this alone that made him gloomy and morose. Inexperienced though he was, he had still a strong sense of the danger of Sibyl's position. This young dandy who was making love to her could mean her no good. He was a gentleman, and he hated him for that, hated him through some curious race-instinct for which he could not account, and which for that reason was all the more dominant within him. He was conscious also of the shallowness and vanity of his mother's nature, and in that saw infinite peril for Sibyl and Sibyl's happiness. Children begin by loving their parents; as they grow older they judge them; sometimes they forgive them.

His mother! He had something on his mind to ask of her, something that he had brooded on for many months of silence. A chance phrase that he had heard at the theatre, a whispered sneer that had reached his ears one night as he waited at the stage-door, had set loose a train of horrible thoughts. He remembered it as if it had been the lash of a hunting-crop across his face. His brows knit together into a wedge-like furrow, and with a twitch of pain he bit his under-lip.

'You are not listening to a word I am saying, Jim,' cried Sibyl, 'and I am making the most delightful plans for your future. Do say something.'

'What do you want me to say?'

'Oh! that you will be a good boy, and not forget us,' she answered, smiling at him.

He shrugged his shoulders. 'You are more likely to forget me, than I am to forget you, Sibyl.'

She flushed. 'What do you mean, Jim?' she asked.

'You have a new friend, I hear. Who is he? Why have you not told me about him? He means you no good.'

'Stop, Jim!' she exclaimed. 'You must not say anything against him. I love him.'

'Why, you don't even know his name,' answered the lad. 'Who is he? I have a right to know.'

'He is called Prince Charming. Don't you like the name? Oh! you silly boy! you should never forget it. If you only saw him, you would think him the most wonderful person in the world. Some day you will meet him: when you come back from Australia. You will like him so much. Everybody likes him, and I . . . love him. I wish you could come to the theatre to-night. He is going to be there, and I am to play Juliet. Oh! how I shall play it! Fancy, Jim, to be in love and play Juliet! To have him sitting there! To play for his delight! I am afraid I may frighten the company, frighten or enthrall them. To be in love is to surpass one's self. Poor dreadful Mr. Isaacs will be shouting "genius" to his loafers at the bar. He has preached me as a dogma; to-night he will announce me as a revelation. I feel it. And it is all his, his only, Prince Charming, my wonderful lover, my god of graces. But I am poor beside him. Poor? What does that matter? When poverty creeps in at the door, love flies in through the window. Our proverbs want re-writing. They were made in winter, and it is summer now; spring-time for me, I think, a very dance of blossoms in blue skies.'

'He is a gentleman,' said the lad, sullenly.

'A Prince!' she cried, musically. 'What more do you want?'

'He wants to enslave you.'

80

'I shudder at the thought of being free.'

'I want you to beware of him.'

'To see him is to worship him, to know him is to trust him.'

'Sibyl, you are mad about him.'

She laughed, and took his arm. 'You dear old Jim, you talk as if you were a hundred. Some day you will be in love yourself. Then you will know what it is. Don't look so sulky. Surely you should be glad to think that, though you are going away, you leave me happier than I have ever been before. Life has been hard for us both, terribly hard and difficult. But it will be different now. You are going to a new world, and I have found one. Here are two chairs; let us sit down and see the smart people go by.'

They took their seats amidst a crowd of watchers. The tulip-beds across the road flamed like throbbing rings of fire. A white dust, tremulous cloud of orris-root it seemed, hung in the panting air. The brightly-coloured parasols danced and dipped like monstrous butterflies.

She made her brother talk of himself, his hopes, his prospects. He spoke slowly and with effort. They passed words to each other as players at a game pass counters. Sibyl felt oppressed. She could not communicate her joy. A faint smile curving that sullen mouth was all the echo she could win. After some time she became silent. Suddenly she caught a glimpse of golden hair and laughing lips, and in an open carriage with two ladies Dorian Gray drove past.

She started to her feet. 'There he is!' she cried.

'Who?' said Jim Vane.

'Prince Charming,' she answered, looking after the victoria.

He jumped up, and seized her roughly by the arm. 'Show him to me. Which is he? Point him out. I must see him!' he exclaimed; but at that moment the Duke of Berwick's four-in-hand came between, and when it had left the space clear, the carriage had swept out of the Park.

'He is gone,' murmured Sibyl, sadly. 'I wish you had seen him.'

'I wish I had, for as sure as there is a God in heaven, if he ever does you any wrong I shall kill him.'

She looked at him in horror. He repeated his words. They cut the air like a dagger. The people round began to gape. A lady standing close to her tittered.

'Come away, Jim; come away,' she whispered. He followed her doggedly, as she passed through the crowd. He felt glad at what he had said.

When they reached the Achilles Statue she turned round. There was pity in her eyes that became laughter on her lips. She shook her head at him. 'You are foolish, Jim, utterly foolish; a bad-tempered boy, that is all. How can you say such horrible things? You don't know what you are talking about. You are simply jealous and unkind. Ah! I wish you would fall in love. Love makes people good, and what you said was wicked.'

'I am sixteen,' he answered, 'and I know what I am about. Mother is no help to you. She doesn't understand how to look after you. I wish now that I was not going to Australia at all. I have a great mind to chuck the whole thing up. I would, if my articles hadn't been signed.'

'Oh, don't be so serious, Jim. You are like one of the heroes of those silly melodramas mother used to be so fond of acting in. I am not going to quarrel with you. I have seen him, and oh! to see him is perfect happiness. We won't quarrel. I know you would never harm anyone I love, would you?'

'Not as long as you love him, I suppose,' was the sullen answer.

'I shall love him for ever!' she cried.

'And he?'

'For ever, too!'

'He had better.'

She shrank from him. Then she laughed and put her hand on his arm. He was merely a boy.

At the Marble Arch they hailed an omnibus, which left them close to their shabby home in the Euston Road. It was after five o'clock, and Sibyl had to lie down for a couple of hours before acting. Jim insisted that she should do so. He said that he would sooner part with her when their mother was not present. She would be sure to make a scene, and he detested scenes of every kind.

In Sibyl's own room, they parted. There was jealousy in the lad's heart, and a fierce, murderous hatred of the stranger who, as it seemed to him, had come between them. Yet, when her arms were flung round his neck, and her fingers strayed through his hair, he softened, and kissed her with real affection. There were tears in his eyes as he went downstairs.

His mother was waiting for him below. She grumbled at his unpunctuality, as he entered. He made no answer, but sat down to his meagre meal. The flies buzzed round the table, and crawled over the stained cloth. Through the rumble of omnibuses, and the clatter of street-cabs, he could hear the droning voice devouring each minute that was left to him.

After some time, he thrust away his plate, and put his head in his hands. He felt that he had a right to know. It should have been told to him before, if it was as he suspected. Leaden with fear, his mother watched him. Words dropped mechanically from her lips. A tattered lace handkerchief twitched in her fingers. When the clock struck six, he got up, and went to the door. Then he turned back, and looked at her. Their eyes met. In hers he saw a wild appeal for mercy. It enraged him.

'Mother, I have something to ask you,' he said. Her

eyes wandered vaguely about the room. She made no answer. 'Tell me the truth. I have a right to know. Were you married to my father?'

She heaved a deep sigh. It was a sigh of relief. The terrible moment, the moment that night and day, for weeks and months, she had dreaded, had come at last, and yet she felt no terror. Indeed in some measure it was a disappointment to her. The vulgar directness of the question called for a direct answer. The situation had not been gradually led up to. It was crude. It reminded her of a bad rehearsal.

'No,' she answered, wondering at the harsh simplicity of life.

'My father was a scoundrel then?' cried the lad, clenching his fists.

She shook her head. 'I knew he was not free. We loved each other very much. If he had lived, he would have made provision for us. Don't speak against him, my son. He was your father, and a gentleman. Indeed he was highly connected.'

An oath broke from his lips. 'I don't care for myself,' he exclaimed, 'but don't let Sibyl . . . It is a gentleman, isn't it, who is in love with her, or says he is? Highly connected, too, I suppose.'

For a moment a hideous sense of humiliation came over the woman. Her head drooped. She wiped her eyes with shaking hands. 'Sibyl has a mother,' she murmured; 'I had none.'

The lad was touched. He went towards her, and stooping down he kissed her. 'I am sorry if I have pained you by asking about my father,' he said, 'but I could not help it. I must go now. Good-bye. Don't forget that you will only have one child now to look after, and believe me that if this man wrongs my sister, I will find out who he is, track him down, and kill him like a dog. I swear it.'

The exaggerated folly of the threat, the passionate gesture that accompanied it, the mad melodramatic words, made life seem more vivid to her. She was familiar with the atmosphere. She breathed more freely, and for the first time for many months she really admired her son. She would have liked to have continued the scene on the same emotional scale, but he cut her short. Trunks had to be carried down, and mufflers looked for. The lodging-house drudge bustled in and out. There was the bargaining with the cabman. The moment was lost in vulgar details. It was with a renewed feeling of disappointment that she waved the tattered lace handkerchief from the window, as her son drove away. She was conscious that a great opportunity had been wasted. She consoled herself by telling Sibyl how desolate she felt her life would be, now that she had only one child to look after. She remembered the phrase. It had pleased her. Of the threat she said nothing. It was vividly and dramatically expressed. She felt that they would all laugh at it some day.

CHAPTER VI

'I SUPPOSE you have heard the news, Basil?' said Lord Henry that evening, as Hallward was shown into a little private room at the Bristol where dinner had been laid for three.

'No, Harry,' answered the artist, giving his hat and coat to the bowing waiter. 'What is it? Nothing about politics, I hope? They don't interest me. There is hardly a single person in the House of Commons worth painting; though many of them would be the better for a little white-washing.'

'Dorian Gray is engaged to be married,' said Lord Henry, watching him as he spoke.

Hallward started, and then frowned. 'Dorian engaged to be married!' he cried. 'Impossible!'

'It is perfectly true.'

'To whom?'

'To some little actress or other.'

'I can't believe it. Dorian is far too sensible.'

'Dorian is far too wise not to do foolish things now and then, my dear Basil.'

'Marriage is hardly a thing that one can do now and then, Harry.'

'Except in America,' rejoined Lord Henry, languidly. 'But I didn't say he was married. I said he was engaged to be married. There is a great difference. I have a distinct remembrance of being married, but I have no recollection at all of being engaged. I am inclined to think that I never was engaged.'

'But think of Dorian's birth, and position, and wealth.

It would be absurd for him to marry so much beneath him.'

'If you want to make him marry this girl tell him that, Basil. He is sure to do it, then. Whenever a man does a thoroughly stupid thing, it is always from the noblest motives.'

'I hope the girl is good, Harry. I don't want to see Dorian tied to some vile creature, who might degrade his nature and ruin his intellect.'

'Oh, she is better than good—she is beautiful,' murmured Lord Henry, sipping a glass of vermouth and orange-bitters. 'Dorian says she is beautiful; and he is not often wrong about things of that kind. Your portrait of him has quickened his appreciation of the personal appearance of other people. It has had that excellent effect, amongst others. We are to see her to-night, if that boy doesn't forget his appointment.'

'Are you serious?'

'Quite serious, Basil. I should be miserable if I thought I should ever be more serious than I am at the present moment.'

'But do you approve of it, Harry?' asked the painter, walking up and down the room, and biting his lip. 'You can't approve of it, possibly. It is some silly infatuation.'

'I never approve, or disapprove, of anything now. It is an absurd attitude to take towards life. We are not sent into the world to air our moral prejudices. I never take any notice of what common people say, and I never interfere with what charming people do. If a personality fascinates me, whatever mode of expression that personality selects is absolutely delightful to me. Dorian Gray falls in love with a beautiful girl who acts Juliet, and proposes to marry her. Why not? If he wedded Messalina he would be none the less interesting. You know I am not a champion of marriage. The real drawback to marriage is that it makes one unselfish. And unselfish people are colourless. They lack individuality. Still, there are certain temperaments that marriage makes more complex. They retain their egotism, and add to it many other egos. They are forced to have more than one life. They become more highly organised, and to be highly organised is, I should fancy, the object of man's existence. Besides, every experience is of value, and, whatever one may say against marriage, it is certainly an experience. I hope that Dorian Gray will make this girl his wife, passionately adore her for six months, and then suddenly become fascinated by someone else. He would be a wonderful study.'

'You don't mean a single word of all that, Harry; you know you don't. If Dorian Gray's life were spoiled, no one would be sorrier than yourself. You are much better than you pretend to be.'

Lord Henry laughed. 'The reason we all like to think so well of others is that we are all afraid for ourselves. The basis of optimism is sheer terror. We think that we are generous because we credit our neighbour with the possession of those virtues that are likely to be a benefit to us. We praise the banker that we may overdraw our account, and find good qualities in the highwayman in the hope that he may spare our pockets. I mean everything that I have said. I have the greatest contempt for optimism. As for a spoiled life, no life is spoiled but one whose growth is arrested. If you want to mar a nature, you have merely to reform it. As for marriage, of course that would be silly, but there are other and more interesting bonds between men and women. I will certainly encourage them. They have the charm of being fashionable. But here is Dorian himself. He will tell you more than I can.'

'My dear Harry, my dear Basil, you must both congratulate me!' said the lad, throwing off his evening cape with its satin-lined wings and shaking each of his friends by the hand in turn. 'I have never been so happy. Of course it is sudden; all really delightful things are. And yet it seems to me to be the one thing I have been looking for all my life.' He was flushed with excitement and pleasure, and looked extraordinarily handsome.

'I hope you will always be very happy, Dorian,' said Hallward, 'but I don't quite forgive you for not having let me know of your engagement. You let Harry know.'

'And I don't forgive you for being late for dinner,' broke in Lord Henry, putting his hand on the lad's shoulder, and smiling as he spoke. 'Come, let us sit down and try what the new *chef* here is like, and then you will tell us how it all came about.'

'There is really not much to tell,' cried Dorian, as they took their seats at the small round table. 'What happened was simply this. After I left you yesterday evening, Harry, I dressed, had some dinner at that little Italian restaurant in Rupert Street you introduced me to, and went down at eight o'clock to the theatre. Sibyl was playing Rosalind. Of course the scenery was dreadful and the Orlando absurd. But Sibyl! You should have seen her! When she came on in her boy's clothes she was perfectly wonderful. She wore a moss-coloured velvet jerkin with cinnamon sleeves, slim brown cross-gartered hose, a dainty little green cap with a hawk's feather caught in a jewel, and a hooded cloak lined with dull red. She had never seemed to me more exquisite. She had all the delicate grace of that Tanagra figurine that you have in your studio, Basil. Her hair clustered round her face like dark leaves round a pale rose. As for her acting—well, you shall see her to-night. She is simply a born artist. I sat in the dingy box absolutely enthralled. I forgot that I was in London and in the nineteenth century. I was away with my love in a forest that

89

no man had ever seen. After the performance was over I went behind, and spoke to her. As we were sitting together, suddenly there came into her eyes a look that I had never seen there before. My lips moved towards hers. We kissed each other. I can't describe to you what I felt at that moment. It seemed to me that all my life had been narrowed to one perfect point of rose-coloured joy. She trembled all over, and shook like a white narcissus. Then she flung herself on her knees and kissed my hands. I feel that I should not tell you all this, but I can't help it. Of course our engagement is a dead secret. She has not even told her own mother. I don't know what my guardians will say. Lord Radley is sure to be furious. I don't care. I shall be of age in less than a year, and then I can do what I like. I have been right, Basil, haven't I, to take my love out of poetry, and to find my wife in Shakespeare's plays? Lips that Shakespeare taught to speak have whispered their secret in my ear. I have had the arms of Rosalind around me, and kissed Juliet on the mouth.'

'Yes, Dorian, I suppose you were right,' said Hallward slowly.

'Have you seen her to-day?' asked Lord Henry.

Dorian Gray shook his head. 'I left her in the forest of Arden, I shall find her in an orchard in Verona.'

Lord Henry sipped his champagne in a meditative manner. 'At what particular point did you mention the word marriage, Dorian? And what did she say in answer? Perhaps you forgot all about it.'

'My dear Harry, I did not treat it as a business transaction, and I did not make any formal proposal. I told her that I loved her, and she said she was not worthy to be my wife. Not worthy! Why, the whole world is nothing to me compared with her.'

'Women are wonderfully practical,' murmured Lord

Henry—'much more practical than we are. In situations of that kind we often forget to say anything about marriage, and they always remind us.'

Hallward laid his hand upon his arm. 'Don't, Harry. You have annoyed Dorian. He is not like other men. He would never bring misery upon anyone. His nature is too fine for that.'

Lord Henry looked across the table. 'Dorian is never annoyed with me,' he answered. 'I asked the question for the best reason possible, for the only reason, indeed, that excuses one for asking any question—simple curiosity. I have a theory that it is always the women who propose to us, and not we who propose to the women. Except, of course, in middle-class life. But then the middle classes are not modern.'

Dorian Gray laughed, and tossed his head. 'You are quite incorrigible, Harry; but I don't mind. It is impossible to be angry with you. When you see Sibyl Vane you will feel that the man who could wrong her would be a beast, a beast without a heart. I cannot understand how anyone can wish to shame the thing he loves. I love Sibyl Vane. I want to place her on a pedestal of gold, and to see the world worship the woman who is mine. What is marriage? An irrevocable vow. You mock at it for that. Ah! don't mock. It is an irrevocable vow that I want to take. Her trust makes me faithful, her belief makes me good. When I am with her, I regret all that you have taught me. I become different from what you have known me to be. I am changed, and the mere touch of Sibyl Vane's hand makes me forget you and all your wrong, fascinating, poisonous, delightful theories.'

'And those are . . .?' asked Lord Henry, helping himself to some salad.

'Oh, your theories about life, your theories about love,

your theories about pleasure. All your theories, in fact, Harry.'

'Pleasure is the only thing worth having a theory about,' he answered, in his slow, melodious voice. 'But I am afraid I cannot claim my theory as my own. It belongs to Nature, not to me. Pleasure is Nature's test, her sign of approval. When we are happy we are always good, but when we are good we are not always happy.'

'Ah! but what do you mean by good?' cried Basil Hallward.

'Yes,' echoed Dorian, leaning back in his chair, and looking at Lord Henry over the heavy clusters of purple-lipped irises that stood in the centre of the table, 'what do you mean by good, Harry?'

'To be good is to be in harmony with one's self,' he replied, touching the thin stem of his glass with his pale, fine-pointed fingers. 'Discord is to be forced to be in harmony with others. One's own life—that is the important thing. As for the lives of one's neighbours, if one wishes to be a prig or a Puritan, one can flaunt one's moral views about them, but they are not one's concern. Besides, Individualism has really the higher aim. Modern morality consists in accepting the standard of one's age. I consider that for any man of culture to accept the standard of his age is a form of the grossest immorality.'

'But, surely, if one lives merely for one's self, Harry, one pays a terrible price for doing so?' suggested the painter.

'Yes, we are overcharged for everything nowadays. I should fancy that the real tragedy of the poor is that they can afford nothing but self-denial. Beautiful sins, like beautiful things, are the privilege of the rich.'

'One has to pay in other ways but money.'

'What sort of ways, Basil?'

'Oh! I should fancy in remorse, in suffering, in . . . well, in the consciousness of degradation.'

Lord Henry shrugged his shoulders. 'My dear fellow, mediæval art is charming, but mediæval emotions are out of date. One can use them in fiction, of course. But then the only things that one can use in fiction are the things that one has ceased to use in fact. Believe me, no civilised man ever regrets a pleasure, and no uncivilised man ever knows what a pleasure is.'

'I know what pleasure is,' cried Dorian Gray. 'It is to adore someone.'

'That is certainly better than being adored,' he answered, toying with some fruits. 'Being adored is a nuisance. Women treat us just as Humanity treats its gods. They worship us, and are always bothering us to do something for them.'

'I should have said that whatever they ask for they had first given to us,' murmured the lad, gravely. 'They create Love in our natures. They have a right to demand it back.'

'That is quite true, Dorian,' cried Hallward.

'Nothing is ever quite true,' said Lord Henry.

'This is,' interrupted Dorian. 'You must admit, Harry, that women give to men the very gold of their lives.'

'Possibly,' he sighed, 'but they invariably want it back in such very small change. That is the worry. Women, as some witty Frenchman once put it, inspire us with the desire to do masterpieces, and always prevent us from carrying them out.'

'Harry, you are dreadful! I don't know why I like you so much.'

'You will always like me, Dorian,' he replied. 'Will you have some coffee, you fellows?—Waiter, bring coffee, and *fine-champagne*, and some cigarettes. No: don't mind the cigarettes; I have some. Basil, I can't allow you to smoke cigars. You must have a cigarette. A cigarette is the perfect type of a perfect pleasure. It is exquisite, and it leaves one unsatisfied. What more can one want? Yes, Dorian, you will always be fond of me. I represent to you all the sins you have never had the courage to commit.'

'What nonsense you talk, Harry!' cried the lad, taking a light from a fire-breathing silver dragon that the waiter had placed on the table. 'Let us go down to the theatre. When Sibyl comes on the stage you will have a new ideal of life. She will represent something to you that you have never known.'

'I have known everything,' said Lord Henry, with a tired look in his eyes, 'but I am always ready for a new emotion. I am afraid, however, that, for me at any rate, there is no such thing. Still, your wonderful girl may thrill me. I love acting. It is so much more real than life. Let us go. Dorian, you will come with me. I am so sorry, Basil, but there is only room for two in the brougham. You must follow us in a hansom.'

They got up and put on their coats, sipping their coffee standing. The painter was silent and preoccupied. There was a gloom over him. He could not bear this marriage, and yet it seemed to him to be better than many other things that might have happened. After a few minutes, they all passed downstairs. He drove off by himself, as had been arranged, and watched the flashing lights of the little brougham in front of him. A strange sense of loss came over him. He felt that Dorian Gray would never again be to him all that he had been in the past. Life had come between them. . . . His eyes darkened, and the crowded, flaring streets became blurred to his eyes. When the cab drew up at the theatre, it seemed to him that he had grown years older.

CHAPTER VII

FOR some reason or other, the house was crowded that night, and the fat Jew manager who met them at the door was beaming from ear to ear with an oily, tremulous smile. He escorted them to their box with a sort of pompous humility, waving his fat jewelled hands, and talking at the top of his voice. Dorian Gray loathed him more than ever. He felt as if he had come to look for Miranda and had been met by Caliban. Lord Henry, upon the other hand, rather liked him. At least he declared he did, and insisted on shaking him by the hand, and assuring him that he was proud to meet a man who had discovered a real genius and gone bankrupt over a poet. Hallward amused himself with watching the faces in the pit. The heat was terribly oppressive, and the huge sunlight flamed like a monstrous dahlia with petals of yellow fire. The youths in the gallery had taken off their coats and waistcoats and hung them over the side. They talked to each other across the theatre, and shared their oranges with the tawdry girls who sat beside them. Some women were laughing in the pit. Their voices were horribly shrill and discordant. The sound of the popping of corks came from the bar.

'What a place to find one's divinity in!' said Lord Henry.

'Yes!' answered Dorian Gray. 'It was here I found her, and she is divine beyond all living things. When she acts you will forget everything. These common, rough people, with their coarse faces and brutal gestures, become quite different when she is on the stage. They sit silently and watch her. They weep and laugh as she wills them to do. She makes them as responsive as a violin. She spiritualises them, and one feels that they are of the same flesh and blood as one's self.'

'The same flesh and blood as one's self! Oh, I hope not!' exclaimed Lord Henry, who was scanning the occupants of the gallery through his opera-glass.

'Don't pay any attention to him, Dorian,' said the painter. 'I understand what you mean, and I believe in this girl. Anyone you love must be marvellous, and any girl that has the effect you describe must be fine and noble. To spiritualise one's age—that is something worth doing. If this girl can give a soul to those who have lived without one, if she can create the sense of beauty in people whose lives have been sordid and ugly, if she can strip them of their selfishness and lend them tears for sorrows that are not their own, she is worthy of all your adoration, worthy of the adoration of the world. This marriage is quite right. I did not think so at first, but I admit it now. The gods made Sibyl Vane for you. Without her you would have been incomplete.'

'Thanks, Basil,' answered Dorian Gray, pressing his hand. 'I knew that you would understand me. Harry is so cynical, he terrifies me. But here is the orchestra. It is quite dreadful, but it only lasts for about five minutes. Then the curtain rises, and you will see the girl to whom I am going to give all my life, to whom I have given everything that is good in me."

A quarter of an hour afterwards, amidst an extraordinary turmoil of applause, Sibyl Vane stepped on to the stage. Yes, she was certainly lovely to look at—one of the loveliest creatures, Lord Henry thought, that he had ever seen. There was something of the fawn in her shy grace and startled eyes. A faint blush, like the shadow of a rose in a mirror of silver, came to her cheeks as she glanced at the crowded, enthusiastic house. She stepped back a few paces, and her lips seemed to tremble. Basil Hallward leaped to his feet and began to applaud. Motionless, and as one in a dream, sat Dorian Gray, gazing at her. Lord Henry peered through his glasses, murmuring, 'Charming! charming!'

The scene was the hall of Capulet's house, and Romeo in his pilgrim's dress had entered with Mercutio and his other friends. The band, such as it was, struck up a few bars of music, and the dance began. Through the crowd of ungainly, shabbily-dressed actors, Sibyl Vane moved like a creature from a finer world. Her body swayed, while she danced, as a plant sways in the water. The curves of her throat were the curves of a white lily. Her hands seemed to be made of cool ivory.

Yet she was curiously listless. She showed no sign of joy when her eyes rested on Romeo. The few words she had to speak:

> Good pilgrim, you do wrong your hand too much,
> Which mannerly devotion shows in this;
> For saints have hands that pilgrims' hands do touch,
> And palm to palm is holy palmers' kiss—

with the brief dialogue that follows, were spoken in a thoroughly artificial manner. The voice was exquisite, but from the point of view of tone it was absolutely false. It was wrong in colour. It took away all the life from the verse. It made the passion unreal.

Dorian Gray grew pale as he watched her. He was puzzled and anxious. Neither of his friends dared to say anything to him. She seemed to them to be absolutely incompetent. They were horribly disappointed.

Yet they felt that the true test of any Juliet is the balcony scene of the second act. They waited for that. If she failed there, there was nothing in her.

She looked charming as she came out in the moonlight. That could not be denied. But the staginess of her acting was unbearable, and grew worse as she went on. Her gestures became absurdly artificial. She over-emphasised everything that she had to say. The beautiful passage:

> Thou knowest the mask of night is on my face,
> Else would a·maiden blush bepaint my cheek
> For that which thou hast heard me speak to-night—

was declaimed with the painful precision of a school-girl who has been taught to recite by some second-rate professor of elocution. When she leaned over the balcony and came to those wonderful lines:

> Although I joy in thee,
> I have no joy of this contract to-night:
> It is too rash, too unadvised, too sudden;
> Too like the lightning, which doth cease to be
> Ere one can say, 'It lightens.' Sweet, good-night!
> This bug of love by summer's ripening breath
> May prove a beauteous flower when next we meet—

she spoke the words as though they conveyed no meaning to her. It was not nervousness. Indeed, so far from being nervous, she was absolutely self-contained. It was simply bad art. She was a complete failure.

Even the common, uneducated audience of the pit and gallery lost their interest in the play. They got restless, and began to talk loudly and to whistle. The Jew manager, who was standing at the back of the dress-circle, stamped and swore with rage. The only person unmoved was the girl herself.

When the second act was over there came a storm of hisses, and Lord Henry got up from his chair and put on his coat. 'She is quite beautiful, Dorian,' he said, 'but she can't act. Let us go.'

'I am going to see the play through,' answered the lad, in

a hard, bitter voice. 'I am awfully sorry that I have made you waste an evening, Harry. I apologise to you both.'

'My dear Dorian, I should think Miss Vane was ill,' interrupted Hallward. 'We will come some other night.'

'I wish she were ill,' he rejoined. 'But she seems to me to be simply callous and cold. She has entirely altered. Last night she was a great artist. This evening she is merely a commonplace, mediocre actress.'

'Don't talk like that about anyone you love, Dorian. Love is a more wonderful thing than Art.'

'They are both simply forms of imitation,' remarked Lord Henry. 'But do let us go. Dorian, you must not stay here any longer. It is not good for one's morals to see bad acting. Besides, I don't suppose you will want your wife to act. So what does it matter if she plays Juliet like a wooden doll? She is very lovely, and if she knows as little about life as she does about acting, she will be a delightful experience. There are only two kinds of people who are really fascinating—people who know absolutely everything, and people who know absolutely nothing. Good heavens, my dear boy, don't look so tragic! The secret of remaining young is never to have an emotion that is unbecoming. Come to the club with Basil and myself. We will smoke cigarettes and drink to the beauty of Sibyl Vane. She is beautiful. What more can you want?'

'Go away, Harry,' cried the lad. 'I want to be alone. Basil, you must go. Ah! can't you see that my heart is breaking?' The hot tears came to his eyes. His lips trembled, and, rushing to the back of the box, he leaned up against the wall, hiding his face in his hands.

'Let us go, Basil,' said Lord Henry, with a strange tenderness in his voice; and the two young men passed out together.

A few moments afterwards the footlights flared up, and

the curtain rose on the third act. Dorian Gray went back to his seat. He looked pale, and proud, and indifferent. The play dragged on, and seemed interminable. Half of the audience went out, tramping in heavy boots, and laughing. The whole thing was a *fiasco*. The last act was played to almost empty benches. The curtain went down on a titter, and some groans.

As soon as it was over, Dorian Gray rushed behind the scenes into the greenroom. The girl was standing there alone, with a look of triumph on her face. Her eyes were lit with an exquisite fire. There was a radiance about her. Her parted lips were smiling over some secret of their own.

When he entered, she looked at him, and an expression of infinite joy came over her. 'How badly I acted to-night, Dorian!' she cried.

'Horribly!' he answered, gazing at her in amazement—'horribly! It was dreadful. Are you ill? You have no idea what it was. You have no idea what I suffered.'

The girl smiled. 'Dorian,' she answered, lingering over his name with long-drawn music in her voice, as though it were sweeter than honey to the red petals of her mouth—'Dorian, you should have understood. But you understand now, don't you?'

'Understand what?' he asked, angrily.

'Why I was so bad to-night. Why I shall always be bad. Why I shall never act well again.'

He shrugged his shoulders. 'You are ill, I suppose. When you are ill you shouldn't act. You make yourself ridiculous. My friends were bored. I was bored.'

She seemed not to listen to him. She was transfigured with joy. An ecstasy of happiness dominated her.

'Dorian, Dorian,' she cried, 'before I knew you, acting was the one reality of my life. It was only in the theatre that I lived. I thought that it was all true. I was Rosalind one night, and Portia the other. The joy of Beatrice was my joy, and the sorrows of Cordelia were mine also. I believed in everything. The common people who acted with me seemed to me to be godlike. The painted scenes were my world. I knew nothing but shadows, and I thought them real. You came—oh, my beautiful love!—and you freed my soul from prison. You taught me what reality really is. To-night, for the first time in my life, I saw through the hollowness, the sham, the silliness of the empty pageant in which I had always played. To-night, for the first time, I became conscious that the Romeo was hideous, and old, and painted, that the moonlight in the orchard was false, that the scenery was vulgar, and that the words I had to speak were unreal, were not my words, were not what I wanted to say. You had brought me something higher, something of which all art is but a reflection. You had made me understand what love really is. My love! my love! Prince Charming! Prince of life! I have grown sick of shadows. You are more to me than all art can ever be. What have I to do with the puppets of a play? When I came on to-night, I could not understand how it was that everything had gone from me. I thought that I was going to be wonderful. I found that I could do nothing. Suddenly it dawned on my soul what it all meant. The knowledge was exquisite to me. I heard them hissing, and I smiled. What could they know of love such as ours? Take me away, Dorian—take me away with you, where we can be quite alone. I hate the stage. I might mimic a passion that I do not feel, but I cannot mimic one that burns me like fire. Oh, Dorian, Dorian, you understand now what it signifies? Even if I could do it, it would be profanation for me to play at being in love. You have made me see that.'

He flung himself down on the sofa, and turned away his face. 'You have killed my love,' he muttered.

She looked at him in wonder, and laughed. He made no answer. She came across to him, and with her little fingers stroked his hair. She knelt down and pressed his hands to her lips. He drew them away, and a shudder ran through him.

Then he leaped up, and went to the door. 'Yes,' he cried, 'you have killed my love. You used to stir my imagination. Now you don't even stir my curiosity. You simply produce no effect. I loved you because you were marvellous, because you had genius and intellect, because you realised the dreams of great poets and gave shape and substance to the shadows of art. You have thrown it all away. You are shallow and stupid. My God! how mad I was to love you! What a fool I have been! You are nothing to me now. I will never see you again. I will never think of you. I will never mention your name. You don't know what you were to me, once. Why . . . Oh, I can't bear to think of it! I wish I had never laid eyes upon you! You have spoiled the romance of my life. How little you can know of love, if you say it mars your art! Without your art you are nothing. I would have made you famous, splendid, magnificent. The world would have worshipped you, and you would have borne my name. What are you now? A third-rate actress with a pretty face.'

The girl grew white and trembled. She clenched her hands together, and her voice seemed to catch in her throat. 'You are not serious, Dorian?' she murmured. 'You are acting.'

'Acting! I leave that to you. You do it so well,' he answered bitterly.

She rose from her knees, and, with a piteous expression of pain in her face, came across the room to him. She put her hand upon his arm, and looked into his eyes. He thrust her back. 'Don't touch me!' he cried.

A low moan broke from her, and she flung herself at his feet, and lay there like a trampled flower. 'Dorian,

Dorian, don't leave me!' she whispered. 'I am so sorry I didn't act well. I was thinking of you all the time. But I will try—indeed, I will try. It came so suddenly across me, my love for you. I think I should never have known it if you had not kissed me—if we had not kissed each other. Kiss me again, my love. Don't go away from me. I couldn't bear it. Oh! don't go away from me. My brother . . . No; never mind. He didn't mean it. He was in jest. . . . But you, oh! can't you forgive me for to-night? I will work so hard, and try to improve. Don't be cruel to me because I love you better than anything in the world. After all, it is only once that I have not pleased you. But you are quite right, Dorian. I should have shown myself more of an artist. It was foolish of me; and yet I couldn't help it. Oh, don't leave me, don't leave me.' A fit of passionate sobbing choked her. She crouched on the floor like a wounded thing, and Dorian Gray, with his beautiful eyes, looked down at her, and his chiselled lips curled in exquisite disdain. There is always something ridiculous about the emotions of people whom one has ceased to love. Sibyl Vane seemed to him to be absurdly melodramatic. Her tears and sobs annoyed him.

'I am going,' he said at last, in his calm, clear voice. 'I don't wish to be unkind, but I can't see you again. You have disappointed me.'

She wept silently, and made no answer, but crept nearer. Her little hands stretched blindly out, and appeared to be seeking for him. He turned on his heel, and left the room. In a few moments he was out of the theatre.

Where he went to he hardly knew. He remembered wandering through dimly-lit streets, past gaunt black-shadowed archways and evil-looking houses. Women with hoarse voices and harsh laughter had called after him. Drunkards had reeled by cursing, and chattering to themselves like monstrous apes. He had seen grotesque children huddled upon doorsteps, and heard shrieks and oaths from gloomy courts.

As the dawn was just breaking he found himself close to Covent Garden. The darkness lifted, and, flushed with faint fires, the sky hollowed itself into a perfect pearl. Huge carts filled with nodding lilies rumbled slowly down the polished empty street. The air was heavy with the perfume of the flowers, and their beauty seemed to bring him an anodyne for his pain. He followed into the market, and watched the men unloading their waggons. A white-smocked carter offered him some cherries. He thanked him, and wondered why he refused to accept any money for them, and began to eat them listlessly. They had been plucked at midnight, and the coldness of the moon had entered into them. A long line of boys carrying crates of striped tulips, and of yellow and red roses, defiled in front of him, threading their way through the huge jade-green piles of vegetables. Under the portico, with its grey sun-bleached pillars, loitered a troop of draggled bareheaded girls, waiting for the auction to be over. Others crowded round the swinging doors of the coffee-house in the Piazza. The heavy cart-horses slipped and stamped upon the rough stones, shaking their bells and trappings. Some of the drivers were lying asleep on a pile of sacks. Iris-necked, and pink-footed, the pigeons ran about picking up seeds.

After a little while, he hailed a hansom, and drove home. For a few moments he loitered upon the doorstep, looking round at the silent Square with its blank, close-shuttered windows, and its staring blinds. The sky was pure opal now, and the roofs of the houses glistened like silver against it. From some chimney opposite a thin wreath of smoke was rising. It curled, a violet riband, through the nacre-coloured air.

In the huge gilt Venetian lantern, spoil of some Doge's barge, that hung from the ceiling of the great oak-panelled hall of entrance, lights were still burning from three flickering jets: thin blue petals of flame they seemed, rimmed with white fire. He turned them out, and, having thrown his hat and cape on the table, passed through the library towards the door of his bedroom, a large octagonal chamber on the ground floor that, in his new-born feeling for luxury, he had just had decorated for himself, and hung with some curious Renaissance tapestries that had been discovered stored in a disused attic at Selby Royal. As he was turning the handle of the door, his eye fell upon the portrait Basil Hallward had painted of him. He started back as if in surprise. Then he went on into his own room, looking somewhat puzzled. After he had taken the buttonhole out of his coat, he seemed to hesitate. Finally he came back, went over to the picture, and examined it. In the dim arrested light that struggled through the cream-coloured silk blinds, the face appeared to him to be a little changed. The expression looked different. One would have said that there was a touch of cruelty in the mouth. It was certainly strange.

He turned round, and, walking to the window, drew up the blind. The bright dawn flooded the room, and swept the fantastic shadows into dusky corners, where they lay shuddering. But the strange expression that he had noticed in the face of the portrait seemed to linger there, to be more intensified even. The quivering, ardent sunlight showed him the lines of cruelty round the mouth as clearly as if he had been looking into a mirror after he had done some dreadful thing.

He winced, and, taking up from the table an oval glass framed in ivory Cupids, one of Lord Henry's many presents to him, glanced hurriedly into its polished depths. No line like that warped his red lips. What did it mean?

He rubbed his eyes, and came close to the picture, and examined it again. There were no signs of any change when he looked into the actual painting, and yet there was no doubt that the whole expression had altered. It was not a mere fancy of his own. The thing was horribly apparent.

He threw himself into a chair, and began to think. Suddenly there flashed across his mind what he had said in Basil Hallward's studio the day the picture had been finished. Yes, he remembered it perfectly. He had uttered a mad wish that he himself might remain young, and the portrait grow old; that his own beauty might be untarnished, and the face on the canvas bear the burden of his passions and his sins; that the painted image might be seared with the lines of suffering and thought, and that he might keep all the delicate bloom and loveliness of his then just conscious boyhood. Surely his wish had not been fulfilled? Such things were impossible. It seemed monstrous even to think of them. And, yet, there was the picture before him, with the touch of cruelty in the mouth.

Cruelty! Had he been cruel? It was the girl's fault, not his. He had dreamed of her as a great artist, had given his love to her because he had thought her great. Then she had disappointed him. She had been shallow and unworthy. And, yet, a feeling of infinite regret came over him, as he thought of her lying at his feet sobbing like a little child. He remembered with what callousness he had watched her. Why had he been made like that? Why had such a soul been given to him? But he had suffered also. During the three terrible hours that the play had lasted, he had lived centuries of pain, æon upon æon of torture. His life was well worth hers. She had marred him for a moment, if he had wounded her for an age. Besides, women were better suited to bear sorrow than men. They lived on their emotions. They only thought of their emotions. When they took lovers, it was merely to have someone with whom they could have scenes. Lord Henry had told him that, and Lord Henry knew what women were. Why should he trouble about Sibyl Vane? She was nothing to him now.

But the picture? What was he to say of that? It held the secret of his life, and told his story. It had taught him to love his own beauty. Would it teach him to loathe his own soul? Would he ever look at it again?

No; it was merely an illusion wrought on the troubled senses. The horrible night that he had passed had left phantoms behind it. Suddenly there had fallen upon his brain that tiny scarlet speck that makes men mad. The picture had not changed. It was folly to think so.

Yet it was watching him, with its beautiful marred face and its cruel smile. Its bright hair gleamed in the early sunlight. Its blue eyes met his own. A sense of infinite pity, not for himself, but for the painted image of himself, came over him. It had altered already, and would alter more. Its gold would wither into grey. Its red and white roses would die. For every sin that he committed, a stain would fleck and wreck its fairness. But he would not sin. The picture, changed or unchanged, would be to him the visible emblem of conscience. He would resist temptation. He would not see Lord Henry any more—would not, at any rate, listen to those subtle poisonous theories that in Basil Hallward's garden had first stirred within him the passion for impossible things. He would go back to Sibyl Vane, make her amends, marry her, try to love her again. Yes, it was his duty to do so. She must have suffered more than he had. Poor child! He had been selfish and cruel to her. The fascination that she had exercised over him would return. They would be happy together. His life with her would be beautiful and pure.

He got up from his chair, and drew a large screen right in

front of the portrait, shuddering as he glanced at it. 'How horrible!' he murmured to himself, and he walked across to the window and opened it. When he stepped out on to the grass, he drew a deep breath. The fresh morning air seemed to drive away all his sombre passions. He thought only of Sibyl. A faint echo of his love came back to him. He repeated her name over and over again. The birds that were singing in the dew-drenched garden seemed to be telling the flowers about her.

CHAPTER VIII

IT was long past noon when he awoke. His valet had crept several times on tiptoe into the room to see if he was stirring, and had wondered what made his young master sleep so late. Finally his bell sounded, and Victor came softly in with a cup of tea, and a pile of letters, on a small tray of old Sèvres china, and drew back the olive-satin curtains, with their shimmering blue lining, that hung in front of the three tall windows.

'Monsieur has well slept this morning,' he said, smiling.

'What o'clock is it, Victor?' asked Dorian Gray, drowsily.

'One hour and a quarter, Monsieur.'

How late it was! He sat up, and, having sipped some tea, turned over his letters. One of them was from Lord Henry, and had been brought by hand that morning. He hesitated for a moment, and then put it aside. The others he opened listlessly. They contained the usual collection of cards, invitations to dinner, tickets for private views, programmes of charity concerts, and the like, that are showered on fashionable young men every morning during the season. There was a rather heavy bill, for a chased silver Louis Quinze toilet-set, that he had not yet had the courage to send on to his guardians, who were extremely old-fashioned people and did not realise that we live in an age when unnecessary things are our only necessities; and there were several very courteously worded communications from Jermyn Street money-lenders offering to advance any sum of money at a moment's notice and at the most reasonable rates of interest.

After about ten minutes he got up, and, throwing on an

elaborate dressing-gown of silk-embroidered cashmere wool, passed into the onyx-paved bathroom. The cool water refreshed him after his long sleep. He seemed to have forgotten all that he had gone through. A dim sense of having taken part in some strange tragedy came to him once or twice, but there was the unreality of a dream about it.

As soon as he was dressed, he went into the library and sat down to a light French breakfast, that had been laid out for him on a small round table close to the open window. It was an exquisite day. The warm air seemed laden with spices. A bee flew in, and buzzed round the blue-dragon bowl that, filled with sulphur-yellow roses, stood before him. He felt perfectly happy.

Suddenly his eye fell on the screen that he had placed in front of the portrait, and he started.

'Too cold for Monsieur?' asked his valet, putting an omelette on the table. 'I shut the window?'

Dorian shook his head. 'I am not cold,' he murmured.

Was it all true? Had the portrait really changed? Or had it been simply his own imagination that had made him see a look of evil where there had been a look of joy? Surely a painted canvas could not alter? The thing was absurd. It would serve as a tale to tell Basil some day. It would make him smile.

And yet, how vivid was his recollection of the whole thing! First in the dim twilight, and then in the bright dawn, he had seen the touch of cruelty round the warped lips. He almost dreaded his valet leaving the room. He knew that when he was alone he would have to examine the portrait. He was afraid of certainty. When the coffee and cigarettes had been brought and the man turned to go, he felt a wild desire to tell him to remain. As the door was closing behind him he called him back. The man stood waiting for his orders. Dorian looked at him for a moment. 'I am not at home to anyone, Victor,' he said, with a sigh. The man bowed and retired.

Then he rose from the table, lit a cigarette, and flung himself down on a luxuriously-cushioned couch that stood facing the screen. The screen was an old one, of gilt Spanish leather, stamped and wrought with a rather florid Louis-Quatorze pattern. He scanned it curiously, wondering if ever before it had concealed the secret of a man's life.

Should he move it aside, after all? Why not let it stay there? What was the use of knowing? If the thing was true, it was terrible. If it was not true, why trouble about it? But what if, by some fate or deadlier chance, eyes other than his spied behind, and saw the horrible change? What should he do if Basil Hallward came and asked to look at his own picture? Basil would be sure to do that. No; the thing had to be examined, and at once. Anything would be better than this dreadful state of doubt.

He got up, and locked both doors. At least he would be alone when he looked upon the mask of his shame. Then he drew the screen aside, and saw himself face to face. It was perfectly true. The portrait had altered.

As he often remembered afterwards, and always with no small wonder, he found himself at first gazing at the portrait with a feeling of almost scientific interest. That such a change should have taken place was incredible to him. And yet it was a fact. Was there some subtle affinity between the chemical atoms, that shaped themselves into form and colour on the canvas, and the soul that was within him? Could it be that what that soul thought, they realised? —that what it dreamed, they made true? Or was there some other, more terrible reason? He shuddered, and felt afraid, and, going back to the couch, lay there, gazing at the picture in sickened horror.

One thing, however, he felt that it had done for him. It had made him conscious how unjust, how cruel, he had been to Sibyl Vane. It was not too late to make reparation for that. She could still be his wife. His unreal and selfish love would yield to some higher influence, would be transformed into some nobler passion, and the portrait that Basil Hallward had painted of him would be a guide to him through life, would be to him what holiness is to some, and conscience to others, and the fear of God to us all. There were opiates for remorse, drugs that could lull the moral sense to sleep. But here was a visible symbol of the degradation of sin. Here was an ever-present sign of the ruin men brought upon their souls.

Three o'clock struck, and four, and the half-hour rang its double chime, but Dorian Gray did not stir. He was trying to gather up the scarlet threads of life, and to weave them into a pattern; to find his way through the sanguine labyrinth of passion through which he was wandering. He did not know what to do, or what to think. Finally, he went over to the table, and wrote a passionate letter to the girl he had loved, imploring her forgiveness, and accusing himself of madness. He covered page after page with wild words of sorrow, and wilder words of pain. There is a luxury in self-reproach. When we blame ourselves we feel that no one else has a right to blame us. It is the confession, not the priest, that gives us absolution. When Dorian had finished the letter, he felt that he had been forgiven.

Suddenly there came a knock to the door, and he heard Lord Henry's voice outside. 'My dear boy, I must see you. Let me in at once. I can't bear your shutting yourself up like this.'

He made no answer at first, but remained quite still. The knocking still continued, and grew louder. Yes, it was better to let Lord Henry in, and to explain to him the new life he was going to lead, to quarrel with him if it became necessary to quarrel, to part if parting was inevitable. He jumped up, drew the screen hastily across the picture, and unlocked the door.

'I am so sorry for it all, Dorian,' said Lord Henry, as he entered. 'But you must not think too much about it.'

'Do you mean about Sibyl Vane?' asked the lad.

'Yes, of course,' answered Lord Henry, sinking into a chair, and slowly pulling off his yellow gloves. 'It is dreadful, from one point of view, but it was not your fault. Tell me, did you go behind and see her, after the play was over?'

'Yes.'

'I felt sure you had. Did you make a scene with her?'

'I was brutal, Harry—perfectly brutal. But it is all right now. I am not sorry for anything that has happened. It has taught me to know myself better.'

'Ah, Dorian, I am so glad you take it in that way! I was afraid I would find you plunged in remorse, and tearing that nice curly hair of yours.'

'I have got through all that,' said Dorian, shaking his head, and smiling. 'I am perfectly happy now. I know what conscience is, to begin with. It is not what you told me it was. It is the divinest thing in us. Don't sneer at it, Harry, any more—at least not before me. I want to be good. I can't bear the idea of my soul being hideous.'

'A very charming artistic basis for ethics, Dorian! I congratulate you on it. But how are you going to begin?'

'By marrying Sibyl Vane.'

'Marrying Sibyl Vane!' cried Lord Henry, standing up, and looking at him in perplexed amazement. 'But, my dear Dorian——'

'Yes, Harry, I know what you are going to say. Something dreadful about marriage. Don't say it. Don't ever say things of that kind to me again. Two days ago I asked

Sibyl to marry me. I am not going to break my word to her. She is to be my wife!'

'Your wife! Dorian! . . . Didn't you get my letter? I wrote to you this morning, and sent the note down, by my own man.'

'Your letter? Oh, yes, I remember. I have not read it yet, Harry. I was afraid there might be something in it that I wouldn't like. You cut life to pieces with your epigrams.'

'You know nothing then?'

'What do you mean?'

Lord Henry walked across the room, and, sitting down by Dorian Gray, took both his hands in his own, and held them tightly. 'Dorian,' he said. 'my letter—don't be frightened—was to tell you that Sibyl Vane is dead.'

A cry of pain broke from the lad's lips, and he leaped to his feet, tearing his hands away from Lord Henry's grasp. 'Dead! Sibyl dead! It is not true! It is a horrible lie! How dare you say it?'

'It is quite true, Dorian,' said Lord Henry, gravely. 'It is in all the morning papers. I wrote down to you to ask you not to see anyone till I came. There will have to be an inquest, of course, and you must not be mixed up in it. Things like that make a man fashionable in Paris. But in London people are so prejudiced. Here, one should never make one's *début* with a scandal. One should reserve that to give an interest to one's old age. I suppose they don't know your name at the theatre? If they don't, it is all right. Did anyone see you going round to her room? That is an important point.'

Dorian did not answer for a few moments. He was dazed with horror. Finally he stammered in a stifled voice, 'Harry, did you say an inquest? What did you mean by that? Did Sibyl——? Oh, Harry, I can't bear it! But be quick. Tell me everything at once.'

'I have no doubt it was not an accident, Dorian, though it must be put in that way to the public. It seems that as she was leaving the theatre with her mother, about half-past twelve or so, she said she had forgotten something upstairs. They waited some time for her, but she did not come down again. They ultimately found her lying dead on the floor of her dressing-room. She had swallowed something by mistake, some dreadful thing they use at theatres. I don't know what it was, but it had either prussic acid or white lead in it. I should fancy it was prussic acid, as she seems to have died instantaneously.

'Harry, Harry, it is terrible!' cried the lad.

'Yes; it is very tragic, of course, but you must not get yourself mixed up in it. I see by the *Standard* that she was seventeen. I should have thought she was almost younger than that. She looked such a child, and seemed to know so little about acting. Dorian, you mustn't let this thing get on your nerves. You must come and dine with me, and afterwards we will look in at the Opera. It is a Patti night, and everybody will be there. You can come to my sister's box. She has got some smart women with her.'

'So I have murdered Sibyl Vane,' said Dorian Gray half to himself—'murdered her as surely as if I had cut her little throat with a knife. Yet the roses are not less lovely for all that. The birds sing just as happily in my garden. And to-night I am to dine with you, and then go on to the Opera, and sup somewhere, I suppose, afterwards. How extraordinarily dramatic life is! If I had read all this in a book, Harry, I think I would have wept over it. Somehow, now that it has happened actually, and to me, it seems far too wonderful for tears. Here is the first passionate love-letter I have ever written in my life. Strange, that my first passionate love-letter should have been addressed to a dead girl. Can they feel, I wonder, those white silent people we call the dead? Sibyl! Can she feel, or know, or listen? Oh, Harry, how I loved her once! It seems years ago to me now. She was everything to me. Then came that dreadful night—was it really only last night?—when she played so badly, and my heart almost broke. She explained it all to me. It was terribly pathetic. But I was not moved a bit. I thought her shallow. Suddenly something happened that made me afraid. I can't tell you what it was, but it was terrible. I said I would go back to her. I felt I had done wrong. And now she is dead. My God! my God! Harry, what shall I do? You don't know the danger I am in, and there is nothing to keep me straight. She would have done that for me. She had no right to kill herself. It was selfish of her.'

'My dear Dorian,' answered Lord Henry, taking a cigarette from his case, and producing a gold-latten matchbox, 'the only way a woman can ever reform a man is by boring him so completely that he loses all possible interest in life. If you had married this girl you would have been wretched. Of course you would have treated her kindly. One can always be kind to people about whom one cares nothing. But she would have soon found out that you were absolutely indifferent to her. And when a woman finds that out about her husband, she either becomes dreadfully dowdy, or wears very smart bonnets that some other woman's husband has to pay for. I say nothing about the social mistake, which would have been abject, which, of course, I would not have allowed, but I assure you that in any case the whole thing would have been an absolute failure.'

'I suppose it would,' muttered the lad, walking up and down the room, and looking horribly pale. 'But I thought it was my duty. It is not my fault that this terrible tragedy has prevented my doing what was right. I remember your saying once that there is a fatality about good resolutions—that they are always made too late. Mine certainly were.'

'Good resolutions are useless attempts to interfere with scientific laws. Their origin is pure vanity. Their result is absolutely *nil*. They give us, now and then, some of those luxurious sterile emotions that have a certain charm for the weak. That is all that can be said for them. They are simply cheques that men draw on a bank where they have no account.'

'Harry,' cried Dorian Gray, coming over and sitting down beside him, 'why is it that I cannot feel this tragedy as much as I want to? I don't think I am heartless. Do you?'

'You have done too many foolish things during the last fortnight to be entitled to give yourself that name, Dorian,' answered Lord Henry, with his sweet, melancholy smile.

The lad frowned. 'I don't like that explanation, Harry,' he rejoined, 'but I am glad you don't think I am heartless. I am nothing of the kind. I know I am not. And yet I must admit that this thing that has happened does not affect me as it should. It seems to me to be simply like a wonderful ending to a wonderful play. It has all the terrible beauty of a Greek tragedy, a tragedy in which I took a great part, but by which I have not been wounded.'

'It is an interesting question,' said Lord Henry, who found an exquisite pleasure in playing on the lad's unconscious egotism— 'an extremely interesting question. I fancy that the true explanation is this. It often happens that the real tragedies of life occur in such an inartistic manner that they hurt us by their crude violence, their absolute incoherence, their absurd want of meaning, their entire lack of style. They affect us just as vulgarity affects us. They give us an impression of sheer brute force, and we revolt against that. Sometimes, however, a tragedy that possesses artistic elements of beauty crosses our lives. If these elements of beauty are real, the whole thing simply appeals to our sense of dramatic effect. Suddenly we find that we are no longer the actors, but the spectators of the play. Or rather we are both. We watch ourselves, and the mere wonder of the spectacle enthralls us. In the present case, what is it that has really happened? Someone has killed herself for love of you. I wish that I had ever had such an experience. It would have made me in love with love for the rest of my life. The people who have adored me—there have not been very many, but there have been some—have always insisted on living on, long after I had ceased to care for them, or they to care for me. They have become stout and tedious, and when I meet them they go in at once for reminiscences. That awful memory of woman! What a fearful thing it is! And what an utter intellectual stagnation it reveals! One should absorb the colour of life, but one should never remember its details. Details are always vulgar.'

'I must sow poppies in my garden,' sighed Dorian.

'There is no necessity,' rejoined his companion. 'Life has always poppies in her hands. Of course, now and then things linger. I once wore nothing but violets all through one season, as a form of artistic mourning for a romance that would not die. Ultimately, however, it did die. I forget what killed it. I think it was her proposing to sacrifice the whole world for me. That is always a dreadful moment. It fills one with the terror of eternity. Well—would you believe it?—a week ago, at Lady Hampshire's, I found myself seated at dinner next the lady in question, and she insisted on going over the whole thing again, and digging up the past, and raking up the future. I had buried my romance in a bed of asphodel. She dragged it out again, and assured me that I had spoiled her life. I am bound to state that she ate an enormous dinner, so I did not feel any anxiety. But what a lack of taste she showed! The one charm of the past is that it is the past. But women never know when the curtain has fallen. They always want a sixth act, and as soon as the interest of the play is entirely over they propose to continue it. If they were allowed their own way, every comedy would have a tragic ending, and every tragedy would culminate in a farce. They are charmingly artificial, but they have no sense of art. You are more fortunate than I am. I assure you, Dorian, that not one of the women I have known would have done for me what Sibyl Vane did for you. Ordinary women always console themselves. Some of them do it by going in for sentimental colours. Never trust a woman who wears mauve, whatever her age may be, or a woman over thirty-five who is fond of pink ribbons. It always means that they have a history. Others find a great consolation in suddenly discovering the good qualities of their husbands. They flaunt their conjugal felicity in one's face, as if it were the most fascinating of sins. Religion consoles some. Its mysteries have all the charm of a flirtation, a woman once told me; and I can quite understand it. Besides, nothing makes one so vain as being told that one is a sinner. Conscience makes egotists of us all. Yes; there is really no end to the consolations that women find in modern life. Indeed, I have not mentioned the most important one.'

'What is that, Harry?' said the lad, listlessly.

'Oh, the obvious consolation. Taking someone else's admirer when one lose one's own. In good society that always whitewashes a woman. But really, Dorian, how different Sibyl Vane must have been from all the women one meets! There is something to me quite beautiful about her death. I am glad I am living in a century when such wonders happen. They make one believe in the reality of the things we all play with, such as romance, passion, and love.'

'I was terribly cruel to her. You forget that.'

'I am afraid that women appreciate cruelty, downright

cruelty, more than anything else. They have wonderfully primitive instincts. We have emancipated them, but they remain slaves looking for their masters, all the same. They love being dominated. I am sure you were splendid. I have never seen you really and absolutely angry, but I can fancy how delightful you looked. And, after all, you said something to me the day before yesterday that seemed to me at the time to be merely fanciful, but that I see now was absolutely true, and it holds the key to everything.'

'What was that, Harry?'

'You said to me that Sibyl Vane represented to you all the heroines of romance—that she was Desdemona one night, and Ophelia the other; that if she died as Juliet, she came to life as Imogen.'

'She will never come to life again now,' muttered the lad, burying his face in his hands.

'No, she will never come to life. She has played her last part. But you must think of that lonely death in the tawdry dressing-room simply as a strange lurid fragment from some Jacobean tragedy, as a wonderful scene from Webster, or Ford, or Cyril Tourneur. The girl never really lived, and so she has never really died. To you at least she was always a dream, a phantom that flitted through Shakespeare's plays and left them lovelier for its presence, a reed through which Shakespeare's music sounded richer and more full of joy. The moment she touched actual life, she marred it, and it marred her, and so she passed away. Mourn for Ophelia, if you like. Put ashes on your head because Cordelia was strangled. Cry out against Heaven because the daughter of Brabantio died. But don't waste your tears over Sibyl Vane. She was less real than they are.'

There was a silence. The evening darkened in the room. Noiselessly, and with silver feet, the shadows crept in from the garden. The colours faded wearily out of things.

After some time Dorian Gray looked up. 'You have explained me to myself, Harry,' he murmured, with something of a sigh of relief. 'I felt all that you have said, but somehow I was afraid of it, and I could not express it to myself. How well you know me! But we will not talk again of what has happened. It has been a marvellous experience. That is all. I wonder if life has still in store for me anything as marvellous.'

'Life has everything in store for you, Dorian. There is nothing that you, with your extraordinary good looks, will not be able to do.'

'But suppose, Harry, I became haggard, and old, and wrinkled? What then?'

'Ah, then,' said Lord Henry, rising to go—'then, my dear Dorian, you would have to fight for your victories. As it is, they are brought to you. No, you must keep your good looks. We live in an age that reads too much to be wise, and that thinks too much to be beautiful. We cannot spare you. And now you had better dress, and drive down to the club. We are rather late, as it is.'

'I think I shall join you at the Opera, Harry. I feel too tired to eat anything. What is the number of your sister's box?'

'Twenty-seven, I believe. It is on the grand tier. You will see her name on the door. But I am sorry you won't come and dine.'

'I don't feel up to it,' said Dorian, listlessly. 'But I am awfully obliged to you for all that you have said to me. You are certainly my best friend. No one has ever understood me as you have.'

'We are only at the beginning of our friendship, Dorian,' answered Lord Henry, shaking him by the hand. 'Good-bye. I shall see you before nine-thirty, I hope. Remember, Patti is singing.'

As he closed the door behind him, Dorian Gray touched the bell, and in a few minutes Victor appeared with the lamps and drew the blinds down. He waited impatiently for him to go. The man seemed to take an interminable time over everything.

As soon as he had left, he rushed to the screen, and drew it back. No; there was no further change in the picture. It had received the news of Sibyl Vane's death before he had known of it himself. It was conscious of the events of life as they occurred. The vicious cruelty that marred the fine lines of the mouth had, no doubt, appeared at the very moment that the girl had drunk the poison, whatever it was. Or was it indifferent to results? Did it merely take cognizance of what passed within the soul? He wondered, and hoped that some day he would see the change taking place before his very eyes, shuddering as he hoped it.

Poor Sibyl! what a romance it had all been! She had often mimicked death on the stage. Then Death himself had touched her, and taken her with him. How had she played that dreadful last scene? Had she cursed him, as she died? No; she had died for love of him, and love would always be a sacrament to him now. She had atoned for everything, by the sacrifice she had made of her life. He would not think any more of what she had made him go through, on that horrible night at the theatre. When he thought of her, it would be as a wonderful tragic figure sent on to the world's stage to show the supreme reality of Love. A wonderful tragic figure? Tears came to his eyes as he remembered her childlike look, and winsome fanciful ways, and shy tremulous grace. He brushed them away hastily, and looked again at the picture.

He felt that the time had really come for making his choice. Or had his choice already been made? Yes, life had decided that for him—life, and his own infinite curiosity about life. Eternal youth, infinite passion, pleasures subtle and secret, wild joys and wilder sins—he was to have all these things. The portrait was to bear the burden of his shame: that was all.

A feeling of pain crept over him as he thought of the desecration that was in store for the fair face on the canvas. Once, in boyish mockery of Narcissus, he had kissed, or feigned to kiss, those painted lips that now smiled so cruelly at him. Morning after morning he had sat before the portrait, wondering at its beauty, almost enamoured of it, as it seemed to him at times. Was it to alter now with every mood to which he yielded? Was it to become a monstrous and loathsome thing, to be hidden away in a locked room, to be shut out from the sunlight that had so often touched to brighter gold the waving wonder of its hair? The pity of it! the pity of it!

For a moment he thought of praying that the horrible sympathy that existed between him and the picture might cease. It had changed in answer to a prayer; perhaps in answer to a prayer it might remain unchanged. And yet, who, that knew anything about Life, would surrender the chance of remaining always young, however fantastic that chance might be, or with what fateful consequences it might be fraught? Besides, was it really under his control? Had it indeed been prayer that had produced the substitution? Might there not be some curious scientific reason for it all? If thought could exercise its influence upon a living organism, might not thought exercise an influence upon dead and inorganic things? Nay, without thought or conscious desire, might not things external to ourselves vibrate in unison with our moods and passions, atom calling to atom in secret love of strange affinity? But the reason was of no importance. He would never again tempt by a prayer any terrible power. If the picture was to alter, it was to alter. That was all. Why inquire too closely into it?

For there would be a real pleasure in watching it. He would be able to follow his mind into its secret places. This portrait would be to him the most magical of mirrors. As it had revealed to him his own body, so it would reveal to him his own soul. And when winter came upon it, he would still be standing where spring trembles on the verge of summer. When the blood crept from its face, and left behind a pallid mask of chalk with leaden eyes, he would keep the glamour of boyhood. Not one blossom of his loveliness would ever fade. Not one pulse of his life would ever weaken. Like the gods of the Greeks, he would be strong, and fleet, and joyous. What did it matter what happened to the coloured image on the canvas? He would be safe. That was everything.

He drew the screen back into its former place in front of the picture, smiling as he did so, and passed into his bedroom, where his valet was already waiting for him. An hour later he was at the Opera, and Lord Henry was leaning over his chair.

CHAPTER IX

As he was sitting at breakfast next morning, Basil Hallward was shown into the room.

'I am so glad I have found you, Dorian,' he said, gravely. 'I called last night, and they told me you were at the Opera. Of course I knew that was impossible. But I wish you had left word where you had really gone to. I passed a dreadful evening, half afraid that one tragedy might be followed by another. I think you might have telegraphed for me when you heard of it first. I read of it quite by chance in a late edition of *The Globe*, that I picked up at the club. I came here at once, and was miserable at not finding you. I can't tell you how heart-broken I am about the whole thing. I know what you must suffer. But where were you? Did you go down and see the girl's mother? For a moment I thought of following you there. They gave the address in the paper. Somewhere in the Euston Road, isn't it? But I was afraid of intruding upon a sorrow that I could not lighten. Poor woman! What a state she must be in! And her only child, too! What did she say about it all?'

'My dear Basil, how do I know?' murmured Dorian Gray, sipping some pale-yellow wine from a delicate gold-beaded bubble of Venetian glass, and looking dreadfully bored. 'I was at the Opera. You should have come on there. I met Lady Gwendolen, Harry's sister, for the first time. We were in her box. She is perfectly charming; and Patti sang divinely. Don't talk about horrid subjects. If one doesn't talk about a thing, it has never happened. It is simply expression, as Harry says, that gives reality to things. I may mention that she was not the woman's only child.

There is a son, a charming fellow, I believe. But he is not on the stage. He is a sailor, or something. And now, tell me about yourself and what you are painting.'

'You went to the Opera?' said Hallward, speaking very slowly, and with a strained touch of pain in his voice 'You went to the Opera while Sibyl Vane was lying dead in some sordid lodging? You can talk to me of other women being charming, and of Patti singing divinely, before the girl you loved has even the quiet of a grave to sleep in? Why, man, there are horrors in store for that little white body of hers!'

'Stop, Basil! I won't hear it!' cried Dorian, leaping to his feet. 'You must not tell me about things, What is done is done. What is past is past.'

'You call yesterday the past?'

'What has the actual lapse of time got to do with it? It is only shallow people who require years to get rid of an emotion. A man who is master of himself can end a sorrow as easily as he can invent a pleasure. I don't want to be at the mercy of my emotions. I want to use them, to enjoy them, and to dominate them.'

'Dorian, this is horrible! Something has changed you completely. You look exactly the same wonderful boy who, day after day, used to come down to my studio to sit for his picture. But you were simple, natural, and affectionate then. You were the most unspoiled creature in the whole world. Now, I don't know what has come over you. You talk as if you had no heart, no pity in you. It is all Harry's influence. I see that.'

The lad flushed up, and, going to the window, looked out for a few moments on the green, flickering, sun-lashed garden. 'I owe a great deal to Harry, Basil,' he said, at last— 'more than I owe to you. You only taught me to be vain.'

'Well, I am punished for that, Dorian—or shall be some day.'

'I don't know what you mean, Basil,' he exclaimed, turning round. 'I don't know what you want. What do you want?'

'I want the Dorian Gray I used to paint,' said the artist sadly.

'Basil,' said the lad, going over to him, and putting his hand on his shoulder, 'you have come too late. Yesterday when I heard that Sibyl Vane had killed herself——'

'Killed herself! Good heavens! is there no doubt about that?' cried Hallward, looking up at him with an expression of horror.

'My dear Basil! Surely you don't think it was a vulgar accident? Of course she killed herself.'

The elder man buried his face in his hands. 'How fearful,' he muttered, and a shudder ran through him.

'No,' said Dorian Gray, 'there is nothing fearful about it. It is one of the great romantic tragedies of the age. As a rule, people who act lead the most commonplace lives. They are good husbands, or faithful wives, or something tedious. You know what I mean—middle-class virtue, and all that kind of thing. How different Sibyl was! She lived her finest tragedy. She was always a heroine. The last night she played—the night you saw her—she acted badly because she had known the reality of love. When she knew its unreality, she died, as Juliet might have died. She passed again into the sphere of art. There is something of the martyr about her. Her death has all the pathetic uselessness of martyrdom, all its wasted beauty. But, as I was saying, you must not think I have not suffered. If you had come in yesterday at a particular moment—about half-past five, perhaps, or a quarter to six—you would have found me in tears. Even Harry, who was here, who brought me the news, in fact, had no idea what I was going through. I suffered immensely. Then it passed away. I cannot repeat an emotion. No one can, except sentimentalists. And you are awfully unjust, Basil. You come down here to console me. That is charming of you. You find me consoled, and you are furious. How like a sympathetic person! You remind me of a story Harry told me about a certain philanthropist who spent twenty years of his life in trying to get some grievance redressed, or some unjust law altered—I forget exactly what it was. Finally he succeeded, and nothing could exceed his disappointment. He had absolutely nothing to do, almost died of *ennui*, and became a confirmed misanthrope. And besides, my dear old Basil, if you really want to console me, teach me rather to forget what has happened, or to see it from the proper artistic point of view. Was it not Gautier who used to write about *la consolation des arts*? I remember picking up a little vellum-covered book in your studio one day and chancing on that delightful phrase. Well, I am not like that young man you told me of when we were down at Marlow together, the young man who used to say that yellow satin could console one for all the miseries of life. I love beautiful things that one can touch and handle. Old brocades, green bronzes, lacquer-work, carved ivories, exquisite surroundings, luxury, pomp, there is much to be got from all these. But the artistic temperament that they create, or at any rate reveal, is still more to me. To become the spectator of one's own life, as Harry says, is to escape the suffering of life. I know you are surprised at my talking to you like this. You have not realised how I have developed. I was a schoolboy when you knew me. I am a man now. I have new passions, new thoughts, new ideas. I am different, but you must not like me less. I am changed, but you must always be my friend. Of course I am very fond of Harry. But I know that you are better than he is. You are not stronger—you are too much afraid of life—but you are better. And how happy we used to be together! Don't leave me, Basil, and don't quarrel with me. I am what I am. There is nothing more to be said.'

The painter felt strangely moved. The lad was infinitely dear to him, and his personality had been the great turning-point in his art. He could not bear the idea of reproaching him any more. After all, his indifference was probably merely a mood that would pass away. There was so much in him that was good, so much in him that was noble.

'Well, Dorian,' he said, at length, with a sad smile, 'I won't speak to you again about this horrible thing, after to-day. I only trust your name won't be mentioned in connection with it. The inquest is to take place this afternoon. Have they summoned you?'

Dorian shook his head and a look of annoyance passed over his face at the mention of the word 'inquest.' There was something so crude and vulgar about everything of the kind. 'They don't know my name,' he answered.

'But surely she did?'

'Only my Christian name, and that I am quite sure she never mentioned to anyone. She told me once that they were all rather curious to learn who I was, and that she invariably told them my name was Prince Charming. It was pretty of her. You must do me a drawing of Sibyl, Basil. I should like to have something more of her than the memory of a few kisses and some broken pathetic words.'

'I will try and do something, Dorian, if it would please you. But you must come and sit to me yourself again. I can't get on without you.'

'I can never sit to you again, Basil. It is impossible!' he exclaimed, starting back.

The painter stared at him. 'My dear boy, what nonsense!' he cried. 'Do you mean to say you don't like what I did of you? Where is it? Why have you pulled the screen in front of it? Let me look at it. It is the best thing I have ever done. Do take the screen away, Dorian. It is simply disgraceful of your servant hiding my work like that. I felt the room looked different as I came in.'

'My servant has nothing to do with it, Basil. You don't imagine I let him arrange my room for me? He settles my flowers for me sometimes—that is all. No; I did it myself. The light was too strong on the portrait.'

'Too strong! Surely not, my dear fellow? It is an admirable place for it. Let me see it.' And Hallward walked towards the corner of the room.

A cry of terror broke from Dorian Gray's lips, and he rushed between the painter and the screen. 'Basil,' he said, looking very pale, 'you must not look at it. I don't wish you to.'

'Not look at my own work! you are not serious. Why shouldn't I look at it?' exclaimed Hallward laughing.

'If you try to look at it, Basil, on my word of honour I will never speak to you again as long as I live. I am quite serious. I don't offer any explanation, and you are not to ask for any. But, remember, if you touch this screen, everything is over between us.'

Hallward was thunderstruck. He looked at Dorian Gray in absolute amazement. He had never seen him like this before. The lad was actually pallid with rage. His hands were clenched, and the pupils of his eyes were like disks of blue fire. He was trembling all over.

'Dorian!'

'Don't speak!'

'But what is the matter? Of course I won't look at it if you don't want me to,' he said, rather coldly, turning on his heel, and going over towards the window. 'But, really, it seems rather absurd that I shouldn't see my own work, especially as I am going to exhibit it in Paris in the autumn. I shall probably have to give it another coat of varnish before that, so I must see it some day, and why not to-day?'

'To exhibit it? You want to exhibit it?' exclaimed Dorian Gray, a strange sense of terror creeping over him. Was the world going to be shown his secret? Were people to gape at the mystery of his life? That was impossible. Something —he did not know what—had to be done at once.

'Yes; I don't suppose you will object to that. George Petit is going to collect all my best pictures for a special exhibition in the Rue de Sèze, which will open the first week in October. The portrait will only be away a month. I should think you could easily spare it for that time. In fact, you are sure to be out of town. And if you keep it always behind a screen, you can't care much about it.'

Dorian Gray passed his hand over his forehead. There were beads of perspiration there. He felt that he was on the brink of a horrible danger. 'You told me a month ago that you would never exhibit it,' he cried. 'Why have you changed your mind? You people who go in for being consistent have just as many moods as others have. The only difference is that your moods are rather meaningless. You can't have forgotten that you assured me most solemnly that nothing in the world would induce you to send it to any exhibition. You told Harry exactly the same thing.' He stopped suddenly, and a gleam of light came into his eyes. He remembered that Lord Henry had said to him once, half seriously and half in jest, 'If you want to have a strange quarter of an hour, get Basil to tell you why he won't exhibit your picture. He told me why he wouldn't, and it was a revelation to me.' Yes, perhaps Basil, too, had his secret. He would ask him and try.

'Basil,' he said, coming over quite close, and looking him straight in the face, 'we have each of us a secret. Let me know yours and I shall tell you mine. What was your reason for refusing to exhibit my picture?'

The painter shuddered in spite of himself. 'Dorian, if I told you, you might like me less than you do, and you would certainly laugh at me. I could not bear your doing either of those two things. If you wish me never to look at your picture again, I am content. I have always you to look at. If you wish the best work I have ever done to be hidden from the world, I am satisfied. Your friendship is dearer to me than any fame or reputation.'

'No, Basil, you must tell me,' insisted Dorian Gray. 'I think I have a right to know.' His feeling of terror had passed away, and curiosity had taken its place. He was determined to find out Basil Hallward's mystery.

'Let us sit down, Dorian,' said the painter, looking troubled. 'Let us sit down. And just answer me one question. Have you noticed in the picture something curious?— something that probably at first did not strike you, but that revealed itself to you suddenly?'

'Basil!' cried the lad, clutching the arms of his chair with trembling hands, and gazing at him with wild, startled eyes.

'I see you did. Don't speak. Wait till you hear what I have to say. Dorian, from the moment I met you, your personality had the most extraordinary influence over me. I was dominated, soul, brain, and power by you. You became to me the visible incarnation of that unseen ideal whose memory haunts us artists like an exquisite dream. I worshipped you. I grew jealous of everyone to whom you spoke. I wanted to have you all to myself. I was only happy when I was with you. When you were away from me you were still present in my art. . . . Of course I never let you know anything about this. It would have been impossible. You would not have understood it. I hardly understood it myself. I only knew that I had seen perfection face to face, and that the world had become wonderful to my eyes—too wonderful, perhaps, for in such mad worships there is peril, the peril of losing them, no less than the peril of keeping them. . . . Weeks and weeks went on, and I grew more and more absorbed in you. Then came a new development. I had drawn you as Paris in dainty armour, and as Adonis with huntsman's cloak and polished boar-spear. Crowned with heavy lotus-blossoms you had sat on the prow of Adrian's barge, gazing across the green turbid Nile. You had leant over the still pool of some Greek woodland, and seen in the water's silent silver the marvel of your own face. And it had all been what art should be, unconscious, ideal, and remote. One day, a fatal day I sometimes think, I determined to paint a wonderful portrait of you as you actually are, not in the costume of dead ages, but in your own dress and in your own time. Whether it was the Realism of the method, or the mere wonder of your own personality, thus directly presented to me without mist or veil, I cannot tell. But I know that as I worked at it, every flake and film of colour seemed to me to reveal my secret. I grew afraid that others would know of my idolatry. I felt, Dorian, that I had told too much, that I had put too much of myself into it. Then it was that I resolved never to allow the picture to be exhibited. You were a little annoyed; but then you did not realise all that it meant to me. Harry, to whom I talked about it, laughed at me. But I did not mind that. When the picture was finished, and I sat alone with it, I felt that I was right. . . . Well, after a few days the thing left my studio, and as soon as I had got rid of the intolerable fascination of its presence it seemed to me that I had been foolish in imagining that I had seen anything in it, more than that you were extremely good-looking, and that I could paint. Even now I cannot help feeling that it is a mistake to think that the passion one feels in creation is ever really shown in the work one creates. Art is always more abstract than we fancy. Form and colour tell us of form and colour—that is all. It often seems to me that art conceals the artist far more completely than it ever reveals him. And so when I got this offer from Paris I determined to make your portrait the principal thing in my exhibition. It never occurred to me that you would refuse. I see now that you were right. The picture cannot be shown. You must not be angry with me, Dorian, for what I have told you. As I said to Harry, once, you are made to be worshipped.'

Dorian Gray drew a long breath. The colour came back to his cheeks, and a smile played about his lips. The peril was over. He was safe for the time. Yet he could not help feeling infinite pity for the painter who had just made this strange confession to him, and wondered if he himself would ever be so dominated by the personality of a friend. Lord Henry had the charm of being very dangerous. But that was all. He was too clever and too cynical to be really fond of. Would there ever be someone who would fill him with a strange idolatry? Was that one of the things that life had in store?

'It is extraordinary to me, Dorian,' said Hallward, 'that you should have seen this in the portrait. Did you really see it?'

'I saw something in it,' he answered, 'something that seemed to me very curious.'

'Well, you don't mind my looking at the thing now?'

Dorian shook his head. 'You must not ask me that, Basil. I could not possibly let you stand in front of that picture.'

'You will some day, surely?'

'Never.'

'Well, perhaps you are right. And now good-bye, Dorian. You have been the one person in my life who has really influenced my art. Whatever I have done that is good, I owe to you. Ah! you don't know what it cost me to tell you all that I have told you.'

'My dear Basil,' said Dorian, 'what have you told me? Simply that you felt that you admired me too much. That is not even a compliment.'

'It was not intended as a compliment. It was a confession. Now that I have made it, something seems to have gone out of me. Perhaps one should never put one's worship into words.'

'It was a very disappointing confession.'

'Why, what did you expect, Dorian? You didn't see anything else in the picture, did you? There was nothing else to see?'

'No; there was nothing else to see. Why do you ask? But you mustn't talk about worship. It is foolish. You and I are friends, Basil, and we must always remain so.'

'You have got Harry,' said the painter, sadly.

'Oh, Harry!' cried the lad, with a ripple of laughter. 'Harry spends his days in saying what is incredible, and his evenings in doing what is improbable. Just the sort of life I would like to lead. But still I don't think I would go to Harry if I were in trouble. I would sooner go to you, Basil.'

'You will sit to me again?'

'Impossible!'

'You spoil my life as an artist by refusing, Dorian. No man came across two ideal things. Few come across one.'

'I can't explain it to you, Basil, but I must never sit to you again. There is something fatal about a portrait. It has a life of its own. I will come and have tea with you. That will be just as pleasant.'

'Pleasanter for you, I am afraid,' murmured Hallward, regretfully. 'And now good-bye. I am sorry you won't let me look at the picture once again. But that can't be helped. I quite understand what you feel about it.'

As he left the room, Dorian Gray smiled to himself. Poor Basil! how little he knew of the true reason! And how strange it was that, instead of having been forced to reveal his own secret, he had succeeded, almost by chance, in wresting a secret from his friend! How much that strange confession explained to him! The painter's absurd fits of jealousy, his wild devotion, his extravagant panegyrics, his curious reticences—he understood them all now, and he felt sorry. There seemed to him to be something tragic in a friendship so coloured by romance.

He sighed, and touched the bell. The portrait must be hidden away at all costs. He could not run such a risk of discovery again. It had been mad of him to have allowed the thing to remain, even for an hour, in a room to which any of his friends had access.

CHAPTER X

WHEN his servant entered, he looked at him steadfastly and wondered if he had thought of peering behind the screen. The man was quite impassive, and waited for his orders. Dorian lit a cigarette, and walked over to the glass and glanced into it. He could see the reflection of Victor's face perfectly. It was like a placid mask of servility. There was nothing to be afraid of, there. Yet he thought it best to be on his guard.

Speaking very slowly, he told him to tell the housekeeper that he wanted to see her, and then to go to the frame-maker and ask him to send two of his men round at once. It seemed to him that as the man left the room his eyes wandered in the direction of the screen. Or was that merely his own fancy?

After a few moments, in her black silk dress, with old-fashioned thread mittens on her wrinkled hands, Mrs. Leaf bustled into the library. He asked her for the key of the schoolroom.

'The old schoolroom, Mr. Dorian?' she exclaimed. 'Why, it is full of dust. I must get it arranged, and put straight before you go into it. It is not fit for you to see, sir. It is not, indeed.'

'I don't want it put straight, Leaf. I only want the key.'

'Well, sir, you'll be covered with cobwebs if you go into it. Why, it hasn't been opened for nearly five years, not since his lordship died.'

He winced at the mention of his grandfather. He had hateful memories of him. 'That does not matter,' he answered. 'I simply want to see the place—that is all. Give me the key.'

'And here is the key, sir,' said the old lady, going over the contents of her bunch with tremulously uncertain hands. 'Here is the key. I'll have it off the bunch in a moment. But you don't think of living up there, sir, and you so comfortable here?'

'No, no,' he cried, petulantly. 'Thank you, Leaf. That will do.'

She lingered for a few moments, and was garrulous over some detail of the household. He sighed, and told her to manage things as she thought best. She left the room, wreathed in smiles.

As the door closed, Dorian put the key in his pocket, and looked round the room. His eyes fell on a large, purple satin coverlet heavily embroidered with gold, a splendid piece of late seventeenth-century Venetian work that his grandfather had found in a convent near Bologna. Yes, that would serve to wrap the dreadful thing in. It had perhaps served often as a pall for the dead. Now it was to hide something that had a corruption of its own, worse than the corruption of death itself—something that would breed horrors and yet would never die. What the worm was to the corpse, his sins would be to the painted image on the canvas. They would mar its beauty, and eat away its grace. They would defile it, and make it shameful. And yet the thing would still live on. It would be always alive.

He shuddered, and for a moment he regretted that he had not told Basil the true reason why he had wished to hide the picture away. Basil would have helped him to resist Lord Henry's influence, and the still more poisonous influences that came from his own temperament. The love that he bore him—for it was really love—had nothing in it that was not noble and intellectual. It was not that mere physical admiration of beauty that is born of the senses, and that dies when the senses tire. It was such love as Michael Angelo had known, and Montaigne, and Winckelmann, and Shakespeare himself. Yes, Basil could have saved him. But it was too late now. The past could always be annihilated. Regret, denial, or forgetfulness could do that. But the future was inevitable. There were passions in him that would find their terrible outlet, dreams that would make the shadow of their evil real.

He took up from the couch the great purple-and-gold texture that covered it, and, holding it in his hands, passed behind the screen. Was the face on the canvas viler than before? It seemed to him that it was unchanged; and yet his loathing of it was intensified. Gold hair, blue eyes, and rose-red lips—they all were there. It was simply the expression that had altered. That was horrible in its cruelty. Compared to what he saw in it of censure or rebuke, how shallow Basil's reproaches about Sibyl Vane had been!—how shallow, and of what little account! His own soul was looking out at him from the canvas and calling him to judgment. A look of pain came across him, and he flung the rich pall over the picture. As he did so, a knock came to the door. He passed out as his servant entered.

'The persons are here, Monsieur.'

He felt that the man must be got rid of at once. He must not be allowed to know where the picture was being taken to. There was something sly about him, and he had thoughtful, treacherous eyes. Sitting down at the writing-table, he scribbled a note to Lord Henry, asking him to send him round something to read, and reminding him that they were to meet at eight-fifteen that evening.

'Wait for an answer,' he said, handing it to him, 'and show the men in here.'

In two or three minutes there was another knock, and Mr. Hubbard himself, the celebrated frame-maker of South Audley Street, came in with a somewhat rough-looking young assistant. Mr. Hubbard was a florid, red-whiskered little man, whose admiration for art was considerably tempered by the inveterate impecuniosity of most of the artists who dealt with him. As a rule, he never left his shop. He waited for people to come to him. But he always made an exception in favour of Dorian Gray. There was something about Dorian that charmed everybody. It was a pleasure even to see him.

'What can I do for you, Mr. Gray?' he said, rubbing his fat freckled hands. 'I thought I would do myself the honour of coming round in person. I have just got a beauty of a frame, sir. Picked it up at a sale. Old Florentine. Came from Fronthill, I believe. Admirably suited for a religious subject, Mr. Gray.'

'I am so sorry you have given yourself the trouble of coming round, Mr. Hubbard. I shall certainly drop in and look at the frame—though I don't go in much at present for religious art—but to-day I only want a picture carried to the top of the house for me. It is rather heavy, so I thought I would ask you to lend me a couple of your men.'

'No trouble at all, Mr. Gray. I am delighted to be of any service to you. Which is the work of art, sir?'

'This,' replied Dorian, moving the screen back. 'Can you move it, covering and all, just as it is? I don't want it to get scratched going upstairs.'

'There will be no difficulty, sir,' said the genial frame-maker, beginning, with the aid of his assistant, to unhook the picture from the long brass chains by which it was suspended. 'And now, where shall we carry it to, Mr. Gray?'

'I will show you the way, Mr. Hubbard, if you will kindly follow me. Or perhaps you had better go in front. I am afraid it is right at the top of the house. We will go up by the front staircase, as it is wider.'

He held the door open for them, and they passed out into the hall and began the ascent. The elaborate character of the frame had made the picture extremely bulky, and now and then, in spite of the obsequious protests of Mr. Hubbard, who had the true tradesman's spirited dislike of seeing a gentleman doing anything useful, Dorian put his hand to it so as to help them.

'Something of a load to carry, sir,' gasped the little man, when they reached the top landing. And he wiped his shiny forehead.

'I am afraid it is rather heavy,' murmured Dorian, as he unlocked the door that opened into the room that was to keep for him the curious secret of his life and hide his soul from the eyes of men.

He had not entered the place for more than four years— not, indeed, since he had used it first as a play-room when he was a child, and then as a study when he grew somewhat older. It was a large, well-proportioned room, which had been specially built by the last Lord Kelso for the use of the little grandson whom, for his strange likeness to his mother, and also for other reasons, he had always hated and desired to keep at a distance. It appeared to Dorian to have but little changed. There was the huge Italian *cassone*, with its fantastically-painted panels and its tarnished gilt mouldings, in which he had so often hidden himself as a boy. There was the satinwood bookcase filled with his dog-eared schoolbooks. On the wall behind it was hanging the same ragged Flemish tapestry, where a faded king and queen were playing chess in a garden, while a company of hawkers rode by, carrying hooded birds on their gauntleted wrists. How well he remembered it all! Every moment of his lonely childhood came back to him as he looked round. He recalled the stainless purity of his boyish life, and it seemed horrible to him that it was here the fatal portrait was to be hidden away.

How little he had thought, in those dead days, of all that was in store for him!

But there was no other place in the house so secure from prying eyes as this. He had the key, and no one else could enter it. Beneath its purple pall, the face painted on the canvas could grow bestial, sodden, and unclean. What did it matter? No one could see it. He himself would not see it. Why should he watch the hideous corruption of his soul? He kept his youth—that was enough. And, besides, might not his nature grow finer, after all? There was no reason that the future should be so full of shame. Some love might come across his life, and purify him, and shield him from those sins that seemed to be already stirring in spirit and in flesh —those curious unpictured sins whose very mystery lent them their subtlety and their charm. Perhaps, some day, the cruel look would have passed away from the scarlet sensitive mouth, and he might show to the world Basil Hallward's masterpiece.

No; that was impossible. Hour by hour, and week by week, the thing upon the canvas was growing old. It might escape the hideousness of sin, but the hideousness of age was in store for it. The cheeks would become hollow or flaccid. Yellow crow's-feet would creep round the fading eyes and make them horrible. The hair would lose its brightness, the mouth would gape or droop, would be foolish or gross, as the mouths of old men are. There would be the wrinkled throat, the cold, blue-veined hands, the twisted body, that he remembered in the grandfather who had been so stern to him in his boyhood. The picture had to be concealed. There was no help for it.

'Bring it in, Mr. Hubbard, please,' he said, wearily, turning round. 'I am sorry I kept you so long. I was thinking of something else.'

'Always glad to have a rest, Mr. Gray,' answered the

frame-maker, who was still gasping for breath. 'Where shall we put it, sir?'

'Oh, anywhere. Here: this will do. I don't want to have it hung up. Just lean it against the wall. Thanks.'

'Might one look at the work of art, sir?'

Dorian started. 'It would not interest you, Mr. Hubbard,' he said, keeping his eye on the man. He felt ready to leap upon him and fling him to the ground if he dared to lift the gorgeous hanging that concealed the secret of his life. 'I shan't trouble you any more now. I am much obliged for your kindness in coming round.'

'Not at all, not at all, Mr. Gray. Ever ready to do anything for you, sir.' And Mr. Hubbard tramped downstairs, followed by the assistant, who glanced back at Dorian with a look of shy wonder in his rough, uncomely face. He had never seen anyone so marvellous.

When the sound of their footsteps had died away, Dorian locked the door, and put the key in his pocket. He felt safe now. No one would ever look upon the horrible thing. No eye but his would ever see his shame.

On reaching the library he found that it was just after five o'clock, and that the tea had been already brought up. On a little table of dark perfumed wood thickly encrusted with nacre, a present from Lady Radley, his guardian's wife, a pretty professional invalid, who had spent the preceding winter in Cairo, was lying a note from Lord Henry, and beside it was a book bound in yellow paper, the cover slightly torn and the edges soiled. A copy of the third edition of *The St. James's Gazette* had been placed on the tea-tray. It was evident that Victor had returned. He wondered if he had met the men in the hall as they were leaving the house, and had wormed out of them what they had been doing. He would be sure to miss the picture—had no doubt missed it already, while he had been laying the tea-things. The screen had not been set back, and a blank space was visible on the wall. Perhaps some night he might find him creeping upstairs and trying to force the door of the room. It was a horrible thing to have a spy in one's house. He had heard of rich men who had been blackmailed all their lives by some servant who had read a letter, or overheard a conversation, or picked up a card with an address, or found beneath a pillow a withered flower or a shred of crumpled lace.

He sighed, and, having poured himself out some tea, opened Lord Henry's note. It was simply to say that he sent him round the evening paper, and a book that might interest him, and that he would be at the club at eight-fifteen. He opened *The St. James's* languidly, and looked through it. A red pencil-mark on the fifth page caught his eye. It drew attention to the following paragraph:

'INQUEST ON AN ACTRESS.—An inquest was held this morning at the Bell Tavern, Hoxton Road, by Mr. Danby, the District Coroner, on the body of Sibyl Vane, a young actress recently engaged at the Royal Theatre, Holborn. A verdict of death by misadventure was returned. Considerable sympathy was expressed for the mother of the deceased, who was greatly affected during the giving of her own evidence, and that of Dr. Birrell, who had made the post-mortem examination of the deceased.'

He frowned, and, tearing the paper in two, went across the room and flung the pieces away. How ugly it all was! And how horribly real ugliness made things! He felt a little annoyed with Lord Henry for having sent him the report. And it was certainly stupid of him to have marked it with red pencil. Victor might have read it. The man knew more than enough English for that.

Perhaps he had read it, and had begun to suspect something.

And, yet, what did it matter? What had Dorian Gray to do with Sibyl Vane's death? There was nothing to fear. Dorian Gray had not killed her.

His eye fell on the yellow book that Lord Henry had sent him. What was it, he wondered. He went towards the little pearl-coloured octagonal stand, that had always looked to him like the work of some strange Egyptian bees that wrought in silver, and taking up the volume, flung himself into an arm-chair, and began to turn over the leaves. After a few minutes he became absorbed. It was the strangest book that he had ever read. It seemed to him that in exquisite raiment, and to the delicate sound of flutes, the sins of the world were passing in dumb show before him. Things that he had dimly dreamed of were suddenly made real to him. Things of which he had never dreamed were gradually revealed.

It was a novel without a plot, and with only one character, being, indeed, simply a psychological study of a certain young Parisian, who spent his life trying to realise in the nineteenth century all the passions and modes of thought that belonged to every century except his own, and to sum up, as it were, in himself the various moods through which the world-spirit had ever passed, loving for their mere artificiality those renunciations that men have unwisely called virtue, as much as those natural rebellions that wise men still call sin. The style in which it was written was that curious jewelled style, vivid and obscure at once, full of *argot* and of archaisms, of technical expressions and of elaborate paraphrases, that characterises the work of some of the finest artists of the French school of *Symbolistes*. There were in it metaphors as monstrous as orchids, and as subtle in colour. The life of the senses was described in the terms of mystical philosophy. One hardly knew at times whether one was reading the spiritual ecstasies of some mediæval saint or the morbid confessions of a modern sinner. It was a poisonous book. The heavy odour of incense seemed to cling about its pages and to trouble the brain. The mere cadence of the sentences, the subtle monotony of their music, so full as it was of complex refrains and movements elaborately repeated, produced in the mind of the lad, as he passed from chapter to chapter, a form of reverie, a malady of dreaming, that made him unconscious of the falling day and creeping shadows.

Cloudless, and pierced by one solitary star, a copper-green sky gleamed through the windows. He read on by its wan light till he could read no more. Then, after his valet had reminded him several times of the lateness of the hour, he got up, and, going into the next room, placed the book on the little Florentine table that always stood at his bedside, and began to dress for dinner.

It was almost nine o'clock before he reached the club, where he found Lord Henry sitting alone, in the morning-room, looking very much bored.

'I am so sorry, Harry,' he cried, 'but really it is entirely your fault. That book you sent me so fascinated me that I forgot how the time was going.'

'Yes; I thought you would like it,' replied his host, rising from his chair.

'I didn't say I liked it, Harry. I said it fascinated me. There is a great difference.'

'Ah, you have discovered that?' murmured Lord Henry. And they passed into the dining-room.

CHAPTER XI

FOR years, Dorian Gray could not free himself from the influence of this book. Or perhaps it would be more accurate to say that he never sought to free himself from it. He procured from Paris no less than nine large-paper copies of the first edition, and had them bound in different colours, so that they might suit his various moods and the changing fancies of a nature over which he seemed, at times, to have almost entirely lost control. The hero, the wonderful young Parisian, in whom the romantic and the scientific temperaments were so strangely blended, became to him a kind of prefiguring type of himself. And, indeed, the whole book seemed to him to contain the story of his own life, written before he had lived it.

In one point he was more fortunate than the novel's fantastic hero. He never knew—never, indeed, had any cause to know—that somewhat grotesque dread of mirrors, and polished metal surfaces, and still water, which came upon the young Parisian so early in his life, and was occasioned by the sudden decay of a beauty that had once, apparently, been so remarkable. It was with an almost cruel joy—and perhaps in nearly every joy, as certainly in every pleasure, cruelty has its place—that he used to read the latter part of the book, with its really tragic, if somewhat over-empha-sised, account of the sorrow and despair of one who had himself lost what in others, and in the world, he had most dearly valued.

For the wonderful beauty that had so fascinated Basil Hallward, and many others besides him, seemed never to leave him. Even those who had heard the most evil things against him, and from time to time strange rumours about his mode of life crept through London and became the chatter of the clubs, could not believe anything to his dishonour when they saw him. He had always the look of one who had kept himself unspotted from the world. Men who talked grossly became silent when Dorian Gray entered the room. There was something in the purity of his face that rebuked them. His mere presence seemed to recall to them the memory of the innocence that they had tarnished. They wondered how one so charming and graceful as he was could have escaped the stain of an age that was at once sordid and sensual.

Often, on returning home from one of those mysterious and prolonged absences that gave rise to such strange conjecture among those who were his friends, or thought that they were so, he himself would creep upstairs to the locked room, open the door with the key that never left him now, and stand, with a mirror, in front of the portrait that Basil Hallward had painted of him, looking now at the evil and ageing face on the canvas, and now at the fair young face that laughed back at him from the polished glass. The very sharpness of the contrast used to quicken his sense of pleasure. He grew more and more enamoured of his own beauty, more and more interested in the corruption of his own soul. He would examine with minute care, and sometimes with a monstrous and terrible delight, the hideous lines that seared the wrinkling forehead, or crawled around the heavy sensual mouth, wondering sometimes which were the more horrible, the signs of sin or the signs of age. He would place his white hands beside the coarse bloated hands of the picture, and smile. He mocked the misshapen body and the failing limbs.

There were moments, indeed, at night, when, lying sleepless in his own delicately-scented chamber, or in the sordid room of the little ill-famed tavern near the Docks, which, under an assumed name, and in disguise, it was his habit to frequent, he would think of the ruin he had brought upon his soul, with a pity that was all the more poignant because it was purely selfish. But moments such as these were rare. That curiosity about life which Lord Henry had first stirred in him, as they sat together in the garden of their friend, seemed to increase with gratification. The more he knew, the more he desired to know. He had mad hungers that grew more ravenous as he fed them.

Yet he was not really reckless, at any rate in his relations to society. Once or twice every month during the winter, and on each Wednesday evening while the season lasted, he would throw open to the world his beautiful house and have the most celebrated musicians of the day to charm his guests with the wonders of their art. His little dinners, in the settling of which Lord Henry always assisted him, were noted as much for the careful selection and placing of those invited, as for the exquisite taste shown in the decoration of the table, with its subtle symphonic arrangements of exotic flowers, and embroidered cloths, and antique plate of gold and silver. Indeed, there were many, especially among the very young men, who saw, or fancied that they saw, in Dorian Gray the true realisation of a type of which they had often dreamed in Eton or Oxford days, a type that was to combine something of the real culture of the scholar with all the grace and distinction and perfect manner of a citizen of the world. To them he seemed to be of the company of those whom Dante describes as having sought to 'make themselves perfect by the worship of beauty.' Like Gautier, he was one for whom 'the visible world existed.'

And, certainly, to him Life itself was the first, the greatest, of the arts, and for it all the other arts seemed to be but a preparation. Fashion, by which what is really fantastic becomes for a moment universal, and Dandyism, which, in its own way, is an attempt to assert the absolute modernity of beauty, had, of course, their fascination for him. His mode of dressing, and the particular styles that from time to time he affected, had their marked influence on the young exquisites of the Mayfair balls and Pall Mall club windows, who copied him in everything that he did, and tried to reproduce the accidental charm of his graceful, though to him only half-serious, fopperies.

For, while he was but too ready to accept the position that was almost immediately offered to him on his coming of age, and found, indeed, a subtle pleasure in the thought that he might really become to the London of his own day what to imperial Neronian Rome the author of the 'Satyricon' once had been, yet in his inmost heart he desired to be something more than a mere *arbiter elegantiarum*, to be consulted on the wearing of a jewel, or the knotting of a necktie, or the conduct of a cane. He sought to elaborate some new scheme of life that would have its reasoned philosophy and its ordered principles, and find in the spiritualising of the senses its highest realisation.

The worship of the senses has often, and with much justice, been decried, men feeling a natural instinct of terror about passions and sensations that seem stronger than themselves, and that they are conscious of sharing with the less highly organised forms of existence. But it appeared to Dorian Gray that the true nature of the senses had never been understood, and that they had remained savage and animal merely because the world had sought to starve them into submission or to kill them by pain, instead of aiming at making them elements of a new spirituality, of which a fine instinct for beauty was to be the dominant characteristic. As he looked back upon man moving through History, he was haunted by a feeling of loss. So much had been surrendered! and to such little purpose! There had been mad wilful rejections, monstrous forms of self-torture and self-denial, whose origin was fear, and whose result was a degradation infinitely more terrible than that fancied degradation from which, in their ignorance, they had sought to escape, Nature, in her wonderful irony, driving out the anchorite to feed with the wild animals of the desert and giving to the hermit the beasts of the field as his companions.

Yes: there was to be, as Lord Henry had prophesied, a new Hedonism that was to recreate life, and to save it from that harsh, uncomely puritanism that is having, in our own day, its curious revival. It was to have its service of the intellect, certainly; yet, it was never to accept any theory or system that would involve the sacrifice of any mode of passionate experience. Its aim, indeed, was to be experience itself, and not the fruits of experience, sweet or bitter as they might be. Of the asceticism that deadens the senses, as of the vulgar profligacy that dulls them, it was to know nothing. But it was to teach man to concentrate himself upon the moments of a life that is itself but a moment.

There are few of us who have not sometimes wakened before dawn, either after one of those dreamless nights that make us almost enamoured of death, or one of those nights of horror and misshapen joy, when through the chambers of the brain sweep phantoms more terrible than reality itself, and instinct with that vivid life that lurks in all grotesques, and that lends to Gothic art its enduring vitality, this art being, one might fancy, especially the art of those whose minds have been troubled with the malady of reverie. Gradually white fingers creep through the curtains, and they appear to tremble. In black fantastic shapes, dumb shadows crawl into the corners of the room, and crouch there. Outside, there is the stirring of birds among the leaves, or the sound of men going forth to their work, or the sigh and sob of the wind coming down from the hills, and wandering round the silent house, as though it feared to wake the sleepers, and yet must needs call forth sleep from her purple cave. Veil after veil of thin dusky gauze is lifted, and by degrees the forms and colours of things are restored to them, and we watch the dawn remaking the world in its antique pattern. The wan mirrors get back their mimic life. The flameless tapers stand where we had left them, and beside them lies the half-cut book that we had been studying, or the wired flower that we had worn at the ball, or the letter that we had been afraid to read, or that we had read too often. Nothing seems to us changed. Out of the unreal shadows of the night comes back the real life that we had known. We have to resume it where we had left off, and there steals over us a terrible sense of the necessity for the continuance of energy in the same wearisome round of stereotyped habits, or a wild longing, it may be, that our eyelids might open some morning upon a world that had been refashioned anew in the darkness for our pleasure, a world in which things would have fresh shapes and colours, and be changed, or have other secrets, a world in which the past would have little or no place, or survive, at any rate, in no conscious form of obligation or regret, the remembrance even of joy having its bitterness, and the memories of pleasure their pain.

It was the creation of such worlds as these that seemed to Dorian Gray to be the true object, or amongst the true objects of life; and in his search for sensations that would be at once new and delightful, and possess that element of strangeness that is so essential to romance, he would often adopt certain modes of thought that he knew to be really alien to his nature, abandon himself to their subtle influences, and then, having, as it were, caught their colour and satisfied his intellectual curiosity, leave them with that curious indifference that is not incompatible with a real ardour of temperament, and that indeed, according to certain modern psychologists, is often a condition of it.

It was rumoured of him once that he was about to join the Roman Catholic communion; and certainly the Roman ritual had always a great attraction for him. The daily sacrifice, more awful really than all the sacrifices of the antique world, stirred him as much by its superb rejection of the evidence of the senses as by the primitive simplicity of its elements and the eternal pathos of the human tragedy that it sought to symbolise. He loved to kneel down on the cold marble pavement, and watch the priest, in his stiff flowered vestment, slowly and with white hands moving aside the veil of the tabernacle, or raising aloft the jewelled lantern-shaped monstrance with that pallid wafer that at times, one would fain think, is indeed the '*panis caelestis*,' the bread of angels, or, robed in the garments of the Passion of Christ, breaking the Host into the chalice, and smiting his breast for his sins. The fuming censers, that the grave boys, in their lace and scarlet, tossed into the air like great gilt flowers, had their subtle fascination for him. As he passed out, he used to look with wonder at the black confessionals, and long to sit in the dim shadow of one of them and listen to men and women whispering through the worn grating the true story of their lives.

But he never fell into the error of arresting his intellectual development by any formal acceptance of creed or system, or of mistaking, for a house in which to live, an inn that is but suitable for the sojourn of a night, or for a few hours of a night in which there are no stars and the moon is in travail. Mysticism, with its marvellous power of making common things strange to us, and the subtle antinomianism that always seems to accompany it, moved him for a season; and for a season he inclined to the materialistic doctrines of the *Darwinismus* movement in Germany, and found a curious pleasure in tracing the thoughts and passions of men to some pearly cell in the brain, or some white nerve in the body, delighting in the conception of the absolute dependence of the spirit on certain physical conditions, morbid or healthy, normal or diseased. Yet, as has been said of him before, no theory of life seemed to him to be of any importance compared with life itself. He felt keenly conscious of how barren all intellectual speculation is when separated from action and experiment. He knew that the senses, no less than the soul, have their spiritual mysteries to reveal.

And so he would now study perfumes, and the secrets of their manufacture, distilling heavily-scented oils, and burning odorous gums from the East. He saw that there was no mood of the mind that had not its counterpart in the sensuous life, and set himself to discover their true relations, wondering what there was in frankincense that made one mystical, and in ambergris that stirred one's passions, and in violets that woke the memory of dead romances, and in musk that troubled the brain, and in champak that stained the imagination; and seeking often to elaborate a real psychology of perfumes, and to estimate the several influences of sweet-smelling roots, and scented pollen-laden flowers, or aromatic balms, and of dark and fragrant woods, of spikenard that sickens, of hovenia that makes men mad, and of aloes that are said to be able to expel melancholy from the soul.

At another time he devoted himself entirely to music, and in a long latticed room, with a vermilion-and-gold ceiling and walls of olive-green lacquer, he used to give curious concerts, in which mad gypsies tore wild music from little zithers, or grave yellow-shawled Tunisians plucked at the strained strings of monstrous lutes, while grinning negroes beat monotonously upon copper drums, and, crouching upon scarlet mats, slim turbaned Indians blew through long pipes of reed or brass, and charmed, or feigned to charm, great hooded snakes and horrible horned adders. The harsh intervals and shrill discords of barbaric music stirred him at times when Schubert's grace, and Chopin's beautiful sorrows, and the mighty harmonies of Beethoven himself, fell unheeded on his ear. He collected together from all parts of the world the strangest instruments that could be found, either in the tombs of dead nations or among the few savage tribes that have survived contact with Western civilisations, and loved to touch and try them. He had the mysterious *juruparis* of the Rio Negro Indians, that women are not allowed to look at, and that even youths may not see till they have been subjected to fasting and scourging, and the earthen jars of the Peruvians that have the shrill cries of birds, and flutes of human bones such as Alfonso de Ovalle heard in Chile, and the sonorous green jaspers that are found near Cuzco and give forth a note of singular sweetness. He had painted gourds filled with pebbles that rattled when they were shaken; the long *clarin* of the Mexicans, into which the performer does not blow, but through which he inhales the air; the harsh *ture* of the Amazon tribes, that is sounded by the sentinels who sit all day long in high trees, and can be heard, it is said, at a distance of three leagues; the *teponaztli*, that has two vibrating tongues of wood, and is beaten with sticks that are smeared with an elastic gum obtained from the milky juice of plants; the *yotl*-bells of the Aztecs, that are hung in clusters like grapes; and a huge cylindrical drum, covered with the skins of great serpents, like the one that Bernal Diaz saw when he went with Cortes into the Mexican temple, and of whose doleful sound he has left us so vivid a description. The fantastic character of these instruments fascinated him, and he felt a curious delight in the thought that Art, like Nature, has her monsters, things of bestial shape and with hideous voices. Yet, after some time, he wearied of them, and would sit in his box at the Opera, either alone or with Lord Henry, listening in rapt pleasure to 'Tannhäuser,' and seeing in the prelude to that great work of art a presentation of the tragedy of his own soul.

On one occasion he took up the study of jewels, and appeared at a costume ball as Anne de Joyeuse, Admiral of France, in a dress covered with five hundred and sixty pearls. This taste enthralled him for years, and, indeed, may be said never to have left him. He would often spend a whole day settling and resetting in their cases the various stones that he had collected, such as the olive-green chrysoberyl that turns red by lamplight, the cymophane with its wire-like line of silver, the pistachio-coloured peridot, rose-pink and wine-yellow topazes, carbuncles of fiery scarlet with tremulous four-rayed stars, flame-red cinnamon-stones, orange and violet spinels, and amethysts with their alternate layers of ruby and sapphire. He loved the red gold of the sunstone, and the moonstone's pearly whiteness, and the broken rainbow of the milky opal. He procured from Amsterdam three emeralds of extraordinary size and richness of colour, and had a turquoise *de la vieille roche* that was the envy of all the connoisseurs.

He discovered wonderful stories, also, about jewels. In Alphonso's 'Clericalis Disciplina' a serpent was mentioned with eyes of real jacinth, and in the romantic history of Alexander, the Conqueror of Emathia was said to have found in the vale of Jordan snakes 'with collars of real emeralds growing on their backs.' There was a gem in the brain of the dragon, Philostratus told us, and 'by the exhibition of golden letters and a scarlet robe' the monster could be thrown into a magical sleep, and slain. According to the great alchemist, Pierre de Boniface, the diamond rendered a man invisible, and the agate of India made him eloquent. The cornelian appeased anger, and the hyacinth provoked sleep, and the amethyst drove away the fumes of wine. The garnet cast out demons, and the hydropicus deprived the moon of her colour. The selenite waxed and waned with the moon, and the meloceus, that discovers thieves, could be affected only by the blood of kids. Leonardus Camillus had seen a white stone taken from the brain of a newly-killed toad, that was a certain antidote against poison. The bezoar, that was found in the heart of the Arabian deer, was a charm that could cure the plague. In the nests of Arabian birds was the aspilates, that, according to Democritus, kept the wearer from any danger by fire.

The King of Ceilan rode through his city with a large ruby in his hand, at the ceremony of his coronation. The gates of the palace of John the Priest were 'made of sardius, with the horn of the horned snake inwrought, so that no man might bring poison within.' Over the gable were 'two golden apples, in which were two carbuncles,' so that the gold might shine by day, and the carbuncles by night. In Lodge's strange romance 'A Margarite of America' it was stated that in the chamber of the queen one could behold 'all the chaste ladies of the world, inchased out of silver, looking through fair mirrours of chrysolites, carbuncles, sapphires, and greene emeraults.' Marco Polo had seen the inhabitants of Zipangu place rose-coloured pearls in the mouths of the dead. A sea-monster had been enamoured of the pearl that the diver brought to King Perozes, and had slain the thief, and mourned for seven moons over its loss. When the Huns lured the king into the great pit, he flung it away—Procopius tells the story—nor was it ever found again, though the Emperor Anastasius offered five hundred-weight of gold pieces for it. The King of Malabar had shown to a certain Venetian a rosary of three hundred and four pearls, one for every god that he worshipped.

When the Duke de Valentinois, son of Alexander VI, visited Louis XII of France, his horse was loaded with gold leaves, according to Brantôme, and his cap had double rows of rubies that threw out a great light. Charles of England had ridden in stirrups hung with four hundred and twenty-one diamonds. Richard II had a coat, valued at thirty thousand marks, which was covered with balas rubies. Hall described Henry VIII, on his way to the Tower previous to his coronation, as wearing 'a jacket of raised gold, the placard embroidered with diamonds and other rich stones, and a great bauderike about his neck of large balasses.' The favourites of James I wore ear-rings of emeralds set in gold fili-grane. Edward II gave to Piers Gaveston a suit of red-gold armour studded with jacinths, a collar of gold roses set with turquoise-stones, and a skull-cap *parsemé* with pearls. Henry II wore jewelled gloves reaching to the elbow, and had a hawk-glove sewn with twelve rubies and fifty-two great orients. The ducal hat of Charles the Rash, the last Duke of Burgundy of his race, was hung with pear-shaped pearls, and studded with sapphires.

How exquisite life had once been! How gorgeous in its pomp and decoration! Even to read of the luxury of the dead was wonderful.

Then he turned his attention to embroideries, and to the tapestries that performed the office of frescoes in the chill rooms of the Northern nations of Europe. As he investigated the subject—and he always had an extraordinary faculty of becoming absolutely absorbed for the moment in whatever he took up—he was almost saddened by the reflection of the ruin that Time brought on beautiful and wonderful things. He, at any rate, had escaped that. Summer followed summer, and the yellow jonquils bloomed and died many times, and nights of horror repeated the story of their shame, but he was unchanged. No winter marred his face or stained his flower-like bloom. How different it was with material things! Where had they passed to? Where was the great crocus-coloured robe on which the gods fought against the giants, that had been worked by brown girls for the pleasure of Athena? Where, the huge velarium that Nero had stretched across the Colosseum at Rome, that Titan sail of purple on which was represented the starry sky, and Apollo driving a chariot drawn by white gilt-reined steeds? He longed to see the curious table-napkins wrought for the Priest of the Sun, on which were displayed all the dainties and viands that could be wanted for a feast; the mortuary cloth of King Chilperic, with its three hundred golden bees; the fantastic robes that excited the indignation of the Bishop of Pontus, and were figured with 'lions, panthers, bears, dogs, forests, rocks, hunters—all, in fact, that a painter can copy from nature'; and the coat that Charles of Orleans once wore, on the sleeves of which were embroidered the verses of a song beginning 'Madame, je suis tout joyeux,' the musical accompaniment of the words being wrought in gold thread, and each note, of square shape in those days, formed with four pearls. He read of the room that was prepared at the palace at Rheims for the use of Queen Joan of Burgundy, and was decorated with 'thirteen hundred and twenty-one parrots, made in broidery, and blazoned with the king's arms, and five hundred and sixty-one butterflies, whose wings were similarly ornamented with the arms of the queen, the whole worked in gold.' Catherine de Médicis had a mourning-bed made for her of black velvet powdered with crescents and suns. Its curtains were of damask, with leafy wreaths and garlands, figured upon a gold and silver ground, and fringed along the edges with broideries of pearls, and it stood in a room hung with rows of the queen's devices in cut black velvet upon cloth of silver. Louis XIV had gold embroidered caryatides fifteen feet high in his apartment. The state bed of Sobieski, King of Poland, was made of Smyrna gold brocade embroidered in turquoises with verses from the Koran. Its supports were of silver gilt, beautifully chased, and profusely set with enamelled and jewelled medallions. It had been taken from the Turkish camp before Vienna, and the standard of Mohammed had stood beneath the tremulous gilt of its canopy.

And so, for a whole year, he sought to accumulate the most exquisite specimens that he could find of textile and embroidered work, getting the dainty Delhi muslins, finely wrought with gold-thread palmates, and stitched over with iridescent beetles' wings; the Dacca gauzes, that from their transparency are known in the East as 'woven air,' and 'running water,' and 'evening dew'; strange figured cloths from Java; elaborate yellow Chinese hangings; books bound in tawny satins or fair blue silks, and wrought with *fleurs de lys*, birds and images; veils of *lacis* worked in Hungary point; Sicilian brocades, and stiff Spanish velvets; Georgian work with its gilt coins, and Japanese *Foukousas* with their green-toned golds and their marvellously-plumaged birds.

He had a special passion, also, for ecclesiastical vestments, as indeed he had for everything connected with the service of the Church. In the long cedar chests that lined the west gallery of his house he had stored away many rare and beautiful specimens of what is really the raiment of the Bride of Christ, who must wear purple and jewels and fine linen that she may hide the pallid macerated body that is worn by the suffering that she seeks for, and wounded by self-inflicted pain. He possessed a gorgeous cope of crimson silk and gold-thread damask, figured with a repeating pattern of golden pomegranates set in six-petalled formal blossoms, beyond which on either side was the pine-apple device wrought in seed-pearls. The orphreys were divided into panels representing scenes from the life of the Virgin, and the coronation of the Virgin was figured in coloured silks upon the hood. This was Italian work of the fifteenth century. Another cope was of green velvet, embroidered with heart-shaped groups of acanthus-leaves, from which spread long-stemmed white blossoms, the details of which were picked out with silver thread and coloured crystals. The morse bore a seraph's head in gold-thread raised work. The orphreys were woven in a diaper of red and gold silk, and were starred with medallions of many saints and martyrs, among whom was St. Sebastian. He had chasubles, also, of amber-coloured silk, and blue silk and gold brocade, and yellow silk damask and cloth of gold, figured with representations of the Passion and Crucifixion of Christ, and embroidered with lions and peacocks and other emblems; dalmatics of white satin and pink silk damask, decorated with tulips and dolphins and *fleurs de lys*; altar frontals of crimson velvet and blue linen; and many corporals, chalice-veils, and sudaria. In the mystic offices to which such things were put, there was something that quickened his imagination.

For these treasures, and everything that he collected in his lovely house, were to be to him means of forgetfulness, modes by which he could escape, for a season, from the fear that seemed to him at times to be almost too great to be borne. Upon the walls of the lonely locked room where he had spent so much of his boyhood, he had hung with his own hands the terrible portrait whose changing features showed him the real degradation of his life, and in front of it had draped the purple-and-gold pall as a curtain. For weeks he would not go there, would forget the hideous painted thing, and get back his light heart, his wonderful joyousness, his passionate absorption in mere existence. Then, suddenly, some night he would creep out of the house, go down to dreadful places near Blue Gate Fields, and stay there, day after day, until he was driven away. On his return he would sit in front of the picture, sometimes loathing it and himself, but filled, at other times, with that pride of individualism that is half the fascination of sin, and smiling with secret pleasure at the misshapen shadow that had to bear the burden that should have been his own.

After a few years he could not endure to be long out of England, and gave up the villa that he had shared at Trouville with Lord Henry, as well as the little white walled-in house at Algiers where they had more than once spent the winter. He hated to be separated from the picture that was such a part of his life, and was also afraid that during his absence someone might gain access to the room, in spite of the elaborate bars that he had caused to be placed upon the door.

He was quite conscious that this would tell them nothing. It was true that the portrait still preserved, under all the foulness and ugliness of the face, its marked likeness to himself; but what could they learn from that? He would laugh at anyone who tried to taunt him. He had not painted it. What was it to him how vile and full of shame it looked? Even if he told them, would they believe it?

Yet he was afraid. Sometimes when he was down at his great house in Nottinghamshire, entertaining the fashionable young men of his own rank who were his chief companions, and astounding the county by the wanton luxury and gorgeous splendour of his mode of life, he would suddenly leave his guests and rush back to town to see that the door had not been tampered with, and that the picture was still there. What if it should be stolen? The mere thought made him cold with horror. Surely the world would know his secret then. Perhaps the world already suspected it.

For, while he fascinated many, there were not a few who distrusted him. He was very nearly blackballed at a West End club of which his birth and social position fully entitled him to become a member, and it was said that on one occasion when he was brought by a friend into the smoking-room of the Churchill, the Duke of Berwick and another gentleman got up in a marked manner and went out. Curious stories became current about him after he had passed his twenty-fifth year. It was rumoured that he had been seen brawling with foreign sailors in a low den in the distant parts of Whitechapel, and that he consorted with thieves and coiners and knew the mysteries of their trade. His extraordinary absences became notorious, and, when he used to reappear again in society, men would whisper to each other in corners, or pass him with a sneer, or look at him with cold searching eyes, as though they were determined to discover his secret.

Of such insolences and attempted slights he, of course, took no notice, and in the opinion of most people his frank debonair manner, his charming boyish smile, and the infinite grace of that wonderful youth that seemed never to leave him, were in themselves a sufficient answer to the calumnies, for so they termed them, that were circulated about him. It was remarked, however, that some of those who had been most intimate with him appeared, after a time, to shun him. Women who had wildly adored him, and for his sake had braved all social censure and set convention at defiance, were seen to grow pallid with shame or horror if Dorian Gray entered the room.

Yet these whispered scandals only increased, in the eyes of many, his strange and dangerous charm. His great wealth was a certain element of security. Society, civilised society at least, is never very ready to believe anything to the detriment of those who are both rich and fascinating. It feels instinctively that manners are of more importance than morals, and, in its opinion, the highest respectability is of much less value than the possession of a good *chef*. And, after all, it is a very poor consolation to be told that the man who has given one a bad dinner, or poor wine, is irreproachable in his private life. Even the cardinal virtues cannot atone for half-cold *entrées*, as Lord Henry remarked once, in a discussion on the subject; and there is possibly a good deal to be said for his view. For the canons of good society are, or should be, the same as the canons of art. Form is absolutely essential to it. It should have the dignity of a ceremony, as well as its unreality, and should combine the insincere character of a romantic play with the wit and beauty that make such plays delightful to us. Is insincerity such a terrible thing? I think not. It is merely a method by which we can multiply our personalities.

Such, at any rate, was Dorian Gray's opinion. He used to wonder at the shallow psychology of those who conceive the Ego in man as a thing simple, permanent, reliable, and of one essence. To him, man was a being with myriad lives and myriad sensations, a complex multiform creature that bore within itself strange legacies of thought and passion, and whose very flesh was tainted with the monstrous maladies of the dead. He loved to stroll through the gaunt cold picture-gallery of his country house and look at the various portraits of those whose blood flowed in his veins. Here was Philip Herbert, described by Francis Osborne, in his *Memoires on the Reigns of Queen Elizabeth and King James*, as one who was 'caressed by the Court for his handsome face, which kept him not long company.' Was it young Herbert's life that he sometimes led? Had some strange poisonous germ crept from body to body till it had reached his own? Was it some dim sense of that ruined grace that had made him so suddenly, and almost without cause, give utterance, in Basil Hallward's studio, to the mad prayer that had so changed his life? Here, in gold-embroidered red doublet, jewelled surcoat, and gilt-edged ruff and wristbands, stood Sir Anthony Sherard, with his silver-and-black armour piled at his feet. What had this man's legacy been? Had the lover of Giovanna of Naples bequeathed him some inheritance of sin and shame? Were his own actions merely the dreams that the dead man had not dared to realise? Here, from the fading canvas, smiled Lady Elizabeth Devereux, in her gauze hood, pearl stomacher, and pink slashed sleeves. A flower was in her right hand, and her left clasped an enamelled collar of white and damask roses. On a table by her side lay a mandolin and an apple. There were large green rosettes upon her little pointed shoes. He knew her life, and the strange stories that were told about her lovers. Had he something of her temperament in him? These oval heavy-lidded eyes seemed to look curiously at him. What of George Willoughby, with his powdered hair and fantastic patches? How evil he looked! The face was saturnine and swarthy, and the sensual lips seemed to be twisted with disdain. Delicate lace ruffles fell over the lean yellow hands that were so over-laden with rings. He had been a macaroni of the eighteenth century, and the friend, in his youth, of Lord Ferrars. What of the second Lord Beckenham, the companion of the Prince Regent in his wildest days, and one of the witnesses at the secret marriage with Mrs. Fitzherbert? How proud and handsome he was, with his chestnut curls and insolent pose! What passions had he bequeathed? The world had looked upon him as infamous. He had led the orgies at Carlton House. The star of the Garter glittered upon his breast. Beside him hung the portrait of his wife, a pallid, thin-lipped woman in black. Her blood, also, stirred within him. How curious it all seemed! And his mother with her Lady Hamilton face, and her moist wine-dashed lips—he knew what he had got from her. He had got from her his beauty, and his passion for the beauty of others. She laughed at him in her loose Bacchante dress. There were vine leaves in her hair. The purple spilled from the cup she was holding. The carnations of the painting had withered, but the eyes were still wonderful in their depth and brilliancy of colour. They seemed to follow him wherever he went.

Yet one had ancestors in literature, as well as in one's own race, nearer perhaps in type and temperament, many of them, and certainly with an influence of which one was more absolutely conscious. There were times when it appeared to Dorian Gray that the whole of history was merely the record of his own life, not as he had lived it in act and circumstance, but as his imagination had created it for him, as it had been in his brain and in his passions. He felt that he had known them all, those strange terrible figures that had passed across the stage of the world and made sin so marvellous, and evil so full of subtlety. It seemed to him that in some mysterious way their lives had been his own.

The hero of the wonderful novel that had so influenced his life had himself known this curious fancy. In the seventh chapter he tells how, crowned with laurel, lest lightning might strike him, he had sat, as Tiberius, in a garden at Capri, reading the shameful books of Elephantis, while dwarfs and peacocks strutted round him, and the flute-player mocked the swinger of the censer; and, as Caligula, had caroused with the green-shirted jockeys in their stables and supped in an ivory manger with a jewel-frontleted horse: and, as Domitian, had wandered through a corridor lined with marble mirrors, looking round with haggard eyes for the reflection of the dagger that was to end his days, and sick with that ennui, that terrible *tædium vitæ*, that comes on those to whom life denies nothing; and had peered through a clear emerald at the red shambles of the. Circus, and then, in a litter of pearl and purple drawn by silver-shod mules, been carried through the Street of Pomegranates to a House of Gold, and heard men cry on Nero Cæsar as he passed by; and, as Elagabalus, had painted his face with colours, and plied the distaff among the women, and brought the Moon from Carthage, and given her in mystic marriage to the Sun.

Over and over again Dorian used to read this fantastic chapter, and the two chapters immediately following, in which, as in some curious tapestries or cunningly-wrought enamels, were pictured the awful and beautiful forms of those whom Vice and Blood and Weariness had made monstrous or mad: Filippo, Duke of Milan, who slew his wife, and painted her lips with a scarlet poison that her lover might suck death from the dead thing he fondled; Pietro Barbi, the Venetian, known as Paul the Second, who sought in his vanity to assume the title of Formosus, and whose tiara, valued at two hundred thousand florins, was bought at the price of a terrible sin; Gian Maria Visconti, who used hounds to chase living men, and whose murdered body was covered with roses by a harlot who had loved him; the Borgia on his white horse, with Fratricide riding beside him, and his mantle stained with the blood of Perotto; Pietro Riario, the young Cardinal Archbishop of Florence, child and minion of Sixtus IV, whose beauty was equalled only by his debauchery, and who received Leonora of Aragon in a pavilion of white and crimson silk, filled with nymphs and centaurs, and gilded a boy that he might serve at the feast as Ganymede or Hylas; Ezzelin, whose melancholy could be cured only by the spectacle of death, and who had a passion for red blood, as other men have for red wine

—the son of the Fiend, as was reported, and one who had cheated his father at dice when gambling with him for his own soul; Giambattista Cibo, who in mockery took the name of Innocent, and into whose torpid veins the blood of three lads was infused by a Jewish doctor; Sigismondo Malatesta, the lover of Isotta, and the lord of Rimini, whose effigy was burned at Rome as the enemy of God and man, who strangled Polyssena with a napkin, and gave poison to Ginevra d'Este in a cup of emerald, and in honour of a shameful passion built a pagan church for Christian worship; Charles VI, who had so wildly adored his brother's wife that a leper had warned him of the insanity that was coming on him, and who, when his brain had sickened and grown strange, could only be soothed by Saracen cards painted with the images of Love and Death and Madness; and, in his trimmed jerkin and jewelled cap and acanthus-like curls, Grifonetto Baglioni, who slew Astorre with his bride, and Simonetto with his page, and whose comeliness was such that, as he lay dying in the yellow piazza of Perugia, those who had hated him could not choose but weep, and Atalanta, who had cursed him, blessed him.

There was a horrible fascination in them all. He saw them at night, and they troubled his imagination in the day. The Renaissance knew of strange manners of poisoning—poisoning by a helmet and a lighted torch, by an embroidered glove and a jewelled fan, by a gilded pomander and by an amber chain. Dorian Gray had been poisoned by a book. There were moments when he looked on evil simply as a mode through which he could realise his conception of the beautiful.

CHAPTER XII

It was on the ninth of November, the eve of his own thirty-eighth birthday, as he often remembered afterwards.

He was walking home about eleven o'clock from Lord Henry's, where he had been dining, and was wrapped in heavy furs, as the night was cold and foggy. At the corner of Grosvenor Square and South Audley Street a man passed him in the mist, walking very fast, and with the collar of his grey ulster turned up. He had a bag in his hand. Dorian recognised him. It was Basil Hallward. A strange sense of fear, for which he could not account, came over him. He made no sign of recognition, and went on quickly in the direction of his own house.

But Hallward had seen him. Dorian heard him first stopping on the pavement, and then hurrying after him. In a few moments his hand was on his arm.

'Dorian! What an extraordinary piece of luck! I have been waiting for you in your library ever since nine o'clock. Finally I took pity on your tired servant, and told him to go to bed, as he let me out. I am off to Paris by the midnight train, and I particularly wanted to see you before I left. I thought it was you, or rather your fur coat, as you passed me. But I wasn't quite sure. Didn't you recognise me?'

'In this fog, my dear Basil? Why, I can't even recognise Grosvenor Square. I believe my house is somewhere about here, but I don't feel at all certain about it. I am sorry you are going away, as I have not seen you for ages. But I suppose you will be back soon?'

'No: I am going to be out of England for six months.

I intend to take a studio in Paris, and shut myself up till I have finished a great picture I have in my head. However, it wasn't about myself I wanted to talk. Here we are at your door. Let me come in for a moment. I have something to say to you.'

'I shall be charmed. But won't you miss your train?' said Dorian Gray, languidly, as he passed up the steps and opened the door with his latchkey.

The lamp-light struggled out through the fog, and Hallward looked at his watch. 'I have heaps of time,' he answered. 'The train doesn't go till twelve-fifteen, and it is only just eleven. In fact, I was on my way to the club to look for you, when I met you. You see, I shan't have any delay about luggage, as I have sent on my heavy things. All I have with me is in this bag, and I can easily get to Victoria in twenty minutes.'

Dorian looked at him and smiled. 'What a way for a fashionable painter to travel! A Gladstone bag, and an ulster! Come in, or the fog will get into the house. And mind you don't talk about anything serious. Nothing is serious nowadays. At least nothing should be.'

Hallward shook his head as he entered, and followed Dorian into the library. There was a bright wood fire blazing in the large open hearth. The lamps were lit, and an open Dutch silver spirit-case stood, with some siphons of soda-water and large cut-glass tumblers, on a little marqueterie table.

'You see your servant made me quite at home, Dorian. He gave me everything I wanted, including your best gold-tipped cigarettes. He is a most hospitable creature. I like him much better than the Frenchman you used to have. What has become of the Frenchman, by the by?'

Dorian shrugged his shoulders. 'I believe he married Lady Radley's maid, and has established her in Paris as an

English dressmaker. *Anglomanie* is very fashionable over there now, I hear. It seems silly of the French, doesn't it? But—do you know?—he was not at all a bad servant. I never liked him, but I had nothing to complain about. One often imagines things that are quite absurd. He was really very devoted to me, and seemed quite sorry when he went away. Have another brandy-and-soda? Or would you like hock-and-seltzer? I always take hock-and-seltzer myself. There is sure to be some in the next room.'

'Thanks, I won't have anything more,' said the painter, taking his cap and coat off, and throwing them on the bag that he had placed in the corner. 'And now, my dear fellow, I want to speak to you seriously. Don't frown like that. You make it so much more difficult for me.'

'What is it all about?' cried Dorian, in his petulant way, flinging himself down on the sofa. 'I hope it is not about myself. I am tired of myself to-night. I should like to be somebody else.'

'It is about yourself,' answered Hallward, in his grave, deep voice, 'and I must say it to you. I shall only keep you half an hour.'

Dorian sighed, and lit a cigarette. 'Half an hour!' he murmured.

'It is not much to ask of you, Dorian, and it is entirely for your own sake that I am speaking. I think it right that you should know that the most dreadful things are being said against you in London.'

'I don't wish to know anything about them. I love scandals about other people, but scandals about myself don't interest me. They have not got the charm of novelty.'

'They must interest you, Dorian. Every gentleman is interested in his good name. You don't want people to talk of you as something vile and degraded. Of course you

171

have your position, and your wealth, and all that kind of thing. But position and wealth are not everything. Mind you, I don't believe these rumours at all. At least, I can't believe them when I see you. Sin is a thing that writes itself across a man's face. It cannot be concealed. People talk sometimes of secret vices. There are no such things. If a wretched man has a vice, it shows itself in the lines of his mouth, the droop of his eyelids, the moulding of his hands even. Somebody—I won't mention his name, but you know him—came to me last year to have his portrait done. I had never seen him before, and had never heard anything about him at the time, though I have heard a good deal since. He offered an extravagant price. I refused him. There was something in the shape of his fingers that I hated. I know now that I was quite right in what I fancied about him. His life is dreadful. But you, Dorian, with your pure, bright, innocent face, and your marvellous untroubled youth—I can't believe anything against you. And yet I see you very seldom, and you never come down to the studio now, and when I am away from you, and I hear all these hideous things that people are whispering about you, I don't know what to say. Why is it, Dorian, that a man like the Duke of Berwick leaves the room of a club when you enter it? Why is it that so many gentlemen in London will neither go to your house nor invite you to theirs? You used to be a friend of Lord Staveley. I met him at dinner last week. Your name happened to come up in conversation, in connection with the miniatures you have lent to the exhibition at the Dudley. Staveley curled his lip, and said that you might have the most artistic tastes, but that you were a man whom no pure-minded girl should be allowed to know, and whom no chaste woman should sit in the same room with. I reminded him that I was a friend of yours, and asked him what he meant. He told me. He told me right out before everybody. It was horrible! Why is your friendship so fatal to young men? There was that wretched boy in the Guards who committed suicide. You were his great friend. There was Sir Henry Ashton, who had to leave England, with a tarnished name. You and he were inseparable. What about Adrian Singleton, and his dreadful end? What about Lord Kent's only son, and his career? I met his father yesterday in St. James's Street. He seemed broken with shame and sorrow. What about the young Duke of Perth? What sort of life has he got now? What gentleman would associate with him?'

'Stop, Basil. You are talking about things of which you know nothing,' said Dorian Gray, biting his lip, and with a note of infinite contempt in his voice. 'You ask me why Berwick leaves a room when I enter it. It is because I know everything about his life, not because he knows anything about mine. With such blood as he has in his veins, how could his record be clean? You ask me about Henry Ashton and young Perth. Did I teach the one his vices, and the other his debauchery? If Kent's silly son takes his wife from the streets what is that to me? If Adrian Singleton writes his friend's name across a bill, am I his keeper? I know how people chatter in England. The middle classes air their moral prejudices over their gross dinner-tables, and whisper about what they call the profligacies of their betters in order to try and pretend that they are in smart society, and on intimate terms with the people they slander. In this country it is enough for a man to have distinction and brains for every common tongue to wag against him. And what sort of lives do these people, who pose as being moral, lead themselves? My dear fellow, you forget that we are in the native land of the hypocrite.'

'Dorian,' cried Hallward, 'that is not the question. England is bad enough, I know, and English society is all wrong. That is the reason why I want you to be fine. You have not been fine. One has a right to judge of a man by the effect he has over his friends. Yours seem to lose all sense of honour, of goodness, of purity. You have filled them with a madness for pleasure. They have gone down into the depths. You led them there. Yes: you led them there, and yet you can smile, as you are smiling now. And there is worse behind. I know you and Harry are inseparable. Surely for that reason, if for none other, you should not have made his sister's name a by-word.'

'Take care, Basil. You go too far.'

'I must speak, and you must listen. You shall listen. When you met Lady Gwendolen, not a breath of scandal had ever touched her. Is there a single decent woman in London now who would drive with her in the Park? Why, even her children are not allowed to live with her. Then there are other stories—stories that you have been seen creeping at dawn out of dreadful houses and slinking in disguise into the foulest dens in London. Are they true? Can they be true? When I first heard them, I laughed. I hear them now, and they make me shudder. What about your country house, and the life that. is led there? Dorian, you don't know what is said about you. I won't tell you that I don't want to preach to you. I remember Harry saying once that every man who turned himself into an amateur curate for the moment always began by saying that, and then proceeded to break his word. I do want to preach to you. I want you to lead such a life as will make the world respect you. I want you to have a clean name and a fair record. I want you to get rid of the dreadful people you associate with. Don't shrug your shoulders like that. Don't be so indifferent. You have a wonderful influence. Let it be for good, not for evil. They say that you corrupt everyone with whom you become intimate, and that it is quite sufficient for you to enter a house, for shame of some kind to follow after. I don't know whether it is so or not. How should I know? But it is said of you. I am told things that it seems impossible to doubt. Lord Gloucester was one of my greatest friends at Oxford. He showed me a letter that his wife had written to him when she was dying alone in her villa at Mentone. Your name was implicated in the most terrible confession I ever read. I told him that it was absurd—that I knew you thoroughly, and that you were incapable of anything of the kind. Know you? I wonder do I know you? Before I could answer that, I should have to see your soul.'

'To see my soul!' muttered Dorian Gray, starting up from the sofa and turning almost white from fear.

'Yes,' answered Hallward, gravely, and with deep-toned sorrow in his voice— 'to see your soul. But only God can do that.'

A bitter laugh of mockery broke from the lips of the younger man. 'You shall see it yourself, to-night!' he cried, seizing a lamp from the table. 'Come: it is your own handiwork. Why shouldn't you look at it? You can tell the world all about it afterwards, if you choose. Nobody would believe you. If they did believe you, they would like me all the better for it. I know the age better than you do, though you will prate about it so tediously. Come, I tell you. You have chattered enough about corruption. Now you shall look on it face to face.'

There was the madness of pride in every word he uttered. He stamped his foot upon the ground in his boyish insolent manner. He felt a terrible joy at the thought that someone else was to share his secret, and that the man who had painted the portrait that was the origin of all his shame was to be burdened for the rest of his life with the hideous memory of what he had done.

'Yes,' he continued, coming closer to him, and looking

steadfastly into his stern eyes, 'I shall show you my soul. You shall see the thing that you fancy only God can see.'

Hallward started back. 'This is blasphemy, Dorian!' he cried. 'You must not say things like that. They are horrible, and they don't mean anything.'

'You think so?' He laughed again.

'I know so. As for what I said to you to-night, I said it for your good. You know I have been always a staunch friend to you.'

'Don't touch me. Finish what you have to say.'

A twisted flash of pain shot across the painter's face. He paused for a moment, and a wild feeling of pity came over him. After all, what right had he to pry into the life of Dorian Gray? If he had done a tithe of what was rumoured about him, how much he must have suffered! Then he straightened himself up, and walked over to the fireplace, and stood there, looking at the burning logs with their frost-like ashes and their throbbing cores of flame.

'I am waiting, Basil,' said the young man, in a hard, clear voice.

He turned round. 'What I have to say is this,' he cried. 'You must give me some answer to these horrible charges that are made against you. If you tell me that they are absolutely untrue from beginning to end, I shall believe you. Deny them, Dorian, deny them! Can't you see what I am going through? My God! don't tell me that you are bad, and corrupt, and shameful.'

Dorian Gray smiled. There was a curl of contempt in his lips. 'Come upstairs, Basil,' he said, quietly. 'I keep a diary of my life from day to day, and it never leaves the room in which it is written. I shall show it to you if you come with me.'

'I shall come with you, Dorian, if you wish it. I see I

have missed my train. That makes no matter. I can go to-morrow. But don't ask me to read anything to-night. All I want is a plain answer to my question.'

'That shall be given to you upstairs. I could not give it here. You will not have to read long.'

CHAPTER XIII

HE passed out of the room, and began the ascent, Basil Hallward following close behind. They walked softly, as men do instinctively at night. The lamp cast fantastic shadows on the wall and staircase. A rising wind made some of the windows rattle.

When they reached the top landing, Dorian set the lamp down on the floor, and taking out the key turned it in the lock. 'You insist on knowing, Basil?' he asked, in a low voice.

'Yes.'

'I am delighted,' he answered, smiling. Then he added, somewhat harshly, 'You are the one man in the world who is entitled to know everything about me. You have had more to do with my life than you think': and, taking up the lamp, he opened the door and went in. A cold current of air passed them, and the light shot up for a moment in a flame of murky orange. He shuddered. 'Shut the door behind you,' he whispered, as he placed the lamp on the table.

Hallward glanced round him, with a puzzled expression. The room looked as if it had not been lived in for years. A faded Flemish tapestry, a curtained picture, an old Italian *cassone*, and an almost empty bookcase—that was all that it seemed to contain, besides a chair and a table. As Dorian Gray was lighting a half-burned candle that was standing on the mantelshelf, he saw that the whole place was covered with dust, and that the carpet was in holes. A mouse ran scuffling behind the wainscoting. There was a damp odour of mildew.

'So you think that it is only God who sees the soul, Basil? Draw that curtain back, and you will see mine.'

The voice that spoke was cold and cruel. 'You are mad, Dorian, or playing a part,' muttered Hallward, frowning.

'You won't? Then I must do it myself,' said the young man; and he tore the curtain from its rod, and flung it on the ground.

An exclamation of horror broke from the painter's lips as he saw in the dim light the hideous face on the canvas grinning at him. There was something in its expression that filled him with disgust and loathing. Good heavens! it was Dorian Gray's own face that he was looking at! The horror, whatever it was, had not yet entirely spoiled that marvellous beauty. There was still some gold in the thinning hair and some scarlet on the sensual mouth. The sodden eyes had kept something of the loveliness of their blue, the noble curves had not yet completely passed away from chiselled nostrils and from plastic throat. Yes, it was Dorian himself. But who had done it? He seemed to recognise his own brushwork, and the frame was his own design. The idea was monstrous, yet he felt afraid. He seized the lighted candle, and held it to the picture. In the left-hand corner was his own name, traced in long letters of bright vermilion.

It was some foul parody, some infamous, ignoble satire. He had never done that. Still, it was his own picture. He knew it, and he felt as if his blood had changed in a moment from fire to sluggish ice. His own picture! What did it mean? Why had it altered? He turned, and looked at Dorian Gray with the eyes of a sick man. His mouth twitched, and his parched tongue seemed unable to articulate. He passed his hand across his forehead. It was dank with clammy sweat.

The young man was leaning against the mantelshelf, watching him with that strange expression that one sees on the faces of those who are absorbed in a play when some great artist is acting. There was neither real sorrow in it nor real joy. There was simply the passion of the spectator, with perhaps a flicker of triumph in his eyes. He had taken the flower out of his coat, and was smelling it, or pretending to do so.

'What does this mean?' cried Hallward, at last. His own voice sounded shrill and curious in his ears.

'Years ago, when I was a boy,' said Dorian Gray, crushing the flower in his hand, 'you met me, flattered me, and taught me to be vain of my good looks. One day you introduced me to a friend of yours, who explained to me the wonder of youth, and you finished the portrait of me that revealed to me the wonder of beauty. In a mad moment, that, even now, I don't know whether I regret or not, I made a wish, perhaps you would call it a prayer . . .'

'I remember it! Oh, how well I remember it! No! the thing is impossible. The room is damp. Mildew has got into the canvas. The paints I used had some wretched mineral poison in them. I tell you the thing is impossible.'

'Ah, what is impossible?' murmured the young man, going over to the window, and leaning his forehead against the cold mist-stained glass.

'You told me you had destroyed it.'

'I was wrong. It has destroyed me.'

'I don't believe it is my picture.'

'Can't you see your ideal in it?' said Dorian, bitterly.

'My ideal, as you call it . . .'

'As you called it.'

'There was nothing evil in it, nothing shameful. You were to me such an ideal as I shall never meet again. This is the face of a satyr.'

'It is the face of my soul.'

'Christ! what a thing I must have worshipped! It has the eyes of a devil.'

'Each of us has Heaven and Hell in him, Basil,' cried Dorian, with a wild gesture of despair.

Hallward turned again to the portrait, and gazed at it. 'My God! if it is true,' he exclaimed, 'and this is what you have done with your life, why, you must be worse even than those who talk against you fancy you to be!' He held the light up again to the canvas, and examined it. The surface seemed to be quite undisturbed, and as he had left it. It was from within, apparently, that the foulness and horror had come. Through some strange quickening of inner life the leprosies of sin were slowly eating the thing away. The rotting of a corpse in a watery grave was not so fearful.

His hand shook. and the candle fell from its socket on the floor, and lay there sputtering. He placed his foot on it and put it out. Then he flung himself into the rickety chair that was standing by the table and buried his face in his hands.

'Good God, Dorian, what a lesson! what an awful lesson!' There was no answer, but he could hear the young man sobbing at the window. 'Pray, Dorian, pray,' he murmured. 'What is it that one was taught to say in one's boyhood? "Lead us not into temptation. Forgive us our sins. Wash away our iniquities." Let us say that together. The prayer of your pride has been answered. The prayer of your repentance will be answered also. I worshipped you too much. I am punished for it. You worshipped yourself too much. We are both punished.'

Dorian Gray turned slowly around, and looked at him with tear-dimmed eyes. 'It is too late, Basil,' he faltered.

'It is never too late, Dorian. Let us kneel down and try if we cannot remember a prayer. Isn't there a verse somewhere, "Though your sins be as scarlet, yet I will make them as white as snow"?'

'Those words mean nothing to me now.'

Hush! don't say that. You have done enough evil in your life. My God! don't you see that accursed thing leering at us?'

Dorian Gray glanced at the picture, and suddenly an uncontrollable feeling of hatred for Basil Hallward came over him, as though it had been suggested to him by the image on the canvas, whispered into his ear by those grinning lips. The mad passions of a hunted animal stirred within him, and he loathed the man who was seated at the table, more than in his whole life he had ever loathed anything. He glanced wildly around. Something glimmered on the top of the painted chest that faced him. His eye fell on it. He knew what it was. It was a knife that he had brought up, some days before, to cut a piece of cord, and had forgotten to take away with him. He moved slowly towards it, passing Hallward as he did so. As soon as he got behind him, he seized it, and turned round. Hallward stirred in his chair as if he was going to rise. He rushed at him, and dug the knife into the great vein that is behind the ear, crushing the man's head down on the table, and stabbing again and again.

There was a stifled groan, and the horrible sound of someone choking with blood. Three times the outstretched arms shot up convulsively, waving grotesque stiff-fingered hands in the air. He stabbed him twice more, but the man did not move. Something began to trickle on the floor. He waited for a moment, still pressing the head down. Then he threw the knife on the table, and listened.

He could hear nothing but the drip, drip on the threadbare carpet. He opened the door and went out on the landing. The house was absolutely quiet. No one was about. For a few seconds he stood bending over the balustrade, and peering down into the black seething well of darkness.

Then he took out the key and returned to the room, locking himself in as he did so.

The thing was still seated in the chair, straining over the table with bowed head, and humped back, and long fantastic arms. Had it not been for the red jagged tear in the neck, and the clotted black pool that was slowly widening on the table, one would have said that the man was simply asleep.

How quickly it had all been done! He felt strangely calm, and, walking over to the window, opened it, and stepped out on the balcony. The wind had blown the fog away, and the sky was like a monstrous peacock's tail, starred with myriads of golden eyes. He looked down, and saw the policeman going his rounds and flashing the long beam of his lantern on the doors of the silent houses. The crimson spot of a prowling hansom gleamed at the corner, and then vanished. A woman in a fluttering shawl was creeping slowly by the railings, staggering as she went. Now and then she stopped, and peered back. Once, she began to sing in a hoarse voice. The policeman strolled over and said something to her. She stumbled away, laughing. A bitter blast swept across the Square. The gas-lamps flickered, and became blue, and the leafless trees shook their black iron branches to and fro. He shivered, and went back, closing the window behind him.

Having reached the door, he turned the key, and opened it. He did not even glance at the murdered man. He felt that the secret of the whole thing was not to realise the situation. The friend who had painted the fatal portrait to which all his misery had been due, had gone out of his life. That was enough.

Then he remembered the lamp. It was a rather curious one of Moorish workmanship, made of dull silver inlaid with arabesques of burnished steel, and studded with coarse turquoises. Perhaps it might be missed by his servant, and questions would be asked. He hesitated for a moment, then he turned back and took it from the table. He could not help seeing the dead thing. How still it was! How horribly white the long hands looked! It was like a dreadful wax image.

Having locked the door behind him, he crept quietly downstairs. The woodwork creaked, and seemed to cry out as if in pain. He stopped several times, and waited. No: everything was still. It was merely the sound of his own footsteps.

When he reached the library, he saw the bag and coat in the corner. They must be hidden away somewhere. He unlocked a secret press that was in the wainscoting, a press in which he kept his own curious disguises, and put them into it. He could easily burn them afterwards. Then he pulled out his watch. It was twenty minutes to two.

He sat down and began to think. Every year—every month, almost—men were strangled in England for what he had done. There had been a madness of murder in the air. Some red star had come too close to the earth. . . . And yet what evidence was there against him? Basil Hallward had left the house at eleven. No one had seen him come in again. Most of the servants were at Selby Royal. His valet had gone to bed. . . . Paris! Yes. It was to Paris that Basil had gone, and by the midnight train, as he had intended. With his curious reserved habits, it would be months before any suspicions would be aroused. Months! Everything could be destroyed long before then.

A sudden thought struck him. He put on his fur coat and hat, and went out into the hall. There he paused, hearing the slow heavy tread of the policeman on the pavement outside, and seeing the flash of the bull's eye reflected in the window. He waited, and held his breath.

After a few moments he drew back the latch, and slipped

out, shutting the door very gently behind him. Then he began ringing the bell. In about five minutes his valet appeared half dressed, and looking very drowsy.

'I am sorry to have had to wake you up, Francis," he said, stepping in; 'but I had forgotten my latchkey. What time is it?'

'Ten minutes past two, sir,' answered the man, looking at the clock and blinking.

'Ten minutes past two? How horribly late! You must wake me at nine to-morrow. I have some work to do.'

'All right, sir.'

'Did anyone call this evening?'

'Mr. Hallward, sir. He stayed here till eleven, and then he went away to catch his train.'

'Oh! I am sorry I didn't see him. Did he leave any message?'

'No, sir, except that he would write to you from Paris, if he did not find you at the club.'

'That will do, Francis. Don't forget to call me at nine to-morrow.'

'No, sir.'

The man shambled down the passage in his slippers.

Dorian Gray threw his hat and coat upon the table, and passed into the library. For a quarter of an hour he walked up and down the room biting his lip, and thinking. Then he took down the Blue Book from one of the shelves, and began to turn over the leaves. 'Alan Campbell, 152, Hertford Street, Mayfair.' Yes; that was the man he wanted.

CHAPTER XIV

AT nine o'clock the next morning his servant came in with a cup of chocolate on a tray, and opened the shutters. Dorian was sleeping quite peacefully, lying on his right side, with one hand underneath his cheek. He looked like a boy who had been tired out with play, or study.

The man had to touch him twice on the shoulder before he woke, and as he opened his eyes a faint smile passed across his lips, as though he had been lost in some delightful dream. Yet he had not dreamed at all. His night had been untroubled by any images of pleasure or of pain. But youth smiles without any reason. It is one of its chiefest charms.

He turned round, and, leaning upon his elbow, began to sip his chocolate. The mellow November sun came streaming into the room. The sky was bright, and there was a genial warmth in the air. It was almost like a morning in May.

Gradually the events of the preceding night crept with silent blood-stained feet into his brain, and reconstructed themselves there with terrible distinctness. He winced at the memory of all that he had suffered, and for a moment the same curious feeling of loathing for Basil Hallward that had made him kill him as he sat in the chair, came back to him, and he grew cold with passion. The dead man was still sitting there, too, and in the sunlight now. How horrible that was! Such hideous things were for the darkness, not for the day.

He felt that if he brooded on what he had gone through he would sicken or ' grow mad. There were sins whose fascination was more in the memory than in the doing of them; strange triumphs that gratified the pride more than the passions, and gave to the intellect a quickened sense of joy, greater than any joy they brought, or could ever bring, to the senses. But this was not one of them. It was a thing to be driven out of the mind, to be drugged with poppies, to be strangled lest it might strangle one itself.

When the half-hour struck, he passed his hand across his forehead, and then got up hastily, and dressed himself with even more than his usual care, giving a good deal of attention to the choice of his necktie and scarf-pin, and changing his rings more than once. He spent a long time also over breakfast, tasting the various dishes, talking to his valet about some new liveries that he was thinking of getting made for the servants at Selby, and going through his correspondence. At some of the letters he smiled. Three of them bored him. One he read several times over, and then tore up with a slight look of annoyance in his face. 'That awful thing, a woman's memory!' as Lord Henry had once said.

After he had drunk his cup of black coffee, he wiped his lips slowly with a napkin, motioned to his servant to wait, and going over to the table sat down and wrote two letters. One he put in his pocket, the other he handed to the valet.

'Take this round to 152, Hertford Street, Francis, and if Mr. Campbell is out of town, get his address.'

As soon as he was alone, he lit a cigarette, and began sketching upon a piece of paper, drawing first flowers, and bits of architecture, and then human faces. Suddenly he remarked that every face that he drew seemed to have a fantastic likeness to Basil Hallward. He frowned, and, getting up, went over to the bookcase and took out a volume at hazard. He was determined that he would not think about what had happened until it became absolutely necessary that he should do so.

When he had stretched himself on the sofa, he looked at the title-page of the book. It was Gautier's *Émaux et Camées*, Charpentier's Japanese-paper edition, with the Jacquemart etching. The binding was of citron-green leather, with a design of gilt trellis-work and dotted pomegranates. It had been given to him by Adrian Singleton. As he turned over the pages his eye fell on the poem about the hand of Lacenaire, the cold yellow hand '*du supplice encore mal lavée*,' with its downy red hairs and its '*doigts de faune*.' He glanced at his own white taper fingers, shuddering slightly in spite of himself, and passed on, till he came to those lovely stanzas upon Venice:

'Sur une gamme chromatique,
    Le sein de perles ruisselant,
La Vénus de l'Adriatique
    Sort de l'eau son corps rose et blanc.

'Les dômes, sur l'azur des ondes
    Suivant la phrase au pur contour,
·S'enflent comme des gorges rondes
    Que soulève un soupir d'amour.

'L'esquif aborde et me dépose,
    Jetant son amarre au pilier,
Devant une façade rose,
    Sur le marbre d'un escalier.'

How exquisite they were! As one read them, one seemed to be floating down the green waterways of the pink and pearl city, seated in a black gondola with silver prow and trailing curtains. The mere lines looked to him like those straight lines of turquoise-blue that follow one as one pushes out to the Lido. The sudden flashes of colour reminded him of the gleam of the opal-and-iris-throated birds that flutter round the tall honey-combed Campanile, or stalk, with such stately grace, through the dim, dust-stained arcades.

Leaning back with half-closed eyes, he kept saying over and over to himself:

> 'Devant une façade rose,
>   Sur le marbre d'un escalier.'

The whole of Venice was in those two lines. He remembered the autumn that he had passed there, and a wonderful love that had stirred him to mad, delightful follies. There was romance in every place. But Venice, like Oxford, had kept the background for romance, and, to the true romantic, background was everything, or almost everything. Basil had been with him part of the time, and had gone wild over Tintoret. Poor Basil! what a horrible way for a man to die!

He sighed, and took up the volume again, and tried to forget. He read of the swallows that fly in and out of the little café at Smyrna where the Hadjis sit counting their amber beads and the turbaned merchants smoke their long tasselled pipes and talk gravely to each other; he read of the Obelisk in the Place de la Concorde that weeps tears of granite in its lonely sunless exile, and longs to be back by the hot lotus-covered Nile, where there are Sphinxes, and rose-red ibises, and white vultures with gilded claws, and crocodiles, with small beryl eyes, that crawl over the green steaming mud; he began to brood over those verses which, drawing music from kiss-stained marble, tell of that curious statue that Gautier compares to a contralto voice, the '*monstre charmant*' that couches in the porphyry-room of the Louvre. But after a time the book fell from his hand. He grew nervous, and a horrible fit of terror came over him. What if Alan Campbell should be out of England? Days would elapse before he could come back. Perhaps he might refuse to come. What could he do then? Every moment was of vital importance. They had been great friends once, five years before—almost inseparable, indeed. Then the intimacy had come suddenly to an end. When they met in society now, it was only Dorian Gray who smiled; Alan Campbell never did.

He was an extremely clever young man, though he had no real appreciation of the visible arts, and whatever little sense of the beauty of poetry he possessed he had gained entirely from Dorian. His dominant intellectual passion was for science. At Cambridge he had spent a great deal of his time working in the Laboratory, and had taken a good class in the Natural Science Tripos of his year. Indeed, he was still devoted to the study of chemistry, and had a laboratory of his own, in which he used to shut himself up all day long, greatly to the annoyance of his mother, who had set her heart on his standing for Parliament, and had a vague idea that a chemist was a person who made up prescriptions. He was an excellent musician, however, as well, and played both the violin and the piano better than most amateurs. In fact, it was music that had first brought him and Dorian Gray together—music and that indefinable attraction that Dorian seemed to be able to exercise whenever he wished, and indeed exercised often without being conscious of it. They had met at Lady Berkshire's the night that Rubinstein played there, and after that used to be always seen together at the Opera, and wherever good music was going on. For eighteen months their intimacy lasted. Campbell was always either at Selby Royal or in Grosvenor Square. To him, as to many others, Dorian Gray was the type of everything that is wonderful and fascinating in life. Whether or not a quarrel had taken place between them no one ever knew. But suddenly people remarked that they scarcely spoke when they met, and that Campbell seemed always to go away early from any party at which Dorian Gray was present. He had changed, too—was strangely melancholy at times, appeared almost to dislike hearing music, and would never himself play, giving as his excuse, when he was called upon, that he was so absorbed in science that he had no time left in which to practise. And this was certainly true. Every day he seemed to become more interested in biology, and his name appeared once or twice in some of the scientific reviews, in connection with certain curious experiments.

This was the man Dorian Gray was waiting for. Every second he kept glancing at the clock. As the minutes went by he became horribly agitated. At last he got up, and began to pace up and down the room, looking like a beautiful caged thing. He took long stealthy strides. His hands were curiously cold.

The suspense became unbearable. Time seemed to him to be crawling with feet of lead, while he by monstrous winds was being swept towards the jagged edge of some black cleft of precipice. He knew what was waiting for him there; saw it indeed, and, shuddering, crushed with dank hands his burning lids as though he would have robbed the very brain of sight, and driven the eyeballs back into their cave. It was useless. The brain had its own food on which it battened, and the imagination, made grotesque by terror, twisted and distorted as a living thing by pain, danced like some foul puppet on a stand, and grinned through moving masks. Then, suddenly, Time stopped for him. Yes: that blind, slow-breathing thing crawled no more, and horrible thoughts, Time being dead, raced nimbly on in front, and dragged a hideous future from its grave, and showed it to him. He stared at it. Its very horror made him stone.

At last the door opened, and his servant entered. He turned glazed eyes upon him.

'Mr. Campbell, sir,' said the man.

A sigh of relief broke from his parched lips, and the colour came back to his cheeks.

'Ask him to come in at once, Francis.' He felt that he was himself again. His mood of cowardice had passed away.

The man bowed, and retired. In a few moments Alan Campbell walked in, looking very stern and rather pale, his pallor being intensified by his coal-black hair and dark eyebrows.

'Alan! this is kind of you. I thank you for coming.'

'I had intended never to enter your house again, Gray. But you said it was a matter of life and death.' His voice was hard and cold. He spoke with slow deliberation. There was a look of contempt in the steady searching gaze that he turned on Dorian. He kept his hands in the pockets of his Astrakhan coat, and seemed not to have noticed the gesture with which he had been greeted.

'Yes: it is a matter of life and death, Alan, and to more than one person. Sit down.'

Campbell took a chair by the table, and Dorian sat opposite to him. The two men's eyes met. In Dorian's there was infinite pity. He knew that what he was going to do was dreadful.

After a strained moment of silence, he leaned across and said, very quietly, but watching the effect of each word upon the face of him he had sent for, 'Alan, in a locked room at the top of this house, a room to which nobody but myself has access, a dead man is seated at a table. He has been dead ten hours now. Don't stir, and don't look at me like that. Who the man is, why he died, how he died, are matters that do not concern you. What you have to do is this——'

'Stop, Gray. I don't want to know anything further. Whether what you have told me is true or not true, doesn't concern me. I entirely decline to be mixed up in your life. Keep your horrible secrets to yourself. They don't interest me any more.'

'Alan, they will have to interest you. This one will have to interest you. I am awfully sorry for you, Alan. But I can't help myself. You are the one man who is able to save me. I am forced to bring you into the matter. I have no option. Alan, you are scientific. You know about chemistry, and things of that kind. You have made experiments. What you have got to do is to destroy the thing that is upstairs— to destroy it so that not a vestige of it will be left. Nobody saw this person come into the house. Indeed, at the present moment he is supposed to be in Paris. He will not be missed for months. When he is missed, there must be no trace of him found here. You, Alan, you must change him, and everything that belongs to him, into a handful of ashes that I may scatter in the air.'

'You are mad, Dorian.'

'Ah! I was waiting for you to call me Dorian.'

'You are mad, I tell you—mad to imagine that I would raise a finger to help you, mad to make this monstrous confession. I will have nothing to do with this matter, whatever it is. Do you think I am going to peril my reputation for you? What is it to me what devil's work you are up to?'

'It was suicide, Alan.'

'I am glad of that. But who drove him to it? You, I should fancy.'

'Do you still refuse to do this for me?'

'Of course I refuse. I will have absolutely nothing to do with it. I don't care what shame comes on you. You deserve it all. I should not be sorry to see you disgraced, publicly disgraced. How dare you ask me, of all men in the world, to mix myself up in this horror? I should have thought you knew more about people's characters. Your friend Lord HenryWotton can't have taught you much about psychology, whatever else he has taught you. Nothing will induce me to stir a step to help you. You have come to the wrong man. Go to some of your friends. Don't come to me.'

'Alan, it was murder. I killed him. You don't know what he had made me suffer. Whatever my life is, he had more to do with the making or the marring of it than poor Harry has had. He may not have intended it, the result was the same.'

'Murder! Good God, Dorian, is that what you have come to? I shall not inform upon you. It is not my business. Besides, without my stirring in the matter, you are certain to be arrested. Nobody ever commits a crime without doing something stupid. But I will have nothing to do with it.'

'You must have something to do with it. Wait, wait a moment; listen to me. Only listen, Alan. All I ask of you is to perform a certain scientific experiment. You go to hospitals and dead-houses, and the horrors that you do there don't affect you. If in some hideous dissecting-room or fetid laboratory you found this man lying on a leaden table with red gutters scooped out in it for the blood to flow through, you would simply look upon him as an admirable subject. You would not turn a hair. You would not believe that you were doing anything wrong. On the contrary, you would probably feel that you were benefiting the human race, or increasing the sum of knowledge in the world, or gratifying intellectual curiosity, or something of that kind. What I want you to do is merely what you have often done before. Indeed, to destroy a body must be far less horrible than what you are accustomed to work at. And, remember, it is the only piece of evidence against me. If it is discovered, I am lost; and it is sure to be discovered unless you help me.'

'I have no desire to help you. You forget that. I am simply indifferent to the whole thing. It has nothing to do with me.'

'Alan, I entreat you. Think of the position I am in. Just before you came I almost fainted with terror. You may know terror yourself some day. No! don't think of that. Look at the matter purely from the scientific point of view. You don't inquire where the dead things on which you experiment come from. Don't inquire now. I have told you too much as it is. But I beg of you to do this. We were friends once, Alan.'

'Don't speak about those days, Dorian: they are dead.'

'The dead linger sometimes. The man upstairs will not go away. He is sitting at the table with bowed head and outstretched arms. Alan! Alan! if you don't come to my assistance I am ruined. Why, they will hang me, Alan! Don't you understand? They will hang me for what I have done.'

'There is no good in prolonging this scene. I absolutely refuse to do anything in the matter. It is insane of you to ask me.'

'You refuse?'

'Yes.'

'I entreat you, Alan.'

'It is useless.'

The same look of pity came into Dorian Gray's eyes. Then he stretched out his hand, took a piece of paper, and wrote something on it. He read it over twice, folded it carefully, and pushed it across the table. Having done this, he got up, and went over to the window.

Campbell looked at him in surprise, and then took up the paper, and opened it. As he read it, his face became ghastly pale, and he fell back in his chair. A horrible sense of sickness came over him. He felt as if his heart was beating itself to death in some empty hollow.

After two or three minutes of terrible silence, Dorian turned round, and came and stood behind him, putting his hand upon his shoulder.

'I am so sorry for you, Alan,' he murmured, 'but you leave me no alternative. I have a letter written already. Here it is. You see the address. If you don't help me, I must send it. If you don't help me, I will send it. You know what the result will be. But you are going to help me. It is impossible for you to refuse now. I tried to spare you. You will do me the justice to admit that. You were stern, harsh, offensive. You treated me as no man has ever dared to treat me—no living man, at any rate. I bore it all. Now it is for me to dictate terms.'

Campbell buried his face in his hands, and a shudder passed through him.

'Yes, it is my turn to dictate terms, Alan. You know what they are. The thing is quite simple. Come, don't work yourself into this fever. The thing has to be done. Face it, and do it.'

A groan broke from Campbell's lips, and he shivered all over. The ticking of the clock on the mantelpiece seemed to him to be dividing Time into separate atoms of agony, each of which was too terrible to be borne. He felt as if an iron ring was being slowly tightened round his forehead, as if the disgrace with which he was threatened had already come upon him. The hand upon his shoulder weighed like a hand of lead. It was intolerable. It seemed to crush him.

'Come, Alan, you must decide at once.'

'I cannot do it,' he said, mechanically, as though words could alter things.

'You must. You have no choice. Don't delay.'

He hesitated a moment. 'Is there a fire in the room upstairs?'

'Yes, there is a gas-fire with asbestos.'

'I shall have to go home and get some things from the laboratory.'

'No, Alan, you must not leave the house. Write out on a sheet of note-paper what you want, and my servant will take a cab and bring the things back to you.'

Campbell scrawled a few lines, blotted them, and addressed an envelope to his assistant. Dorian took the note up and read it carefully. Then he rang the bell, and gave it to his valet, with orders to return as soon as possible, and to bring the things with him.

As the hall door shut, Campbell started nervously, and, having got up from the chair, went over to the chimney-piece. He was shivering with a kind of ague. For nearly twenty minutes, neither of the men spoke. A fly buzzed noisily about the room, and the ticking of the clock was like the beat of a hammer.

As the chime struck one, Campbell turned round, and, looking at Dorian Gray, saw that his eyes were filled with tears. There was something in the purity and refinement of that sad face that seemed to enrage him. 'You are infamous, absolutely infamous!' he muttered.

'Hush, Alan: you have saved my life,' said Dorian.

'Your life? Good heavens! what a life that is! You have gone from corruption to corruption, and now you have culminated in crime. In doing what I am going to do, what you force me to do, it is not of your life that I am thinking.'

'Ah, Alan,' murmured Dorian, with a sigh, 'I wish you had a thousandth part of the pity for me that I have for you.' He turned away as he spoke, and stood looking out at the garden. Campbell made no answer.

After about ten minutes a knock came to the door, and the servant entered, carrying a large mahogany chest of chemicals, with a long coil of steel and platinum wire and two rather curiously-shaped iron clamps.

'Shall I leave the things here, sir?' he asked Campbell.

'Yes,' said Dorian. 'And I am afraid, Francis, that I have another errand for you. What is the name of the man at Richmond who supplies Selby with orchids?'

'Harden, sir.'

'Yes—Harden. You must go down to Richmond at once, see Harden personally, and tell him to send twice as many orchids as I ordered, and to have as few white ones as possible. In fact, I don't want any white ones. It is a lovely day, Francis, and Richmond is a very pretty place, otherwise I wouldn't bother you about it.'

'No, trouble, sir. At what time shall I be back?'

Dorian looked at Campbell. 'How long will your experiment take, Alan?' he said, in a calm, indifferent voice. The presence of a third person in the room seemed to give him extraordinary courage.

Campbell frowned, and bit his lip. 'It will take about five hours,' he answered.

'It will be time enough, then, if you are back at half-past seven, Francis. Or stay: just leave my things out for dressing. You can have the evening to yourself. I am not dining at home, so I shall not want you.'

'Thank you, sir,' said the man, leaving the room.

'Now, Alan, there is not a moment to be lost. How heavy this chest is! I'll take it for you. You bring the other things.' He spoke rapidly, and in an authoritative manner. Campbell felt dominated by him. They left the room together.

When they reached the top landing, Dorian took out the key and turned it in the lock. Then he stopped, and a troubled look came into his eyes. He shuddered. 'I don't think I can go in, Alan,' he murmured.

'It is nothing to me. I don't require you,' said Campbell coldly.

Dorian half opened the door. As he did so, he saw the face of his portrait leering in the sunlight. On the floor in front of it the torn curtain was lying. He remembered that the night before he had forgotten, for the first time in his life, to hide the fatal canvas, and was about to rush forward, when he drew back with a shudder.

What was that loathsome red dew that gleamed, wet and glistening, on one of the hands, as though the canvas had sweated blood? How horrible it was!—more horrible, it seemed to him for the moment, than the silent thing that he knew was stretched across the table, the thing whose grotesque misshapen shadow on the spotted carpet showed him that it had not stirred, but was still there, as he had left it.

He heaved a deep breath, opened the door a little wider, and with half-closed eyes and averted head walked quickly in, determined that he would not look even once upon the dead man. Then, stooping down, and taking up the gold and purple hanging, he flung it right over the picture.

There he stopped, feeling afraid to turn round, and his eyes fixed themselves on the intricacies of the pattern before him. He heard Campbell bringing in the heavy chest, and the irons, and the other things that he had required for his dreadful work. He began to wonder if he and Basil Hallward had ever met, and, if so, what they had thought of each other.

'Leave me now,' said a stern voice behind him.

He turned and hurried out, just conscious that the dead man had been thrust back into the chair, and that Campbell was gazing into a glistening yellow face. As he was going downstairs he heard the key being turned in the lock.

It was long after seven when Campbell came back into the library. He was pale, but absolutely calm. 'I have done what you asked me to do,' he muttered. 'And now, good-bye. Let us never see each other again.'

'You have saved me from ruin, Alan. I cannot forget that,' said Dorian, simply.

As soon as Campbell had left, he went upstairs. There was a horrible smell of nitric acid in the room. But the thing that had been sitting at the table was gone.

CHAPTER XV

THAT evening, at eight-thirty, exquisitely dressed and wearing a large buttonhole of Parma violets, Dorian Gray was ushered into Lady Narborough's drawing-room by bowing servants. His forehead was throbbing with maddened nerves, and he felt wildly excited, but his manner as he bent over his hostess's hand was as easy and graceful as ever. Perhaps one never seems so much at one's ease as when one has to play a part. Certainly no one looking at Dorian Gray that night could have believed that he had passed through a tragedy as horrible as any tragedy of our age. Those finely-shaped fingers could never have clutched a knife for sin, nor those smiling lips have cried out on God and goodness. He himself could not help wondering at the calm of his demeanour, and for a moment felt keenly the terrible pleasure of a double life.

It was a small party, got up rather in a hurry by Lady Narborough, who was a very clever woman, with what Lord Henry used to describe as the remains of really remarkable ugliness. She had proved an excellent wife to one of our most tedious ambassadors, and having buried her husband properly in a marble mausoleum, which she had herself designed, and married off her daughters to some rich, rather elderly men, she devoted herself now to the pleasures of French fiction, French cookery, and French *esprit* when she could get it.

Dorian was one of her special favourites, and she always told him that she was extremely glad she had not met him in early life. 'I know, my dear, I should have fallen madly in love with you,' she used to say, 'and thrown my bonnet right over the mills for your sake. It is most fortunate that you were not thought of at the time. As it was, our bonnets were so unbecoming, and the mills were so occupied in trying to raise the wind, that I never had even a flirtation with anybody. However, that was all Narborough's fault. He was dreadfully short-sighted, and there is no pleasure in taking in a husband who never sees anything.'

Her guests this evening were rather tedious. The fact was, as she explained to Dorian, behind a very shabby fan, one of her married daughters had come up quite suddenly to stay with her, and, to make matters worse, had actually brought her husband with her. 'I think it is most unkind of her, my dear,' she whispered. 'Of course I go and stay with them every summer after I come from Homburg, but then an old woman like me must have fresh air sometimes, and besides, I really wake them up. You don't know what an existence they lead down there. It is pure unadulterated country life. They get up early, because they have so much to do, and go to bed early because they have so little to think about. There has not been a scandal in the neighbourhood since the time of Queen Elizabeth, and consequently they all fall asleep after dinner. You shan't sit next either of them. You shall sit by me, and amuse me.'

Dorian murmured a graceful compliment, and looked round the room. Yes: it was certainly a tedious party. Two of the people he had never seen before, and the others consisted of Ernest Harrowden, one of those middle-aged mediocrities so common in London clubs who have no enemies, but are thoroughly disliked by their friends; Lady Ruxton, an over-dressed woman of forty-seven, with a hooked nose, who was always trying to get herself compromised, but was so peculiarly plain that to her great disappointment no one would ever believe anything against her; Mrs. Erlynne, a pushing nobody, with a delightful lisp, and Venetian-red hair; Lady Alice Chapman, his hostess's daughter, a dowdy dull girl, with one of those characteristic British faces, that, once seen, are never remembered; and her husband, a red-cheeked, white-whiskered creature who, like so many of his class, was under the impression that inordinate joviality can atone for an entire lack of ideas.

He was rather sorry he had come, till Lady Narborough, looking at the great ormolu gilt clock that sprawled in gaudy curves on the mauve-draped mantelshelf, exclaimed: 'How horrid of Henry Wotton to be so late! I sent round to him this morning on chance, and he promised faithfully not to disappoint me.'

It was some consolation that Harry was to be there, and when the door opened and he heard his slow musical voice lending charm to some insincere apology, he ceased to feel bored.

But at dinner he could not eat anything. Plate after plate went away untasted. Lady Narborough kept scolding him for what she called 'an insult to poor Adolphe, who invented the *menu* specially for you,' and now and then Lord Henry looked across at him, wondering at his silence and abstracted manner. From time to time the butler filled his glass with champagne. He drank eagerly, and his thirst seemed to increase.

'Dorian,' said Lord Henry, at last, as the *chaud-froid* was being handed round, 'what is the matter with you to-night? You are quite out of sorts.'

'I believe he is in love,' cried Lady Narborough, 'and that he is afraid to tell me for fear I should be jealous. He is quite right. I certainly should.'

'Dear Lady Narborough,' murmured Dorian, smiling, 'I have not been in love for a whole week—not, in fact, since Madame de Ferrol left town.'

'How you men can fall in love with that woman!' exclaimed the old lady. 'I really cannot understand it.'

'It is simply because she remembers you when you were a little girl, Lady Narborough,' said Lord Henry. 'She is the one link between us and your short frocks.'

'She does not remember my short frocks at all, Lord Henry. But I remember her very well at Vienna thirty years ago, and how *décolletée* she was then.'

'She is still *décolletée*,' he answered, taking an olive in his long fingers; 'and when she is in a very smart gown she looks like an *édition de luxe* of a bad French novel. She is really wonderful, and full of surprises. Her capacity for family affection is extraordinary. When her third husband died, her hair turned quite gold from grief.'

'How can you, Harry!' cried Dorian.

'It is a most romantic explanation,' laughed the hostess. 'But her third husband, Lord Henry! You don't mean to say Ferrol is the fourth.'

'Certainly, Lady Narborough.'

'I don't believe a word of it.'

'Well, ask Mr. Gray. He is one of her most intimate friends.'

'Is it true, Mr. Gray?'

'She assures me so, Lady Narborough,' said Dorian. 'I asked her whether, like Marguerite de Navarre, she had their hearts embalmed and hung at her girdle. She told me she didn't, because none of them had had any hearts at all.'

'Four husbands! Upon my word that is *trop de zèle*.'

'*Trop d'audace*, I tell her,' said Dorian.

'Oh! she is audacious enough for anything, my dear. And what is Ferrol like? I don't know him.'

'The husbands of very beautiful women belong to the criminal classes,' said Lord Henry, sipping his wine.

Lady Narborough hit him with her fan. 'Lord Henry, I

am not at all surprised that the world says that you are extremely wicked.'

'But what world says that?' asked Lord Henry, elevating his eyebrows. 'It can only be the next world. This world and I are on excellent terms.'

'Everybody I know says you are very wicked,' cried the old lady, shaking her head.

Lord Henry looked serious for some moments. 'It is perfectly monstrous,' he said, at last, 'the way people go about nowadays saying things against one behind one's back that are absolutely and entirely true.'

'Isn't he incorrigible?' cried Dorian, leaning forward in his chair.

'I hope so,' said his hostess, laughing. 'But really if you all worship Madame de Ferrol in this ridiculous way, I shall have to marry again so as to be in the fashion.'

'You will never marry again, Lady Narborough,' broke in Lord Henry. 'You were far too happy. When a woman marries again it is because she detested her first husband. When a man marries again, it is because he adored his first wife. Women try their luck; men risk theirs.'

'Narborough wasn't perfect,' cried the old lady.

'If he had been, you would not have loved him, my dear lady,' was the rejoinder. 'Women love us for our defects. If we have enough of them they will forgive us everything, even our intellects. You will never ask me to dinner again, after saying this, I am afraid, Lady Narborough; but it is quite true.'

'Of course it is true, Lord Henry. If we women did not love you for your defects, where would you all be? Not one of you would ever be married. You would be a set of unfortunate bachelors. Not, however, that that would alter you much. Nowadays all the married men live like bachelors, and all the bachelors like married men.'

'*Fin de siècle*,' murmured Lord Henry.

'*Fin du globe*,' answered his hostess.

'I wish it were *fin du globe*,' said Dorian, with a sigh. 'Life is a great disappointment.'

'Ah, my dear,' cried Lady Narborough, putting on her gloves, 'don't tell me that you have exhausted Life. When a man says that one knows that Life has exhausted him. Lord Henry is very wicked, and I sometimes wish that I had been; but you are made to be good—you look so good. I must find you a nice wife. Lord Henry, don't you think that Mr. Gray should get married?'

'I am always telling him so, Lady Narborough,' said Lord Henry, with a bow.

'Well, we must look out for a suitable match for him. I shall go through Debrett carefully to-night, and draw out a list of all the eligible young ladies.'

'With their ages, Lady Narborough?' asked Dorian.

'Of course, with their ages, slightly edited. But nothing must be done in a hurry. I want it to be what *The Morning Post* calls a suitable alliance, and I want you both to be happy.'

'What nonsense people talk about happy marriages!' exclaimed Lord Henry. 'A man can be happy with any woman as long as he does not love her.'

'Ah! what a cynic you are!' cried the old lady, pushing back her chair, and nodding to Lady Ruxton. 'You must come and dine with me soon again. You are really an admirable tonic, much better than what Sir Andrew prescribes for me. You must tell me what people you would like to meet, though. I want it to be a delightful gathering.'

'I like men who have a future, and women who have a past,' he answered. 'Or do you think that would make it a petticoat party?'

'I fear so,' she said, laughing, as she stood up. 'A thousand pardons, my dear Lady Ruxton,' she added. 'I didn't see you hadn't finished your cigarette.'

'Never mind, Lady Narborough. I smoke a great deal too much. I am going to limit myself, for the future.'

'Pray don't, Lady Ruxton,' said Lord Henry. 'Moderation is a fatal thing. Enough is as bad as a meal. More than enough is as good as a feast.'

Lady Ruxton glanced at him curiously. 'You must come and explain that to me some afternoon, Lord Henry. It sounds a fascinating theory,' she murmured, as she swept out of the room.

'Now, mind you don't stay too long over your politics and scandal,' cried Lady Narborough from the door. 'If you do, we are sure to squabble upstairs.'

The men laughed, and Mr. Chapman got up solemnly from the foot of the table and came up to the top. Dorian Gray changed his seat, and went and sat by Lord Henry. Mr. Chapman began to talk in a loud voice about the situation in the House of Commons. He guffawed at his adversaries. The word *doctrinaire*—word full of terror to the British mind—reappeared from time to time between his explosions. An alliterative prefix served as an ornament of oratory. He hoisted the Union Jack on the pinnacles of Thought. The inherited stupidity of the race—sound English common sense he jovially termed it—was shown to be the proper bulwark for Society.

A smile curved Lord Henry's lips, and he turned round and looked at Dorian.

'Are you better, my dear fellow?' he asked. 'You seemed rather out of sorts at dinner.'

'I am quite well, Harry. I am tired. That is all.'

'You were charming last night. The little Duchess is quite devoted to you. She tells me she is going down to Selby.'

'She has promised to come on the twentieth.'

'Is Monmouth to be there too?'

'Oh, yes, Harry.'

'He bores me dreadfully, almost as much as he bores her. She is very clever, too clever for a woman. She lacks the indefinable charm of weakness. It is the feet of clay that make the gold of the image precious. Her feet are very pretty, but they are not feet of clay. White porcelain feet, if you like. They have been through the fire, and what fire does not destroy, it hardens. She has had experiences.'

'How long has she been married?' asked Dorian.

'An eternity, she tells me. I believe, according to the peerage, it is ten years, but ten years with Monmouth must have been like eternity, with time thrown in. Who else is coming?'

'Oh, the Willoughbys, Lord Rugby and his wife, our hostess, Geoffrey Clouston, the usual set. I have asked Lord Grotrian.'

'I like him,' said Lord Henry. 'A great many people don't, but I find him charming. He atones for being occasionally somewhat over-dressed, by being always absolutely over-educated. He is a very modern type.'

'I don't know if he will be able to come, Harry. He may have to go to Monte Carlo with his father.'

'Ah! what a nuisance people's people are! Try and make him come. By the way, Dorian, you ran off very early last night. You left before eleven. What did you do afterwards? Did you go straight home?'

Dorian glanced at him hurriedly, and frowned. 'No, Harry,' he said at last, 'I did not get home till nearly three.'

'Did you go to the club?'

'Yes,' he answered. Then he bit his lip. 'No, I don't mean that. I didn't go to the club. I walked about. I forget what

I did. . . . How inquisitive you are, Harry! You always want to know what one has been doing. I always want to forget what I have been doing. I came in at half-past two, if you wish to know the exact time. I had left my latchkey at home, and my servant had to let me in. If you want any corroborative evidence on the subject you can ask him.'

Lord Henry shrugged his shoulders. 'My dear fellow, as if I cared! Let us go up to the drawing-room. No sherry, thank you, Mr. Chapman. Something has happened to you, Dorian. Tell me what it is. You are not yourself to-night.'

'Don't mind me, Harry. I am irritable, and out of temper. I shall come round and see you to-morrow or next day. Make my excuses to Lady Narborough. I shan't go upstairs. I shall go home. I must go home.'

'All right, Dorian. I dare say I shall see you to-morrow at tea-time. The Duchess is coming.'

'I will try to be there, Harry,' he said, leaving the room. As 'he drove back to his own house he was conscious that the sense of terror he thought he had strangled had come back to him. Lord Henry's casual questioning had made him lose his nerve for the moment, and he wanted his nerve still. Things that were dangerous had to be destroyed. He winced. He hated the idea of even touching them.

Yet it had to be done. He realised that, and when he had locked the door of his library, he opened the secret press into which he had thrust Basil Hallward's coat and bag. A huge fire was blazing. He piled another log on it. The smell of the singeing clothes and burning leather was horrible. It took him three-quarters of an hour to consume everything. At the end he felt faint and sick, and having lit some Algerian pastilles in a pierced copper brazier, he bathed his hands and forehead with a cool musk-scented vinegar.

Suddenly he started. His eyes grew strangely bright, and he gnawed nervously at his under-lip. Between two of the windows stood a large Florentine cabinet, made out of ebony, and inlaid with ivory and blue lapis. He watched it as though it were a thing that could fascinate and make afraid, as though it held something that he longed for and yet almost loathed. His breath quickened. A mad craving came over him. He lit a cigarette and then threw it away. His eyelids drooped till the long-fringed lashes almost touched his cheek. But he still watched the cabinet. At last he got up from the sofa on which he had been lying, went over to it, and, having unlocked it, touched some hidden spring. A triangular drawer passed slowly out. His fingers moved instinctively towards it, dipped in, and closed on something. It was a small Chinese box of black and gold-dust lacquer, elaborately wrought, the sides patterned with curved waves, and the silken cords hung with round crystals and tasselled in plaited metal threads. He opened it. Inside was a green paste, waxy in lustre, the odour curiously heavy and persistent.

He hesitated for some moments, with a strangely immobile smile upon his face. Then shivering, though the atmosphere of the room was terribly hot, he drew himself up, and glanced at the clock. It was twenty minutes to twelve. He put the box back, shutting the cabinet doors as he did so, and went into his bedroom.

As midnight was striking bronze blows upon the dusky air, Dorian Gray dressed commonly, and with a muffler wrapped round his throat, crept quietly out of the house. In Bond Street he found a hansom with a good horse. He hailed it, and in a low voice gave the driver an address.

The man shook his head. 'It is too far for me,' he muttered.

'Here is a sovereign for you,' said Dorian. 'You shall have another if you drive fast.'

'All right, sir,' answered the man, 'you will be there in an hour,' and after his fare had got in he turned his horse round, and drove rapidly towards the river.

CHAPTER XVI

A COLD rain began to fall, and the blurred street-lamps looked ghastly in the dripping mist. The public-houses were just closing, and dim men and women were clustering in broken groups round their doors. From some of the bars came the sound of horrible laughter. In others, drunkards brawled and screamed.

Lying back in the hansom, with his hat pulled over his forehead, Dorian Gray watched with listless eyes the sordid shame of the great city, and now and then he repeated to himself the words that Lord Henry had said to him on the first day they had met, 'To cure the soul by means of the senses, and the senses by means of the soul.' Yes, that was the secret. He had often tried it, and would try it again now. There were opium-dens, where one could buy oblivion, dens of horror where the memory of old sins could be destroyed by the madness of sins that were new.

The moon hung low in the sky like a yellow skull. From time to time a huge misshapen cloud stretched a long arm across and hid it. The gas-lamps grew fewer, and the streets more narrow and gloomy. Once the man lost his way, and had to drive back half a mile. A steam rose from the horse as it splashed up the puddles. The side-windows of the hansom were clogged with a grey-flannel mist.

'To cure the soul by means of the senses, and the senses by means of the soul!' How the words rang in his ears! His soul, certainly, was sick to death. Was it true that the senses could cure it? Innocent blood had been spilt. What could atone for that? Ah! for that there was no atonement; but though forgiveness was impossible, forgetfulness was possible still, and he was determined to forget, to stamp the thing out, to crush it as one would crush the adder that had stung one. Indeed, what right had Basil to have spoken to him as he had done? Who had made him a judge over others? He had said things that were dreadful, horrible, not to be endured.

On and on plodded the hansom, going slower, it seemed to him, at each step. He thrust up the trap, and called to the man to drive faster. The hideous hunger for opium began to gnaw at him. His throat burned, and his delicate hands twitched nervously together. He struck at the horse madly with his stick. The driver laughed, and whipped up. He laughed in answer, and the man was silent.

The way seemed interminable, and the streets like the black web of some sprawling spider. The monotony became unbearable, and, as the mist thickened, he felt afraid.

Then they passed by lonely brickfields. The fog was lighter here, and he could see the strange bottle-shaped kilns with their orange fan-like tongues of fire. A dog barked as they went by, and far away in the darkness some wandering sea-gull screamed. The horse stumbled in a rut, then swerved aside, and broke into a gallop.

After some time they left the clay road, and rattled again over rough-paven streets. Most of the windows were dark, but now and then fantastic shadows were silhouetted against some lamp-lit blind. He watched them curiously. They moved like monstrous marionettes, and made gestures like live things. He hated them. A dull rage was in his heart. As they turned a corner a woman yelled something at them from an open door, and two men ran after the hansom for about a hundred yards. The driver beat at them with his whip.

It is said that passion makes one think in a circle. Certainly with hideous iteration the bitten lips of Dorian Gray shaped and reshaped those subtle words that dealt with soul and sense, till he had found in them the full expression, as it were, of his mood, and justified, by intellectual approval, passions that without such justification would still have dominated his temper. From cell to cell of his brain crept the one thought; and the wild desire to live, most terrible of all man's appetites, quickened into force each trembling nerve and fibre. Ugliness that had once been hateful to him because it made things real, became dear to him now for that very reason. Ugliness was the one reality. The coarse brawl, the loathsome den, the crude violence of disordered life, the very vileness of thief and outcast, were more vivid, in their intense actuality of impression, than all the gracious shapes of Art, the dreamy shadows of Song. They were what he needed for forgetfulness. In three days he would be free.

Suddenly the man drew up with a jerk at the top of a dark lane. Over the low roofs and jagged chimney stacks of the houses rose the black masts of ships. Wreaths of white mist clung like ghostly sails to the yards.

'Somewhere about here, sir, ain't it?' he asked huskily through the trap.

Dorian started, and peered round. 'This will do,' he answered, and, having got out hastily, and given the driver the extra fare he had promised him, he walked quickly in the direction of the quay. Here and there a lantern gleamed at the stern of some huge merchantman. The light shook and splintered in the puddles. A red glare came from an outward-bound steamer that was coaling. The slimy pavement looked like a wet mackintosh.

He hurried on towards the left, glancing back now and then to see if he was being followed. In about seven or eight minutes he reached a small shabby house, that was wedged in between two gaunt factories. In one of the top windows stood a lamp. He stopped, and gave a peculiar knock.

After a little time he heard steps in the passage, and the chain being unhooked. The door opened quietly, and he went in without saying a word to the squat misshapen figure that flattened itself into the shadow as he passed. At the end of the hall hung a tattered green curtain that swayed and shook in the gusty wind which had followed him in from the street. He dragged it aside, and entered a long, low room which looked as if it had once been a third-rate dancing-saloon. Shrill flaring gas-jets, dulled and distorted in the fly-blown mirrors that faced them, were ranged round the walls. Greasy reflectors of ribbed tin backed them, making quivering discs of light. The floor was covered with ochre-coloured sawdust, trampled here and there into mud, and stained with dark rings of spilt liquor. Some Malays were crouching by a little charcoal stove playing with bone counters, and showing their white teeth as they chattered. In one corner, with his head buried in his arms, a sailor sprawled over a table, and by the tawdrily-painted bar that ran across one complete side stood two haggard women mocking an old man who was brushing the sleeves of his coat with an expression of disgust. 'He thinks he's got red ants on him,' laughed one of them, as Dorian passed by. The man looked at her in terror and began to whimper.

At the end of the room there was a little staircase, leading to a darkened chamber. As Dorian hurried up its three rickety steps, the heavy odour of opium met him. He heaved a deep breath, and his nostrils quivered with pleasure. When he entered, a young man with smooth yellow hair, who was bending over a lamp, lighting a long thin pipe, looked up at him, and nodded in a hesitating manner.

'You here, Adrian?' muttered Dorian.

'Where else should I be?' he answered, listlessly. 'None of the chaps will speak to me now.'

'I thought you had left England.'

'Darlington is not going to do anything. My brother paid the bill at last. George doesn't speak to me either. . . . I don't care,' he added, with a sigh. 'As long as one has this stuff, one doesn't want friends. I think I have had too many friends.'

Dorian winced, and looked round at the grotesque things that lay in such fantastic postures on the ragged mattresses. The twisted limbs, the gaping mouths, the staring lustreless eyes, fascinated him. He knew in what strange heavens they were suffering, and what dull hells were teaching them the secret of some new joy. They were better off than he was. He was prisoned in thought. Memory, like a horrible malady, was eating his soul away. From time to time he seemed to see the eyes of Basil Hallward looking at him. Yet he felt he could not stay. The presence of Adrian Singleton troubled him. He wanted to be where no one would know who he was. He wanted to escape from himself.

'I am going on to the other place,' he said, after a pause.

'On the wharf?'

'Yes.'

'That mad-cat is sure to be there. They won't have her in this place now.'

Dorian shrugged his shoulders. 'I am sick of women who love one. Women who hate one are much more interesting. Besides, the stuff is better.'

'Much the same.'

'I like it better. Come and have something to drink. I must have something.'

'I don't want anything,' murmured the young man.

'Never mind.'

Adrian Singleton rose up wearily, and followed Dorian to the bar. A half-caste, in a ragged turban and a shabby ulster, grinned a hideous greeting as he thrust a bottle of brandy and two tumblers in front of them. The women sidled up, and began to chatter. Dorian turned his back on them, and said something in a low voice to Adrian Singleton.

A crooked smile, like a Malay crease, writhed across the face of one of the women. 'We are very proud to-night,' she sneered.

'For God's sake don't talk to me,' cried Dorian, stamping his foot on the ground. 'What do you want? Money? Here it is. Don't ever talk to me again.'

Two red sparks flashed for a moment in the woman's sodden eyes, then flickered out, and left them dull and glazed. She tossed her head, and raked the coins off the counter with greedy fingers. Her companion watched her enviously.

'It's no use,' sighed Adrian Singleton. 'I don't care to go back. What does it matter? I am quite happy here.'

'You will write to me if you want anything, won't you?' said Dorian, after a pause.

'Perhaps.'

'Good night, then.'

'Good night,' answered the young man, passing up the steps, and wiping his parched mouth with a handkerchief.

Dorian walked to the door with a look of pain in his face. As he drew the curtain aside a hideous laugh broke from the painted lips of the woman who had taken his money. 'There goes the devil's bargain!' she hiccoughed, in a hoarse, voice.

'Curse you!' he answered, 'don't call me that.'

She snapped her fingers. 'Prince Charming is what you like to be called, ain't it?' she yelled after him.

The drowsy sailor leapt to his feet as she spoke, and looked wildly round. The sound of the shutting of the hall door fell on his ear. He rushed out as if in pursuit.

Dorian Gray hurried along the quay through the drizzling rain. His meeting with Adrian Singleton had strangely moved him, and he wondered if the ruin of that young life was really to be laid at his door, as Basil Hallward had said to him with such infamy of insult. He bit his lip, and for a few seconds his eyes grew sad. Yet, after all, what did it matter to him? One's days were too brief to take the burden of another's errors on one's shoulders. Each man lived his own life, and paid his own price for living it. The only pity was one had to pay so often for a single fault. One had to pay over and over again, indeed. In her dealings with man Destiny never closed her accounts.

There are moments, psychologists tell us, when the passion for sin, or for what the world calls sin, so dominates a nature, that every fibre of the body, as every cell of the brain, seems to be instinct with fearful impulses. Men and women at such moments lose the freedom of their will. They move to their terrible end as automatons move. Choice is taken from them, and conscience is either killed, or, if it lives at all, lives but to give rebellion its fascination, and disobedience its charm. For all sins, as theologians weary not of reminding us, are sins of disobedience. When that high spirit, that morning-star of evil, fell from heaven, it was as a rebel that he fell.

Callous, concentrated on evil, with stained mind, and soul hungry for rebellion, Dorian Gray hastened on, quickening his step as he went, but as he darted aside into a dim archway, that had served him often as a short cut to the ill-famed place where he was going, he felt himself suddenly seized from behind, and before he had time to defend himself he was thrust back against the wall, with a brutal hand round his throat.

He struggled madly for life, and by a terrible effort wrenched the tightening fingers away. In a second he heard the click of a revolver, and saw the gleam of a polished barrel pointing straight at his head, and the dusky form of a short thick-set man facing him.

'What do you want?' he gasped.

'Keep quiet,' said the man. 'If you stir, I shoot you.'

'You are mad. What have I done to you?'

'You wrecked the life of Sibyl Vane,' was the answer, 'and Sibyl Vane was my sister. She killed herself. I know it. Her death is at your door. I swore I would kill you in return. For years I have sought you. I had no clue, no trace. The two people who could have described you were dead. I knew nothing of you but the pet name she used to call you. I heard it to-night by chance. Make your peace with God, for to-night you are going to die.'

Dorian Gray grew sick with fear. 'I never knew her,' he stammered. 'I never heard of her. You are mad.'

'You had better confess your sin, for as sure as I am James Vane, you are going to die.' There was a horrible moment. Dorian did not know what to say or do. 'Down on your knees!' growled the man. 'I give you one minute to make your peace— no more. I go on board to-night for India, and I must do my job first. One minute. That's all.'

Dorian's arms fell to his side. Paralysed with terror, he did not know what to do. Suddenly a wild hope flashed across his brain. 'Stop,' he cried. 'How long ago is it since your sister died? Quick, tell me!'

'Eighteen years,' said the man. 'Why do you ask me? What do years matter?'

'Eighteen years,' laughed Dorian Gray, with a touch of triumph in his voice. 'Eighteen years! Set me under the lamp and look at my face!'

James Vane hesitated for a moment, not understanding what was meant. Then he seized Dorian Gray and dragged him from the archway.

Dim and wavering as was the wind-blown light, yet it served to show him the hideous error, as it seemed, into which he had fallen, for the face of the man he had sought to kill had all the bloom of boyhood, all the unstained purity of youth. He seemed little more than a lad of twenty summers. hardly older, if older indeed at all, than his sister had been when they had parted. so many years ago. It was obvious that this was not the man who had destroyed her life.

He loosened his hold and reeled back. 'My God! my God!' he cried, 'and I would have murdered you!'

Dorian Gray drew a long breath. 'You have been on the brink of committing a terrible crime, my man,' he said, looking at him sternly. 'Let this be a warning to you not to take vengeance into your own hands.'

'Forgive me, sir,' muttered James Vane. 'I was deceived. A chance word I heard in that damned den set me on the wrong track.'

'You had better go home, and put that pistol away, or you may get into trouble," said Dorian, turning on his heel, and going slowly down the street.

James Vane stood on the pavement in horror. He was trembling from head to foot. After a little while a black shadow .that had been creeping along the dripping wall, moved out into the light and came close to him with stealthy footsteps. He felt a hand laid on his arm and looked round with a start. It was one of the women who had been drinking at the bar.

'Why didn't you kill him?' she hissed out, putting her haggard face quite close to his. 'I knew you were following him when you rushed out from Daly's. You fool! You should have killed him. He has lots of money, and he's as bad as bad.'

'He is not the man I am looking for,' he answered, 'and I want no man's money. I want a man's life. The man whose life I want must be nearly forty now. This one is little more than a boy. Thank God, I have not got his blood upon my hands.'

The woman gave a bitter laugh. 'Little more than a boy!' she sneered. 'Why, man, it's nigh on eighteen years since Prince Charming made me what I am.'

'You lie!' cried James Vane.

She raised her hand up to heaven. 'Before God I am telling the truth,' she cried.

'Before God?'

'Strike me dumb if it ain't so. He is the worst one that comes here. They say he has sold himself to the devil for a pretty face. It's nigh on eighteen years since I met him. He hasn't changed much since then. I have though,' she added, with a sickly leer.

'You swear this?'

'I swear it,' came in hoarse echo from her flat mouth. 'But don't give me away to him,' she whined; 'I am afraid of him. Let me have some money for my night's lodging.'

He broke from her with an oath, and rushed to the corner of the street, but Dorian Gray had disappeared. When he looked back, the woman had vanished also.

CHAPTER XVII

A WEEK later Dorian Gray was sitting in the conservatory at Selby Royal talking to the pretty Duchess of Monmouth, who with her husband, a jaded-looking man of sixty, was amongst his guests. It was tea-time, and the mellow light of the huge lace-covered lamp that stood on the table lit up the delicate china and hammered silver of the service at which the Duchess was presiding. Her white hands were moving daintily among the cups, and her full red lips were smiling at something that Dorian had whispered to her. Lord Henry was lying back in a silk-draped wicker chair looking at them. On a peach-coloured divan sat Lady Narborough pretending to listen to the Duke's description of the last Brazilian beetle that he had added to his collection. Three young men in elaborate smoking-suits were handing tea-cakes to some of the women. The house-party consisted of twelve people, and there were more expected to arrive on the next day.

'What are you two talking about?' said Lord Henry, strolling over to the table, and putting his cup down. 'I hope Dorian has told you about my plan for rechristening everything, Gladys. It is a delightful idea.'

'But I don't want to be rechristened, Harry,' rejoined the Duchess, looking up at him with her wonderful eyes. 'I am quite satisfied with my own name, and I am sure Mr. Gray should be satisfied with his.'

'My dear Gladys, I would not alter either name for the world. They are both perfect. I was thinking chiefly of flowers. Yesterday I cut an orchid, for my buttonhole. It was a marvellous spotted thing, as effective as the seven deadly sins. In a thoughtless moment I asked one of the gardeners what it was called. He told me it was a fine specimen of *Robinsoniana*, or something dreadful of that kind. It is a sad truth, but we have lost the faculty of giving lovely names to things. Names are everything. I never quarrel with actions. My one quarrel is with words. That is the reason I hate vulgar realism in literature. The man who could call a spade a spade should be compelled to use one. It is the only thing he is fit for.'

'Then what should we call you, Harry?' she asked.

'His name is Prince Paradox,' said Dorian.

'I recognise him in a flash,' exclaimed the Duchess.

'I won't hear of it,' laughed Lord Henry, sinking into a chair. 'From a label there is no escape! I refuse the title.'

'Royalties may not abdicate,' fell as a warning from pretty lips.

'You wish me to defend my throne, then?'

'Yes.'

'I give the truths of to-morrow.'

'I prefer the mistakes of to-day,' she answered.

'You disarm me, Gladys,' he cried, catching the wilfulness of her mood.

'Of your shield, Harry: not of your spear.'

'I never tilt against Beauty,' he said, with a wave of his hand.

'That is your error, Harry, believe me. You value beauty far too much.'

'How can you say that? I admit that I think that it is better to be beautiful than to be good. But on the other hand no one is more ready than I am to acknowledge that it is better to be good than to be ugly.'

'Ugliness is one of the seven deadly sins, then?' cried the Duchess. 'What becomes of your simile about the orchid?'

'Ugliness is one of the seven deadly virtues, Gladys. You, as a good Tory, must not underrate them. Beer, the Bible, and the seven deadly virtues have made our England what she is.'

'You don't like your country, then?' she asked.

'I live in it.'

'That you may censure it the better.'

'Would you have me take the verdict of Europe on it?' he inquired.

'What do they say of us?'

'That Tartuffe has emigrated to England and opened a shop.'

'Is that yours, Harry?'

'I give it to you.'

'I could not use it. It is too true.'

'You need not be afraid. Our countrymen never recognise a description.'

'They are practical.'

'They are more cunning than practical. When they make up their ledger, they balance stupidity by wealth, and vice by hypocrisy.'

'Still, we have done great things.'

'Great things have been thrust on us, Gladys.'

'We have carried their burden.'

'Only as far as the Stock Exchange.'

She shook her head. 'I believe in the race,' she cried.

'It represents the survival of the pushing.'

'It has development.'

'Decay fascinates me more.'

'What of Art?' she asked.

'It is a malady.'

'Love?'

'An illusion.'

'Religion?'

'The fashionable substitute for Belief.'

'You are a sceptic.'

'Never! Scepticism is the beginning of Faith.'

'What are you?'

'To define is to limit.'

'Give me a clue.'

'Threads snap. You would lose your way in the labyrinth.'

'You bewilder me. Let us talk of someone else.'

'Our host is a delightful topic. Years ago he was christened Prince Charming.'

'Ah! don't remind me of that,' cried Dorian Gray.

'Our host is rather horrid this evening,' answered the Duchess, colouring. 'I believe he thinks that Monmouth married me on purely scientific principles as the best specimen he could find of a modern butterfly.'

'Well, I hope he won't stick pins into you, Duchess,' laughed Dorian.

'Oh! my maid does that already, Mr. Gray, when she is annoyed with me.'

'And what does she get annoyed with you about, Duchess?'

'For the most trivial things, Mr. Gray, I assure you. Usually because I come in at ten minutes to nine and tell her that I must be dressed by half-past eight.'

'How unreasonable of her! You should give her warning.'

'I daren't, Mr. Gray. Why, she invents hats for me. You remember the one I wore at Lady Hilstone's garden-party? You don't, but it is nice of you to pretend that you do. Well, she made it out of nothing. All good hats are made out of nothing.'

'Like all good reputations, Gladys,' interrupted Lord Henry. 'Every effect that one produces gives one an enemy. To be popular one must be a mediocrity.'

'Not with women,' said the Duchess, shaking her head;

'and women rule the world. I assure you we can't bear mediocrities. We women, as someone says, love with our ears, just as you men love with your eyes, if you ever love at all.'

'It seems to me that we never do anything else,' murmured Dorian.

'Ah! then, you never really love, Mr. Gray,' answered the Duchess, with mock sadness.

'My dear Gladys!' cried Lord Henry. 'How can you say that? Romance lives by repetition, and repetition converts an appetite into an art. Besides, each time that one loves is the only time one has ever loved. Difference of object does not alter singleness of passion. It merely intensifies it. We can have in life but one great experience at best, and the secret of life is to reproduce that experience as often as possible.'

'Even when one has been wounded by it, Harry?' asked the Duchess, after a pause.

'Especially when one has been wounded by it,' answered Lord Henry.

The Duchess turned and looked at Dorian Gray with a curious expression in her eyes. 'What do you say to that, Mr. Gray?' she inquired.

Dorian hesitated for a moment. Then he threw his head back and laughed. 'I always agree with Harry, Duchess.'

'Even when he is wrong?'

'Harry is never wrong, Duchess.'

'And does his philosophy make you happy?'

'I have never searched for happiness. Who wants happiness? I have searched for pleasure.'

'And found it, Mr. Gray?'

'Often. Too often.'

The Duchess sighed. 'I am searching for peace,' she said, 'and if I don't go and dress, I shall have none this evening.'

'Let me get you some orchids, Duchess,' cried Dorian, starting to his feet, and walking down the conservatory.

'You are flirting disgracefully with him,' said Lord Henry to his cousin. 'You had better take care. He is very fascinating.'

'If he were not, there would be no battle.'

'Greek meets Greek, then?'

'I am on the side of the Trojans. They fought for a woman.'

'They were defeated.'

'There are worse things than capture,' she answered.

'You gallop with a loose rein.'

'Pace gives life,' was the *riposte*.

'I shall write it in my diary to-night.'

'What?'

'That a burnt child loves the fire.'

'I am not even singed. My wings are untouched.'

'You use them for everything, except flight.'

'Courage has passed from men to women. It is a new experience for us.'

'You have a rival.'

'Who?'

He laughed. 'Lady Narborough,' he whispered. 'She perfectly adores him.'

'You fill me with apprehension. The appeal to Antiquity is fatal to us who are romanticists.'

'Romanticists! You have all the methods of science.'

'Men have educated us.'

'But not explained you.'

'Describe us as a sex,' was her challenge.

'Sphinxes without secrets.'

She looked at him, smiling. 'How long Mr. Gray is!' she said. 'Let us go and help him. I have not yet told him the colour of my frock.'

'Ah! you must suit your frock to his flowers, Gladys.'

'That would be a premature surrender.'

'Romantic Art begins with its climax.'

'I must keep an opportunity for retreat.'

'In the Parthian manner?'

'They found safety in the desert. I could not do that.'

'Women are not always allowed a choice,' he answered, but hardly had he finished the sentence before from the far end of the conservatory came a stifled groan, followed by the dull sound of a heavy fall. Everybody started up. The Duchess stood motionless in horror. And with fear in his eyes Lord Henry rushed through the flapping palms to find Dorian Gray lying face downwards on the tiled floor in a death-like swoon.

He was carried at once into the blue drawing-room, and laid upon one of the sofas. After a short time he came to himself, and looked round with a dazed expression.

'What has happened?' he asked. 'Oh! I remember. Am I safe here, Harry?' He began to tremble.

'My dear Dorian,' answered Lord Henry, 'you merely fainted. That was all. You must have overtired yourself. You had better not come down to dinner. I will take your place.'

'No, I will come down,' he said, struggling to his feet. 'I would rather come down. I must not be alone.'

He went to his room and dressed. There was a wild recklessness of gaiety in his manner as he sat at table, but now and then a thrill of terror ran through him when he remembered that, pressed against the window of the conservatory, like a white handkerchief, he had seen the face of James Vane watching him.

CHAPTER XVIII

THE next day he did not leave the house, and, indeed, spent most of the time in his own room, sick with a wild terror of dying, and yet indifferent to life itself. The consciousness of being hunted, snared, tracked down, had begun to dominate him. If the tapestry did but tremble in the wind, he shook. The dead leaves that were blown against the leaded panes seemed to him like his own wasted resolutions and wild regrets. When he closed his eyes, he saw again the sailor's face peering through the mist-stained glass, and horror seemed once more to lay its hand upon his heart.

But perhaps it had been only his fancy that had called vengeance out of the night, and set the hideous shapes of punishment before him. Actual life was chaos, but there was something terribly logical in the imagination. It was the imagination that set remorse to dog the feet of sin. It was the imagination that made each crime bear its misshapen brood. In the common world of fact the wicked were not punished, nor the good rewarded. Success was given to the strong, failure thrust upon the weak. That was all. Besides, had any stranger been prowling round the house he would have been seen by the servants or the keepers. Had any footmarks been found on the flower-beds, the gardeners would have reported it. Yes: it had been merely fancy. Sibyl Vane's brother had not come back to kill him. He had sailed away in his ship to founder in some winter sea. From him, at any rate, he was safe. Why, the man did not know who he was, could not know who he was. The mask of youth had saved him.

And yet if it had been merely an illusion, how terrible

it was to think that conscience could raise such fearful phantoms, and give them visible form, and make them move before one! What sort of life would his be, if day and night, shadows of his crime were to peer at him from silent corners, to mock him from secret places, to whisper in his ear as he sat at the feast, to wake him with icy fingers as he lay asleep! As the thought crept through his brain, he grew pale with terror, and the air seemed to him to have become suddenly colder. Oh! in what a wild hour of madness he had killed his friend! How ghastly the mere memory of the scene! He saw it all again. Each hideous detail came back to him with added horror. Out of the black cave of Time, terrible and swathed in scarlet, rose the image of his sin. When Lord Henry came in at six o'clock, he found him crying as one whose heart will break.

It was not till the third day that he ventured to go out. There was something in the clear, pine-scented air of that winter morning that seemed to bring him back his joyousness and his ardour for life. But it was not merely the physical conditions of environment that had caused the change. His own nature had revolted against the excess of anguish that had sought to maim and mar the perfection of its calm. With subtle and finely-wrought temperaments it is always so. Their strong passions must either bruise or bend. They either slay the man, or themselves die. Shallow sorrows and shallow loves live on. The loves and sorrows that are great are destroyed by their own plenitude. Besides, he had convinced himself that he had been the victim of a terror-stricken imagination, and looked back now on his fears with something of pity and not a little of contempt.

After breakfast he walked with the Duchess for an hour in the garden, and then drove across the park to join the shooting-party. The crisp frost lay like salt upon the grass.

The sky was an inverted cup of blue metal. A thin film of ice bordered the flat reed-grown lake.

At the corner of the pine-wood he caught sight of Sir Geoffrey Clouston, the Duchess's brother, jerking two spent cartridges out of his gun. He jumped from the cart, and having told the groom to take the mare home, made his way towards his guest through the withered bracken and rough undergrowth.

'Have you have good sport, Geoffrey?' he asked.

'Not very good, Dorian. I think most of the birds have gone to the open. I dare say it will be better after lunch, when we get to new ground.'

Dorian strolled along by his side. The keen aromatic air, the brown and red lights that glimmered in the wood, the hoarse cries of the beaters ringing out from time to time, and the sharp snaps of the guns that followed, fascinated him, and filled him with a sense of delightful freedom. He was dominated by the carelessness of happiness, by the high indifference of joy.

Suddenly from a lumpy tussock of old grass, some twenty yards in front of them, with black-tipped ears erect, and long hinder limbs throwing it forward, started a hare. It bolted for a thicket of alders. Sir Geoffrey put his gun to his shoulder, but there was something in the animal's grace of movement that strangely charmed Dorian Gray, and he cried out. at once, 'Don't shoot it, Geoffrey. Let it live.'

'What nonsense, Dorian!' laughed his companion, and as the hare bounded into the thicket he fired. There were two cries heard, the cry of a hare in pain, which is dreadful, the cry of a man in agony, which is worse.

'Good heavens! I have hit a beater!' exclaimed Sir Geoffrey. 'What an ass the man was to get in front of the guns! Stop shooting there!' he called out at the top of his voice. 'A man is hurt.'

The head-keeper came running up with a stick in his hand.

'Where, sir? Where is he?' he shouted. At the same time the firing ceased along the line.

'Here,' answered Sir Geoffrey, angrily, hurring towards the thicket. 'Why on earth don't you keep your men back? Spoiled my shooting for the day.'

Dorian watched them as they plunged into the alder-clump, brushing the lithe, swinging branches aside. In a few moments they emerged, dragging a body after them into the sunlight. He turned away in horror. It seemed to him that misfortune followed wherever he went. He heard Sir Geoffrey ask if the man was really dead, and the affirmative answer of the keeper. The wood seemed to him to have become suddenly alive with faces. There was the trampling of myriad feet, and the low buzz of voices. A great copper-breasted pheasant came beating through the boughs overhead.

After a few moments, that were to him, in his perturbed state, like endless hours of pain, he felt a hand laid on his shoulder. He started, and looked round.

'Dorian,' said Lord Henry, 'I had better tell them that the shooting is stopped for to-day. It would not look well to go on.'

'I wish it were stopped for ever, Harry,' he answered bitterly. 'The whole thing is hideous and cruel. Is the man . . .?'

He could not finish the sentence.

'I am afraid so,' rejoined Lord Henry. 'He got the whole charge of shot in his chest. He must have died almost instantaneously. Come; let us go home.'

They walked side by side in the direction of the avenue for nearly fifty yards without speaking. Then Dorian looked at Lord Henry and said, with a heavy sigh, 'It is a bad omen, Harry, a very bad omen.'

'What is?' asked Lord Henry. 'Oh, this accident, I suppose. My dear fellow, it can't be helped. It was the man's own fault. Why did he get in front of the guns? Besides, it's nothing to us. It is rather awkward for Geoffrey, of course. It does not do to pepper beaters. It makes people think that one is a wild shot. And Geoffrey is not; he shoots very straight. But there is no use talking about the matter.'

Dorian shook his head. 'It is a bad omen, Harry. I feel as if something horrible were going to happen to some of us. To myself, perhaps,' he added, passing his hand over his eyes, with a gesture of pain.

The elder man laughed. 'The only horrible thing in the world is *ennui*, Dorian. That is the one sin for which there is no forgiveness. But we are not likely to suffer from it, unless these fellows keep chattering about this thing at dinner. I must tell them that the subject is to be tabooed. As for omens, there is no such thing as an omen. Destiny does not send us heralds. She is too wise or too cruel for that. Besides, what on earth could happen to you, Dorian? You have everything in the world that a man can want. There is no one who would not be delighted to change places with you.'

'There is no one with whom I would not change places, Harry. Don't laugh like that. I am telling you the truth. The wretched peasant who has just died is better off than I am. I have no terror of Death. It is the coming of Death that terrifies me. Its monstrous wings seem to wheel in the leaden air around me. Good heavens! don't you see a man moving behind the trees there, watching me, waiting for me?'

Lord Henry looked in the direction in which the trembling gloved hand was pointing. 'Yes,' he said, smiling, 'I see the gardener waiting for you. I suppose he wants to ask you what flowers you wish to have on the table to-night. How absurdly nervous you are, my dear fellow! You must come and see my doctor, when we get back to town.'

Dorian heaved a sigh of relief as he saw the gardener approaching. The man touched his hat, glanced for a moment at Lord Henry in a hesitating manner, and then produced a letter, which he handed to his master. 'Her Grace told me to wait for an answer,' he murmured.

Dorian put the letter into his pocket. 'Tell her Grace that I am coming in,' he said, coldly. The man turned round, and went rapidly in the direction of the house.

'How fond women are of doing dangerous things!' laughed Lord Henry. 'It is one of the qualities in them that I admire most. A woman will flirt with anybody in the world as long as other people are looking on.'

'How fond you are of saying dangerous things, Harry! In the present instance you are quite astray. I like the Duchess very much, but I don't love her.'

'And the Duchess loves you very much, but she likes you less, so you are excellently matched.'

'You are talking scandal, Harry, and there is never any basis for scandal.'

'The basis of every scandal is an immoral certainty,' said Lord Henry, lighting a cigarette.

'You would sacrifice anybody, Harry, for the sake of an epigram.'

'The world goes to the altar of its own accord,' was the answer.

'I wish I could love,' cried Dorian Gray, with a deep note of pathos in his voice. 'But I seem to have lost the passion, and forgotten the desire. I am too much concentrated on myself. My own personality has become a burden to me. I want to escape, to go away, to forget. It was silly of me to come down here at all. I think I shall send a wire to

Harvey to have the yacht got ready. On a yacht one is safe.'

'Safe from what, Dorian? You are in some trouble. Why not tell me what it is? You know I would help you'.

'I can't tell you, Harry,' he answered, sadly. 'And I dare say it is only a fancy of mine. This unfortunate accident has upset me. I have a horrible presentiment that something of the kind may happen to me.'

'What nonsense!'

'I hope it is, but I can't help feeling it. Ah! here is the Duchess, looking like Artemis in a tailor-made gown. You see we have come back, Duchess.'

'I have heard all about it, Mr. Gray,' she answered. 'Poor Geoffrey is terribly upset. And it seems that you asked him not to shoot the hare. How curious!'

'Yes, it was very curious. I don't know what made me say it. Some whim, I suppose. It looked the loveliest of little live things. But I am sorry they told you about the man. It is a hideous subject.'

'It is an annoying subject,' broke in Lord Henry. 'It has no psychological value at all. Now if Geoffrey had done the thing on purpose, how interesting he would be! I should like to know someone who had committed a real murder.'

'How horrid of you, Harry!' cried the Duchess. 'Isn't it, Mr. Gray? Harry, Mr. Gray is ill again. He is going to faint.'

Dorian drew himself up with an effort, and smiled. 'It is nothing, Duchess,' he murmured; 'my nerves are dreadfully out of order. That is all. I am afraid I walked too far this morning. I didn't hear what Harry said. Was it very bad? You must tell me some other time. I think I must go and lie down. You will excuse me, won't you?'

They had reached the great flight of steps that led from

the conservatory on to the terrace. As the glass door closed behind Dorian, Lord Henry turned and looked at the Duchess with his slumberous eyes. 'Are you very much in love with him?' he asked.

She did not answer for some time, but stood gazing at the landscape. 'I wish I knew,' she said at last.

He shook his head. 'Knowledge would be fatal. It is the uncertainty that charms one. A mist makes things wonderful.'

'One may lose one's way.'

'All ways end at the same point, my dear Gladys.'

'What is that?'

'Disillusion.'

'It was my *début* in life,' she sighed.

'It came to you crowned.'

'I am tired of strawberry leaves.'

'They become you.'

'Only in public.'

'You would miss them,' said Lord Henry.

'I will not part with a petal.'

'Monmouth has ears.'

'Old age is dull of hearing.'

'Has he never been jealous?'

'I wish he had been.'

He glanced about as if in search of something. 'What are you looking for?' she inquired.

'The button from your foil,' he answered. 'You have dropped it.'

She laughed. 'I have still the mask.'

'It makes your eyes lovelier,' was his reply.

She laughed again. Her teeth showed like white seeds in a scarlet fruit.

Upstairs, in his own room, Dorian Gray was lying on a sofa, with terror in every tingling fibre of his body. Life had suddenly become too hideous a burden for him to bear. The dreadful death of the unlucky beater, shot in the thicket like a wild animal, had seemed to him to prefigure death for himself also. He had nearly swooned at what Lord Henry had said in a chance mood of cynical jesting.

At five o'clock he rang his bell for his servant and gave him orders to pack his things for the night-express to town, and to have the brougham at the door by eight-thirty. He was determined not to sleep another night at Selby Royal. It was an ill-omened place. Death walked there in the sunlight. The grass of the forest had been spotted with blood.

Then he wrote a note to Lord Henry, telling him that he was going up to town to consult his doctor, and asking him to entertain his guests in his absence. As he was putting it into the envelope, a knock came to the door, and his valet informed him that the head-keeper wished to see him. He frowned, and bit his lip. 'Send him in,' he muttered, after some moments' hesitation.

As soon as the man entered Dorian pulled his cheque-book out of a drawer, and spread it out before him.

'I suppose you have come about the unfortunate accident of this morning, Thornton?' he said, taking up a pen.

'Yes, sir,' answered the gamekeeper.

'Was the poor fellow married? Had he any people dependent on him?' asked Dorian, looking bored. 'If so, I should not like them to be left in want, and will send them any sum of money you may think necessary.'

'We don't know who he is, sir. That is what I took the liberty of coming to you about.'

'Don't know who he is?' said Dorian, listlessly. 'What do you mean? Wasn't he one of your men?'

'No, sir. Never saw him before. Seems like a sailor, sir.'

The pen dropped from Dorian Gray's hand, and he felt as if

his heart had suddenly stopped beating. 'A sailor?' he cried out. 'Did you say a sailor?'

'Yes, sir. He looks as if he had been a sort of sailor; tattooed on both arms, and that kind of thing.'

'Was there anything found on him?' said Dorian, leaning forward and looking at the man with startled eyes. 'Anything that would tell his name?'

'Some money, sir—not much, and a six-shooter. There was no name of any kind. A decent-looking man, sir, but rough-like. A sort of sailor, we think.'

Dorian started to his feet. A terrible hope fluttered past him. He clutched at it madly. 'Where is the body?' he exclaimed. 'Quick! I must see it at once.'

'It is in an empty stable in the Home Farm, sir. The folk don't like to have that sort of thing in their houses. They say a corpse brings bad luck.'

'The Home Farm! Go there at once and meet me. Tell one of the grooms to bring my horse round. No. Never mind. I'll go to the stables myself. It will save time.'

In less than a quarter of an hour Dorian Gray was galloping down the long avenue as hard as he could go. The trees seemed to sweep past him in spectral procession, and wild shadows to fling themselves across his path. Once the mare swerved at a white gate-post and nearly threw him. He lashed her across the neck with his crop. She cleft the dusky air like an arrow. The stones flew from her hoofs.

At last he reached the Home Farm. Two men were loitering in the yard. He leapt from the saddle and threw the reins to one of them. In the farthest stable a light was glimmering. Something seemed to tell him that the body was there, and he hurried to the door, and put his hand upon the latch.

There he paused for a moment, feeling that he was on the brink of a discovery that would either make or mar his life. Then he thrust the door open, and entered.

On a heap of sacking in the far corner was lying the dead body of a man dressed in a coarse shirt and a pair of blue trousers. A spotted handkerchief had been placed over the face. A coarse candle, stuck in a bottle, sputtered beside it.

Dorian Gray shuddered. He felt that his could not be the hand to take the handkerchief away, and called out to one of the farm-servants to come to him.

'Take that thing off the face. I wish to see it,' he said, clutching at the doorpost for support.

When the farm-servant had done so, he stepped forward. A cry of joy broke from his lips. The man who had been shot in the thicket was James Vane.

He stood there for some minutes looking at the dead body. As he rode home, his eyes were full of tears, for he knew he was safe.

CHAPTER XIX

'THERE is no use your telling me that you are going to be good,' cried Lord Henry, dipping his white fingers into a red copper bowl filled with rose-water. 'You're quite perfect. Pray, don't change.'

Dorian Gray shook his head. 'No, Harry, I have done too many dreadful things in my life. I am not going to do any more. I began my good actions yesterday.'

'Where were you yesterday?'

'In the country, Harry. I was staying at a little inn by myself.'

'My dear boy,' said Lord Henry, smiling, 'anybody can be good in the country. There are no temptations there. That is the reason why people who live out of town are so absolutely uncivilised. Civilisation is not by any means an easy thing to attain to. There are only two ways by which man can reach it. One is by being cultured, the other by being corrupt. Country people have no opportunity of being either, so they stagnate.'

'Culture and corruption,' echoed Dorian. 'I have known something of both. It seems terrible to me now that they should ever be found together. For I have a new ideal, Harry. I am going to alter. I think I have altered.'

'You have not yet told me what your good action was. Or did you say you had done more than one?' asked his companion, as he spilt into his plate a little crimson pyramid of seeded strawberries, and through a perforated shell-shaped spoon snowed white sugar upon them.

'I can tell you, Harry. It is not a story I could tell to anyone else. I spared somebody. It sounds vain, but you understand what I mean. She was quite beautiful, and wonderfully like Sibyl Vane. I think it was that which first attracted me to her. You remember Sibyl, don't you? How long ago that seems! Well, Hetty was not one of our own class, of course. She was simply a girl in a village. But I really loved her. I am quite sure that I loved her. All during this wonderful May that we have been having, I used to run down and see her two or three times a week. Yesterday she met me in a little orchard. The apple-blossoms kept tumbling down on her hair, and she was laughing. We were to have gone away together this morning at dawn. Suddenly I determined to leave her as flower-like as I had found her.'

'I should think the novelty of the emotion must have given you a thrill of real pleasure, Dorian,' interrupted Lord Henry. 'But I can finish your idyll for you. You gave her good advice, and broke her heart. That was the beginning of your reformation.'

'Harry, you are horrible! You mustn't say these dreadful things. Hetty's heart is not broken. Of course she cried, and all that. But there is no disgrace upon her. She can live, like Perdita, in her garden of mint and marigold.'

'And weep over a faithless Florizel,' said Lord Henry, laughing, as he leant back in his chair. 'My dear Dorian, you have the most curiously boyish moods. Do you think this girl will ever be really contented now with anyone of her own rank? I suppose she will be married some day to a rough carter or a grinning ploughman. Well, the fact of having met you, and loved you, will teach her to despise her husband, and she will be wretched. From a moral point of view, I cannot say that I think much of your great renunciation. Even as a beginning, it is poor. Besides, how do you know that Hetty isn't floating at the present moment in some star-lit mill-pond, with lovely water-lilies round her, like Ophelia?'

'I can't bear this, Harry! You mock at everything, and then suggest the most serious tragedies. I am sorry I told you now. I don't care what you say to me. I know I was right in acting as I did. Poor Hetty! As I rode past the farm this morning, I saw her white face at the window, like a spray of jasmine. Don't let us talk about it any more, and don't try to persuade me that the first good action I have done for years, the first little bit of self-sacrifice I have ever known, is really a sort of sin. I want to be better. I am going to be better. Tell me something about yourself. What is going on in town? I have not been to the club for days.'

'The people are still discussing poor Basil's disappearance.'

'I should have thought they had got tired of that by this time,' said Dorian, pouring himself out some wine and frowning slightly.

'My dear boy, they have only been talking about it for six weeks, and the British public are really not equal to the mental strain of having more than one topic every three months. They have been very fortunate lately, however. They have had my own divorce-case, and Alan Campbell's suicide. Now they have got the mysterious disappearance of an artist. Scotland Yard still insists that the man in the grey ulster who left for Paris by the midnight train on the ninth of November was poor Basil, and the French police declare that Basil never arrived in Paris at all. I suppose in about a fortnight we shall be told that he has been seen in San Francisco. It is an odd thing, but everyone who disappears is said to be seen at San Francisco. It must be a delightful city, and possess all the attractions of the next world.'

'What do you think has happened to Basil?' asked Dorian, holding up his Burgundy against the light, and wondering how it was that he could discuss the matter so calmly.

'I have not the slightest idea. If Basil chooses to hide

himself, it is no business of mine. If he is dead, I don't want to think about him. Death is the only thing that ever terrifies me. I hate it.'

'Why?' said the younger man, wearily.

'Because,' said Lord Henry, passing beneath his nostrils the gilt trellis of an open vinaigrette box, 'one can survive everything nowadays except that. Death and vulgarity are the only two facts in the nineteenth century that one cannot explain away. Let us have our coffee in the music-room, Dorian. You must play Chopin to me. The man with whom my wife ran away played Chopin exquisitely. Poor Victoria! I was very fond of her. The house is rather lonely without her. Of course married life is merely a habit, a bad habit. But then one regrets the loss even of one's worst habits. Perhaps one regrets them the most. They are such an essential part of one's personality.'

Dorian said nothing, but rose from the table and, passing into the next room, sat down to the piano and let his fingers stray across the white and black ivory of the keys. After the coffee had been brought in, he stopped, and, looking over at Lord Henry, said, 'Harry, did it ever occur to you that Basil was murdered?'

Lord Henry yawned. 'Basil was very popular, and always wore a Waterbury watch. Why should he have been murdered? He was not clever enough to have enemies. Of course he had a wonderful genius for painting. But a man can paint like Velasquez and yet be as dull as possible. Basil was really·rather dull. He only interested me once, and that was when he told me, years ago, that he had a wild adoration for you, and that you were the dominant motive of his art.'

'I was very fond of Basil,' said Dorian with a note of sadness in his voice. 'But don't people say that he was murdered?'

'Oh, some of the papers do. It does not seem to me to be at all probable. I know there are dreadful places in Paris, but Basil was not the sort of man to have gone to them. He had no curiosity. It was his chief defect.'

'What would you say, Harry, if I told you that I had murdered Basil?' said the younger man. He watched him intently after he had spoken.

'I would say, my dear fellow, that you were posing for a character that doesn't suit you. All crime is vulgar, just as all vulgarity is crime. It is not in you, Dorian, to commit a murder. I am sorry if I hurt your vanity by saying so, but I assure you it is true. Crime belongs exclusively to the lower orders. I don't blame them in the smallest degree. I should fancy that crime was to them what art is to us, simply a method of procuring extraordinary sensations.'

'A method of procuring sensations? Do you think, then, that a man who has once committed a murder could possibly do the same crime again? Don't tell me that.'

'Oh! anything becomes a pleasure if one does it too often,' cried Lord Henry, laughing. 'That is one of the most important secrets of life. I should fancy, however, that murder is always a mistake. One should never do anything that one cannot talk about after dinner. But let us pass from poor Basil. I wish I could believe that he had come to such a really romantic end as you suggest; but I can't. I dare say he fell into the Seine off an omnibus, and that the conductor hushed up the scandal. Yes: I should fancy that was his end. I see him lying now on his back under those dull-green waters with the heavy barges floating over him, and long weeds catching in his hair. Do you know, I don't think he would have done much more good work. During the last ten years his painting had gone off very much.'

Dorian heaved a sigh, and Lord Henry strolled across the room and began to stroke the head of a curious Java parrot, a large grey-plumaged bird, with pink crest and tail, that was balancing itself upon a bamboo perch. As his pointed fingers touched it, it dropped the white scurf of crinkled lids over black glass-like eyes, and began to sway backwards and forwards.

'Yes,' he continued, turning round, and taking his handkerchief out of his pocket; 'his painting had quite gone off. It seemed to me to have lost something. It had lost an ideal. When you and he ceased to be great friends, he ceased to be a great artist. What was it separated you? I suppose he bored you. If so, he never forgave you. It's a habit bores have. By the way, what has become of that wonderful portrait he did of you? I don't think I have ever seen it since he finished it. Oh! I remember your telling me years ago that you had sent it down to Selby, and that it had got mislaid or stolen on the way. You never got it back? What a pity! It was really a masterpiece. I remember I wanted to buy it. I wish I had now. It belonged to Basil's best period. Since then, his work was that curious mixture of bad painting and good intentions that always entitles a man to be called a representative British artist. Did you advertise for it? You should.'

'I forget,' said Dorian. 'I suppose I did. But I never really liked it. I am sorry I sat for it. The memory of the thing is hateful to me. Why do you talk of it? It used to remind me of those curious lines in some play—*Hamlet*, I think— how do they run?

> '"Like the painting of a sorrow,
> A face without a heart."

Yes: that is what it was like.'

Lord Henry laughed. 'If a man treats life artistically, his brain is his heart,' he answered, sinking into an armchair.

Dorian Gray shook his head, and struck some soft chords on the piano. '"Like the painting of a sorrow,"' he repeated. '"a face without a heart."'

The elder man lay back and looked at him with half-closed eyes. 'By the way, Dorian,' he said, after a pause, '"what does it profit a man if he gain the whole world and lose"—how does the quotation run?—"his own soul"?'

The music jarred and Dorian Gray started, and stared at his friend. 'Why do you ask me that, Harry?'

'My dear fellow,' said Lord Henry, elevating his eyebrows in surprise, 'I asked you because I thought you might be able to give me an answer. That is all. I was going through the Park last Sunday, and close by the Marble Arch there stood a little crowd of shabby-looking people listening to some vulgar street-preacher. As I passed by, I heard the man yelling out that question to his audience. It struck me as being rather dramatic. London is very rich in curious effects of that kind. A wet Sunday, an uncouth Christian in a mackintosh, a ring of sickly white faces under a broken roof of dripping umbrellas, and a wonderful phrase flung into the air by shrill, hysterical lips—it was really very good in its way, quite a suggestion. I thought of telling the prophet that Art had a soul, but that man had not. I am afraid, however, he would not have understood me.'

'Don't, Harry. The soul is a terrible reality. It can be bought, and sold, and bartered away. It can be poisoned, or made perfect. There is a soul in each one of us. I know it.'

'Do you feel quite sure of that, Dorian?'

'Quite sure.'

'Ah! then it must be an illusion. The things one feels absolutely certain about are never true. That is the fatality of Faith, and the lesson of Romance. How grave you are! Don't be so serious. What have you or I to do with the superstitions of our age? No: we have given up our belief in the soul. Play me something. Play me a nocturne, Dorian, and, as you play, tell me, in a low voice, how you have kept your youth. You must have some secret. I am only ten years older than you are, and I am wrinkled, and worn, and yellow. You are really wonderful, Dorian. You have never looked more charming than you do to-night. You remind me of the day I saw you first. You were rather cheeky, very shy, and absolutely extraordinary. You have changed, of course, but not in appearance. I wish you would tell me your secret. To get back my youth I would do anything in the world, except take exercise, get up early, or be respectable. Youth! There is nothing like it. It's absurd to talk of the ignorance of youth. The only people to whose opinions I listen now with any respect are people much younger than myself. They seem in front of me. Life has revealed to them her latest wonder. As for the aged, I always contradict the aged. I do it on principle. If you ask them their opinion on something that happened yesterday, they solemnly give you the opinions current in 1820, when people wore high stocks, believed in everything, and knew absolutely nothing. How lovely that thing you are playing is! I wonder did Chopin write it at Majorca, with the sea weeping round the villa, and the salt spray dashing against the panes? It is marvellously romantic. What a blessing it is that there is one art left to us that is not imitative! Don't stop. I want music to-night. It seems to me that you are the young Apollo, and that I am Marsyas listening to you. I have sorrows, Dorian, of my own, that even you know nothing of. The tragedy of old age is not that one is old, but that one is young. I am amazed sometimes at my own sincerity. Ah, Dorian, how happy you are! What an exquisite life you have had! You have drunk deeply of everything. You have crushed the grapes against your palate. Nothing has been hidden from you. And it has all been to you no more than the sound of music. It has not marred you. You are still the same.'

'I am not the same, Harry.'

'Yes: you are the same. I wonder what the rest of your life will be. Don't spoil it by renunciations. At present you are a perfect type. Don't make yourself incomplete. You are quite flawless now. You need not shake your head: you know you are. Besides, Dorian, don't deceive yourself. Life is not governed by will or intention. Life is a question of nerves, and fibres, and slowly built-up cells in which thought hides itself and passion has its dreams. You may fancy yourself safe, and think yourself strong. But a chance tone of colour in a room or a morning sky, a particular perfume that you had once loved and that brings subtle memories with it, a line from a forgotten poem that you had come across again, a cadence from a piece of music that you had ceased to play—I tell you, Dorian, that it is on things like these that our lives depend. Browning writes about that somewhere; but our own senses will imagine them for us. There are moments when the odour of *lilas blanc* passes suddenly across me, and I have to live the strangest month of my life over again. I wish I could change places with you, Dorian. The world has cried out against us both, but it has always worshipped you. It always will worship you. You are the type of what the age is searching for, and what it is afraid it has found. I am so glad that you have never done anything, never carved a statue, or painted a picture, or produced anything outside of yourself! Life has been your art. You have set yourself to music. Your days are your sonnets.'

Dorian rose up from the piano and passed his hand through his hair. 'Yes, life has been exquisite,' he murmured, 'but I am not going to have the same life, Harry. And you must not say these extravagant things to me. You don't know everything about me. I think that if you did, even you would turn from me. You laugh. Don't laugh.'

'Why have you stopped playing, Dorian? Go back and give me the nocturne over again. Look at that great honey-coloured moon that hangs in the dusky air. She is waiting for you to charm her, and if you play she will come closer to the earth. You won't? Let us go to the club, then. It has been a charming evening, and we must end it charmingly. There is someone at White's who wants immensely to know you —young Lord Poole, Bournemouth's eldest son. He has already copied your neckties, and has begged me to introduce him to you. He is quite delightful, and rather reminds me of you.'

'I hope not,' said Dorian, with a sad look in his eyes. 'But I am tired to-night, Harry. I shan't go to the club. It is nearly eleven, and I want to go to bed early.'

'Do stay. You have never played so well as to-night. There was something in your touch that was wonderful. It had more expression than I had ever heard from it before.'

'It is because I am going to be good,' he answered, smiling. 'I am a little changed already.'

'You cannot change to me, Dorian,' said Lord Henry. 'You and I will always be friends.'

'Yet you poisoned me with a book once. I should not forgive that. Harry, promise me that you will never lend that book to anyone. It does harm.'

'My dear boy, you are really beginning to moralise. You will soon be going about like the converted, and the revivalist, warning people against all the sins of which you have grown tired. You are much too delightful to do that. Besides, it is no use. You and I are what we are, and will be what we will be. As for being poisoned by a book, there is no such thing as that. Art has no influence upon action. It annihilates the desire to act. It is superbly sterile. The books that the world calls immoral are books that show the world its own shame. That is all. But we won't discuss literature. Come round to-morrow. I am going to ride at eleven. We might go together, and I will take you to lunch afterwards with Lady Branksome. She is a charming woman, and wants to consult you about some tapestries she is thinking of buying. Mind you come. Or shall we lunch with our little Duchess? She says she never sees you now. Perhaps you are tired of Gladys? I thought you would be. Her clever tongue gets on one's nerves. Well, in any case, be here at eleven.'

'Must I really come, Harry?'

'Certainly. The Park is quite lovely now. I don't think there have been such lilacs since the year I met you.'

'Very well. I shall be here at eleven,' said Dorian. 'Good night, Harry.' As he reached the door he hesitated for a moment, as if he had something more to say. Then he sighed and went out.

CHAPTER XX

IT was a lovely night, so warm that he threw his coat over his arm, and did not even put his silk scarf round his throat. As he strolled home, smoking his cigarette, two young men in evening dress passed him. He heard one of them whisper to the other, 'That is Dorian Gray.' He remembered how pleased he used to be when he was pointed out, or stared at, or talked about. He was tired of hearing his own name now. Half the charm of the little village where he had been so often lately was that no one knew who he was. He had often told the girl whom he had lured to love him that he was poor, and she had believed him. He had told her once that he was wicked, and she had laughed at him, and answered that wicked people were always very old and very ugly. What a laugh she had!—just like a thrush singing. And how pretty she had been in her cotton dresses and her large hats! She knew nothing, but she had everything that he had lost.

When he reached home, he found his servant waiting up for him. He sent him to bed, and threw himself down on the sofa in the library, and began to think over some of the things that Lord Henry had said to him.

Was it really true that one could never change? He felt a wild longing for the unstained purity of his boyhood—his rose-white boyhood, as Lord Henry had once called it. He knew that he had tarnished himself, filled his mind with corruption, and given horror to his fancy; that he had been an evil influence to others, and had experienced a terrible joy in being so; and that, of the lives that had crossed his own, it had been the fairest and the most full of promise that he had brought to shame. But was it all irretrievable? Was there no hope for him?

Ah! in what a monstrous moment of pride and passion he had prayed that the portrait should bear the burden of his days, and he keep the unsullied splendour of eternal youth! All his failure had been due to that. Better for him that each sin of his life had brought its sure, swift penalty along with it. There was purification in punishment. Not 'Forgive us our sins,' but 'Smite us for our iniquities' should be the prayer of a man to a most just God.

The curiously-carved mirror that Lord Henry had given to him, so many years ago now, was standing on the table, and the white-limbed Cupids laughed round it as of old. He took it up, as he had done on that night of horror, when he had first noted the change in the fatal picture, and with wild, tear-dimmed eyes looked into its polished shield. Once, someone who had terribly loved him had written to him a mad letter, ending with these idolatrous words: 'The world is changed because you are made of ivory and gold. The curves of your lips rewrite history.' The phrases came back to his memory, and he repeated them over and over to himself. Then he loathed his own beauty, and, flinging the mirror on the floor, crushed it into silver splinters beneath his heel. It was his beauty that had ruined him, his beauty and the youth that he had prayed for. But for those two things, his life might have been free from stain. His beauty had been to him but a mask, his youth but a mockery. What was youth at best? A green, an unripe time, a time of shallow moods and sickly thoughts. Why had he worn its livery? Youth had spoiled him.

It was better not to think of the past. Nothing could alter that. It was of himself, and of his own future, that he had to think. James Vane was hidden in a nameless grave in Selby churchyard. Alan Campbell had shot himself one night in his laboratory, but had not revealed the secret that he had been forced to know. The excitement, such as it was, over Basil Hallward's disappearance would soon pass away. It was already waning. He was perfectly safe there. Nor, indeed, was it the death of Basil Hallward that weighed most upon his mind. It was the living death of his own soul that troubled him. Basil had painted the portrait that had marred his life. He could not forgive him that. It was the portrait that had done everything. Basil had said things to him that were unbearable, and that he had yet borne with patience. The murder had been simply the madness of a moment. As for Alan Campbell, his suicide had been his own act. He had chosen to do it. It was nothing to him.

A new life! That was what he wanted. That was what he was waiting for. Surely he had begun it already. He had spared one innocent thing, at any rate. He would never again tempt innocence. He would be good.

As he thought of Hetty Merton, he began to wonder if the portrait in the locked room had changed. Surely it was not still so horrible as it had been? Perhaps if his life became pure, he would be able to expel every sign of evil passion from the face. Perhaps the signs of evil had already gone away. He would go and look.

He took the lamp from the table and crept upstairs. As he unbarred the door a smile of joy flitted across his strangely young-looking face and lingered for a moment about his lips. Yes, he would be good, and the hideous thing that he had hidden away would no longer be a terror to him. He felt as if the load had been lifted from him already.

He went in quietly, locking the door behind him, as was his custom, and dragged the purple hanging from the portrait. A cry of pain and indignation broke from him. He could see no change, save that in the eyes there was a look of cunning, and in the mouth the curved wrinkle of the hypocrite. The thing was still loathsome—more loathsome, if possible, than before—and the scarlet dew that spotted the hand seemed brighter, and more like blood newly spilt. Then he trembled. Had it been merely vanity that had made him do his one good deed? Or the desire for a new sensation, as Lord Henry had hinted, with his mocking laugh? Or that passion to act a part that sometimes makes us do things finer than we are ourselves? Or, perhaps, all these? And why was the red stain larger than it had been? It seemed to have crept like a horrible disease over the wrinkled fingers. There was blood on the painted feet, as though the thing had dripped—blood even on the hand that had not held the knife. Confess? Did it mean that he was to confess? To give himself up, and be put to death? He laughed. He felt that the idea was monstrous. Besides, even if he did confess, who would believe him? There was no trace of the murdered man anywhere. Everything belonging to him had been destroyed. He himself had burned what had been below-stairs. The world would simply say that he was mad. They would shut him up if he persisted in his story. . . . Yet it was his duty to confess, to suffer public shame, and to make public atonement. There was a God who called upon men to tell their sins to earth as well as to heaven. Nothing that he could do would cleanse him till he had told his own sin. His sin? He shrugged his shoulders. The death of Basil Hallward seemed very little to him. He was thinking of Hetty Merton. For it was an unjust mirror, this mirror of his soul that he was looking at. Vanity? Curiosity? Hypocrisy? Had there been nothing more in his renunciation than that? There had been something more. At least he thought so. But who could tell? . . . No. There had been nothing more. Through vanity he had spared her. In hypocrisy he had worn the mask of goodness.

'Mr. Dorian Gray's, sir,' answered the policeman.

They looked at each other, as they walked away, and sneered. One of them was Sir Henry Ashton's uncle.

Inside, in the servants' part of the house, the half-clad domestics were talking in low whispers to each other. Old Mrs. Leaf was crying and wringing her hands. Francis was as pale as death.

After about a quarter of an hour, he got the coachman and one of the footmen and crept upstairs. They knocked, but there was no reply. They called out. Everything was still. Finally, after vainly trying to force the door, they got on the roof, and dropped down on to the balcony. The windows yielded easily: their bolts were old.

When they entered they found, hanging upon the wall, a splendid portrait of their master as they had last seen him, in all the wonder of his exquisite youth and beauty. Lying on the floor was a dead man, in evening dress, with a knife in his heart. He was withered, wrinkled, and loathsome of visage. It was not till they had examined the rings that they recognised who it was.

THE END

For curiosity's sake he had tried the denial of self. He recognised that now.

But this murder—was it to dog him all his life? Was he always to be burdened by his past? Was he really to confess? Never. There was only one bit of evidence left against him. The picture itself—that was evidence. He would destroy it. Why had he kept it so long? Once it had given him pleasure to watch it changing and growing old. Of late he had felt no such pleasure. It had kept him awake at night. When he had been away, he had been filled with terror lest other eyes should look upon it. It had brought melancholy across his passions. Its mere memory had marred many moments of joy. It had been like conscience to him. Yes, it had been conscience. He would destroy it.

He looked round, and saw the knife that had stabbed Basil Hallward. He had cleaned it many times, till there was no stain left upon it. It was bright, and glistened. As it had killed the painter, so it would kill the painter's work, and all that that meant. It would kill the past, and when that was dead he would be free. It would kill this monstrous soul-life, and, without its hideous warnings, he would be at peace. He seized the thing, and stabbed the picture with it.

There was a cry heard, and a crash. The cry was so horrible in its agony that the frightened servants woke, and crept out of their rooms. Two gentlemen, who were passing in the Square below, stopped, and looked up at the great house. They walked on till they met a policeman, and brought him back. The man rang the bell several times, but there was no answer. Except for a light in one of the top windows, the house was all dark. After a time, he went away and stood in an adjoining portico and watched.

'Whose house is that, constable?' asked the elder of the two gentlemen.

255